T0283138

WHEN RUSSIA DID DEMOCRACY

'The Russian people have long deserved
a monument in their own lifetimes.'

Alexander Lebed

WHEN RUSSIA DID DEMOCRACY

From St Vladimir to Tsar Putin

Kenneth MacInnes

AMBERLEY

First published 2023

Amberley Publishing
The Hill, Stroud
Gloucestershire, GL5 4EP

www.amberley-books.com

Copyright © Kenneth MacInnes, 2023

The right of Kenneth MacInnes to be identified as the Author of this work has been
asserted in accordance with the Copyright, Designs and Patents Act 1988.

All rights reserved. No part of this book may be reprinted or reproduced or utilised in any
form or by any electronic, mechanical or other means, now known or hereafter invented,
including photocopying and recording, or in any information storage or retrieval system,
without the permission in writing from the Publishers.

British Library Cataloguing in Publication Data.
A catalogue record for this book is available from the British Library.

ISBN 978 1 3981 0544 7 (hardback)
ISBN 978 1 3981 0545 4 (ebook)

1 2 3 4 5 6 7 8 9 10

Typesetting by SJmagic DESIGN SERVICES, India.
Printed in the UK.

Contents

Introduction

'"Democracy is not for Russians." Whether that claim comes from the
right or the left, it is still balderdash.'

Mikhail Gorbachev

'Russia has always had a unique capacity to surprise.'

Margaret Thatcher

In March 1995, the fourteen members of Russia's central electoral
commission met to elect their chairman. Voting was secret and the only
name on the ballot paper was the incumbent, Nikolai Ryabov, who had
been appointed by President Boris Yeltsin in 1993. The rules stated that
those in favour of his candidacy should make 'a mark' in the box next
to his name. No mark would render the ballot paper invalid. There were
no instructions on how to cast a vote against. One of the members of
the commission, Professor Yevgeny Kolyushin, wanted to vote against
Ryabov and so he wrote the word *nyet* ('no') clearly in the box. After the
votes were counted, he was astonished to learn that the chairman had
been re-elected... unanimously! When he complained and demanded an
investigation, it was found that the tellers had interpreted the word 'no'
in his box as 'a mark' – which meant 'yes'...

This story perfectly illustrates an oft-repeated phrase, commonly attributed
to Stalin, though actually originating with Napoleon III: 'I care not who
casts the votes of a nation, provided I can count them.' It would also seem to
reinforce a widely held belief, particularly in the light of the extended period
of authoritarianism under Vladimir Putin, that Russians are 'unsuited' to
democracy and 'European values'. Respected journalist and broadcaster
Vladimir Pozner told an American audience in 2018 that 'Russia never, in its
entire thousand years, never had democracy.' But is this the case?

My first encounter with Russian democracy came in 1985, when studying the history of the 1917 revolutions at school. I was haunted by the poignant last sentence in our textbook on the Constituent Assembly, which was shut down by the Bolsheviks in 1918 after only one sitting: 'And so ended Russia's one-day experiment with democracy.' But there was an unexpected sequel that year, when Mikhail Gorbachev became Soviet leader and, in an unplanned series of events, ushered in a period of real democracy in Russia.

Between the end of the Soviet Union in 1991 and the election of Vladimir Putin in 2000, no one ever knew who was going to win a Russian election – not even the president himself. There was an incredible range of parties representing the entire political spectrum – liberals, communists, nationalists, environmentalists, fascists, social democrats, conservatives, technocrats, anarchists, monarchists and sometimes even combinations of ideologies, such as 'national bolshevism'. There were parties for women – even one for abandoned women – and single-issue groups, such as the Beer Lovers' Party.

The nineties were an exciting period as Russians made up for all the time lost since that one day in 1918 – confirming a popular Russian saying that 'no matter how well you feed a wolf, he'll still hanker after the forest.' While there were many bitter campaigns and contested elections, smears and fraud, violence and assassinations, even the shelling of parliament by order of the president in 1993, most of the political fighting was done via the ballot box or on the television networks.

Throughout these years, I studied and worked in St Petersburg, so this project began as a desire to relive that brief decade between Communism and Putinism. As Trotsky wrote in his memoirs, the last person to ask what happened during a revolution is the one who witnessed it. This book was to be about rediscovering and analysing Russia in the 1990s, only this time from the outside, filtered through the later experience of working for the House of Commons (whose members were once described by Ivan the Terrible as 'trading peasants'). But when I started digging deeper, I found that the earlier history of Russian parliamentarianism and popular representation was even richer.

The medieval republic of Novgorod was, for almost four centuries, the world's largest democracy and one of the most democratic parts of Europe. Between 1136 and 1478, 'parties' competed in elections and every executive post was elected; princes, prime ministers, archbishops and civil servants only held office for as long as they enjoyed public confidence. In the sixteenth and seventeenth centuries, the Land Assembly (*Zemsky sobor*) elected Russian tsars and represented a larger proportion of the population than Westminster Palace in England. In more modern times, the Russian Empire was the first place in Europe where women gained political equality (Gurian Republic in 1905) and voted in local elections (Latvia in 1905) and national elections (Finland in 1907).

The elections to the Constituent Assembly in November 1917 were, at the time, the greatest ever display of democracy, when over fifty million men and women voted under the freest electoral law ever written. By this time, Russia was the world's leading democracy and contributed to the growth of liberty and equality in neighbouring countries. The following month saw the creation of the first democratic state in Central Asia (Turkestan Autonomy) and the first Turkic republic (Crimean Democratic Republic). Muslim women voted for the first time in the Crimea in spring 1917 – ahead of the rest of Russia in summer 1917 – while a Buddhist theocracy in the Far East gave the vote to everyone over the age of fifteen in 1919 – at a time when only some women double that age could vote in Britain.

Russians have had no problems winning elections in foreign democracies. The first four presidents of Israel – and six prime ministers – were born in the Russian Empire. Even a member of the Romanov dynasty – Paul Ilyinsky, a great-grandson of Tsar Alexander II – was elected mayor of Palm Beach in Florida in the 1990s. So why is Russia rightfully proud of her military victories against invaders and pioneering conquest of space, yet not of the central role of the Council of the Whole Land in liberating the nation in 1612 or of being the first country to canvass voters from aeroplanes in 1917? All this history, from the Early Slavic assemblies chronicled by Byzantine historians to the events of August 1991, contradicts the myths that the Russian people have always lived in servility and that, in the words of Pyotr Chaadayev, 'there is something in our blood which repels all true progress.'

Alas, such myths are often perpetuated by Russia's own leaders, who – like us – generally associate democracy with the West. But this is not true, as the first democratic states emerged not in Greece or even in Europe, but in Asia – in the Middle East and India. Before 3,000 BC, the kings of Sumer were elected and had to share power with a bicameral legislature. This system of a monarch ruling alongside a popular assembly was then adopted by Babylon. Democratic republics were established in India before the sixth century BC and existed in modern Pakistan and Afghanistan at the time of Alexander the Great. Even the Mongol khans were 'elected' at an assembly called a *kurultai*, including Genghis Khan himself in 1206.

Just as the Greeks adopted their alphabet from the Phoenicians, so were their political ideas shaped by their interaction with the Middle East in the eighth century BC, when the Greek city-states (*poleis*) started to develop. The future Russian lands were exposed to Greek democracy after *poleis* were established in the areas to the north of the Black Sea. Chersonesus in the Crimea (*Tauris*) was a direct democracy during much of the classical period, before falling to oligarchic rule at the time of the Romans.

Russia adopted much of her culture, including the alphabet and religion, from Greece. The Greek language gave Russia her two words for 'democracy' – *demokratiya* and the calque *narodovlastiye* (literally 'people power'). Unfortunately, by this time Greece was the Byzantine Empire. Orthodox Christianity upheld the absolute rule of the 'caesar' anointed by God, ensuring that an Oliver Cromwell could never really emerge in Russia. During the reign of Emperor Justinian I in the mid-sixth century AD – which is roughly where this book begins – the word *demokratia* meant a riot or 'mob rule'.

This is a history of Russia viewed solely through the prism of democracy. A lack of space means that many pivotal events which affected the lives of millions, such as the national triumphs over Napoleon and Hitler or the mass repressions under Stalin and Ivan the Terrible, are often reduced to a single sentence. Peter the Great (who limited democracy) is given approximately the same attention as Fyodor III (his elder half-brother who increased democracy). For similar reasons, the narrative focuses on central power and does not explore in detail the democratic traditions and institutions of marginal communities, such as the Cossacks. While it is true that elections are not the cause but the result of democracy, voting is one of its most visible forms and so claims a considerable share of the book – especially in the guise of the phenomenon known as the 'campaign circus', which was already visible in the elections of 1598 and 1613.

I have tried to tell the story of how 'Russia did democracy' throughout her history. The aim is not to guide or lead in any direction, but to present some lesser-known facts and let readers draw their own conclusions (that is, after all, democracy). And possibly also think about our own democratic deficits and whether, after a thousand years of uninterrupted parliamentary history, our modern system is any better at representing, legislating, scrutinising and holding public servants to account.

Introduction

This book would not have been possible without the prior work of all the great historians whose writings I widely consulted, from Procopius and Nestor through Nikolai Karamzin and Ivan Belyaev to Vasily Klyuchevsky and Lev Protasov. Their immense labours have been complemented by the kind assistance of many outstanding and erudite scholars, researchers, artists, friends and experts, to whom I acknowledge my immense gratitude for being so responsive, generous, gracious and helpful in my endeavours. They are, in no particular order, Professor Jeffrey Sachs, Ralph Murphine, Walter Clinton, Professor Sarah Oates, Professor Nina Khrushcheva, Sheelagh Graham, Vyacheslav Nikonov of the State Duma, Fabian Theurer of the Friedrich-Naumann-Stiftung für die Freiheit, Alex Kireev of the *Electoral Geography* website, Vladimir Zamyatin, Alexey Titkov, DJL, Michelle Cowan, Roo, Professor Alexander Drikker (†), Anthony Baker M.Litt. and Yury Gerlovin. All muddles, mistakes and misconceptions are mine, based on Paul Winterton's handy assertion that 'there are no experts on Russia, merely varying degrees of ignorance.'

Russia followed the Julian (Old Style) calendar until 31 January 1918. The following day, the Bolsheviks switched to the Gregorian (New Style) calendar, which was by that time thirteen days ahead of Russia, so 1 February became 14 February 1918. All dates before the change are given in the Old Style, except for a few internationally significant events in the West, when both dates are given through a dividing slash. Russian names and words are transliterated using the Library of Congress system as closely as possible, although the overriding principle in the main text has been to follow established tradition (so 'Raisa Gorbachev' instead of 'Gorbacheva'). Well-known names are given in their more familiar anglicised versions (eg. 'Michael Romanov' or 'Leo Tolstoy'). This principle also governs the occasional occurrence of Ukrainian and Belarusian (or Belorussian) names, which are given in the more traditional format for established historical terms ('Kievan Rus'), but try to use the local spellings in all other cases ('Oleksandrivsk' rather than 'Alexandrovsk'). To aid pronunciation, some less familiar names are spelt as phonetically as possible (e.g. 'Mogilyov' rather than 'Mogilev').

Kenneth MacInnes
Kippford, Solway Firth

1

'Sovereign Democracy' – Medieval Rus

'It is liberty which is ancient and despotism which is modern.'

Germaine de Staël

The birth of the Russian state is commonly dated to 862 AD, when a Scandinavian prince called Rurik is said to have been invited to rule over the people of Novgorod. According to the Primary Chronicle, the inhabitants of this vast territory told him: 'Our land is great and abundant, but there is no order in it.' But if Rurik had dreams of dictatorial powers, he was in for a shock – because the East Slavic tribes inhabiting these lands had parliaments long before they had any organised state.

As Byzantine historian Procopius of Caesarea wrote in the sixth century, the early Slavs were governed by popular assemblies: 'For these nations... are not ruled by one man, but they have lived from of old under democracy, and consequently everything which involves their welfare, whether for good or for ill, is referred to the people.'[1] Their assembly was called a *veche*, from the Old Slavonic *vete*, which is also the root of the modern word *soviet* (meaning 'council' or 'advice'). The earliest recorded mention of the word is in the *Strategicon* – a military manual written by Byzantine emperor Maurice in the late sixth century.

All land-owning adult males were automatically members of the *veche*. Everyone had an equal right to speak and vote – rich or poor, young or old, Slavic or non-Slavic. Each town and village had its own *veche*. Supreme power in the land belonged to the *veche* based in the largest community, to which all lesser assemblies were subordinated. In the first half of the ninth century, the Primary Chronicle describes the Khazars exacting tribute from the Slavic Polans, who hold an assembly before agreeing to their demands. Later, in 1176, the Suzdal Chronicle reports: 'From of old, the people of Novgorod, of Smolensk, of Kiev, of Polotsk and of all the lands have assembled for council in *veches*.'[2]

Rurik died in 879 and was succeeded by Oleg, who left Novgorod and travelled south down the River Dnieper in 882. There he discovered the much richer town of Kiev, which he used as a base for bringing the other East Slavic tribes under his control. The city eventually became the capital of a federation of principalities known as Kievan Rus, which stretched all the way 'from the Varangians to the Greeks' – meaning from Scandinavia to the Byzantine Empire.

In 907, Oleg raided Constantinople from the sea and secured a favourable trade agreement with the Byzantine Empire. In a later Rus-Byzantine treaty signed in 945, the common people are listed in the opening sentence as a separate political entity: 'Our Grand Prince Igor, and his boyars, and all the Russian people, have sent us...' Close commercial ties with Byzantium led to the adoption of their Orthodox religion, first by Igor's widow Olga – Russia's first female ruler and, according to the Primary Chronicle, 'wisest of all persons'[3] – and then by her grandson, Grand Prince Vladimir, who converted the whole nation in 988.

'*Sovereign Lord Novgorod the Great*'

'Who can stand against God and Novgorod the Great?'

Popular medieval saying

Medieval Novgorod was an enormous colonial empire, covering the entire northern part of European Russia. At its greatest extent, this huge state stretched from the Baltic Sea in the west to the White Sea in the north and into Siberia in the east. Throughout this vast land – from the bustling trading posts in the south to the sparsely inhabited forests of the north – democracy reigned and sovereign power belonged to the people.

All executive positions in Novgorod were elected – from the prince and archbishop right down to the elders of every street and church. There were no set periods of office – governors, commanders and administrators remained in their posts for as long as they enjoyed public confidence. Some held office for many years and even died in the post, while others were replaced after several months. Whenever an official displeased the people, a *veche* was called and he was dismissed and replaced with a newly elected official.

Smaller towns and villages elected officials at their own assemblies, which were like a miniature version of the main *veche* in the city of Novgorod. The congregation of each church even had a *veche*, which elected the priest, sexton, verger and elders. In this way, Novgorod solved the problem of how to apply the advantages of direct democracy – previously thought possible only in a city-state – across a vast republic.

When Oleg became an independent prince in Kiev in 882, he came to an agreement with the people of Novgorod. The city would pay him tribute and he would leave a governor (*posadnik*) to reign on his behalf. Later, Novgorod was traditionally ruled by whoever was heir to the throne of the 'grand prince' in Kiev. Novgorod was proud of this status and when, in 972, Svyatoslav proposed replacing his son with ordinary officials, the people of Novgorod warned him: 'We know how to find another prince.'

When Grand Prince Vladimir died in 1015, his son, Yaroslav the Wise, was reigning on his behalf in Novgorod. Yaroslav's half-brother Svyatopolk seized power in Kiev, killing three of his other brothers. Yaroslav defeated him in 1019 with the help of the Novgorodians, who were rewarded with new freedoms and privileges. Novgorod now became independent of Kievan Rus and was free to choose its own prince – as long as he was a descendant of Yaroslav. The payment of tribute to the grand prince of Kiev, originally initiated by Oleg, was abolished.

This relationship lasted over a hundred years, before things changed again in the twelfth century. By this time, Kievan Rus had fragmented into a much looser federation of semi-independent princedoms, while Novgorod was growing in wealth and power. In 1126, the prince of Novgorod lost the right to appoint his own *posadnik*. The post was now elected by the *veche* and became almost completely independent of the prince.

Ten years later, military defeat sparked a revolution, bringing further democratic benefits for the people.[4] In 1135, Prince Vsevolod Mstislavich led the Novgorodians to defeat against the combined Rostov-Suzdal armies at the Battle of Mount Zhdanaya. The Nikon Chronicle reports: 'Many good and brave men of Novgorod were slaughtered, and much Christian blood was shed.' The dead included the *posadnik* and other prominent officials – but not Prince Vsevolod, who fled the field of battle 'in front of all'.

On 28 May 1136, the people of Novgorod rose up against the prince, who was imprisoned in the bishop's residence for seven weeks 'along with his wife and children and mother-in-law'. On 15 July 1136, the *veche* met to decide his fate. They voted to expel him from the city and to reduce the post of prince to what was effectively an elected figurehead. This was the birth date of the Republic of Novgorod.

Prince Vsevolod was replaced by Svyatoslav Olgovich, who was driven out in 1138, 'having sat two years less three months'. In 1141, 'the people of Novgorod sat without a prince for nine months.' The next man to be chosen, Svyatoslav Vsevolodovich was 'let go' after a few weeks and replaced by Rostislav, who was overthrown in 1142 and 'imprisoned in the bishop's residence, having sat for four months.'[5]

In 1154, Novgorod again expelled its prince, Yaroslav, and replaced him with another, Rostislav. He promptly left to reign in Kiev, leaving his son David in his place. But 'the men of Novgorod were indignant... and they showed the road to his son.' In 1157, following a riot, David's successor Mstislav had to flee under cover of the night. The next prince, Svyatoslav Rostislavich, was driven out in 1160 – 'the princess they let enter the convent of St Barbara' – only to be restored after just 'one year short of a week', when his rival and supplanter was 'fetched away'.[6]

Even the legendary St Alexander Nevsky, who led Novgorod to victory over the Swedes at the Battle of the Neva in 1240, was expelled later that same year, 'having quarrelled with the men of Novgorod'. Fortunately, he was recalled the following year and led the Novgorodians to another military triumph, this time against the Teutonic Knights at the Battle on the Ice in 1242.

There were further changes in 1156, when the prince lost the right to appoint the bishop of Novgorod. After the death of Niphont – who was accused of having 'robbed the treasury and gone to Constantinople' – all bishops were elected by the *veche* and only after their election sent to Kiev for ordainment by the metropolitan. The first elected bishop was Arkady in 1156. In 1165, during the tenure of his successor, John II, the rank of bishop was raised to archbishop – a sign of Novgorod's growing importance and its political independence.

When electing an archbishop, the *veche* selected three candidates from among the local clergy (this could even be a simple monk) and the winner was then 'chosen by God' – meaning by lot drawn by a child or a blind man. The *veche* also had a process for removing an archbishop who had displeased the people. In 1211, Archbishop Mitrofan was blamed for a devastating fire and banished from the city. Seventeen years later,

Archbishop Arseny was held responsible for a long spell of rainy weather and dismissed in 1228.[7]

This unique fusion of Russian Orthodoxy and democracy appears to have worked remarkably well, as seventeen of the thirty bishops elected during Novgorod's republican period were later canonised as Russian saints. Democracy also influenced religious architecture in Novgorod – churches built before the twelfth century had special galleries for the nobility, while those constructed later just used one common space.

In 1228, the *veche* brought in a new rule for all princes elected to the throne of Novgorod. The prince now had to sign a contract promising to uphold the historical rights and freedoms of the republic. This document stipulated all the conditions of his office, ranging from not being allowed to extradite Novgorodians to other domains to how often he could fish in Lake Ladoga (only every third summer). The prince was not permitted to levy taxes, interfere in politics or replace officials.

As long as the prince kept these conditions, he still had a lot of power and was second only to the *veche*. He could command the army, declare war, sign peace, send and receive embassies – all with the agreement of the *veche*. The prince had the authority to summon a *veche*, pass sentences and even issue laws in his own name, just so long as they did not infringe upon the rights and liberties of 'Sovereign Lord Novgorod the Great'.

Responsible Government
'Novgorod had a popular government; the people in the assembly at the *veche* were the true rulers.'

Alexander Radischev

The next elected post beneath the prince was the *posadnik*. He was the head of government and, like the prince, had both executive and judicial powers. He handled domestic and international affairs, commanded the army alongside the prince and acted as a judge. The *posadnik* chaired the *veche* and conducted negotiations with foreign states on behalf of Novgorod. The post was roughly similar to that of a prime minister combined with speaker in a modern parliamentary republic.

While princes and archbishops were simply banished, an unpopular *posadnik* was lucky to escape with his life. In 1388, 'three of the quarters of the St Sophia Side rose against the *posadnik* Esif Zakharinich and, summoning a *veche* at St Sophia, they went like a large army, every one armed, to his dwelling and took his house and demolished his rooms. And

16

posadnik Esif fled across the river.'[8] This might sound like mob justice, but it was actually an officially prescribed punishment, known as *potok i grablenie* ('wholesale pillage'). The offender and the rest of his family were chased out of town, while his property was confiscated and shared out among the rest of the population. Although anarchic, the punishment was democratic and a good check on corruption in medieval Russia.

The third most important post in the republic was the chiliarch or 'thousandman' (*tysyatsky*), who commanded a military force of a thousand men. This official was also responsible for collecting taxes, resolving disputes with foreign traders, supervising fortifications and acting as an ambassador. When dealing with Novgorod, foreigners translated the post of *tysyatsky* as *dux* (duke). The *tysyatsky* was the deputy and assistant of the *posadnik* at the *veche*, where his duties were keeping order and submitting the business (a combination of the roles of serjeant-at-arms and leader of the house in the British parliament). To ensure that all classes were represented in government, the *posadnik* was generally chosen from among the boyars (the upper nobility) and rich merchants, while the *tysyatsky* was elected from among the lower classes.

The next rank of official was the *sotsky* (constable or headman). There were ten of them in the city of Novgorod and one or two in smaller towns. The *sotsky* dispatched embassies to neighbouring states and participated in military campaigns, heading the troops from their tenth part of Novgorod. The *sotsky* was followed by the elder (*starosta*). This was the oldest elected office in Novgorod and had existed since the days before Rurik. All of these positions meant that the prince was not just under the nominal control of the *veche*. His power was held in check by an entire hierarchy of elected officials, who together constituted responsible government in Novgorod. (See plate section.)

Parliamentary Sovereignty

'That bell on the *veche* tower served freedom alone.'

Mikhail Lermontov

The supreme authority over all elected officials and the entire territory of the Republic of Novgorod was the *veche*. This was the only organ of power which was not elected, as every male citizen was automatically a member, with one vote. The only exception was the clergy, who were not allowed to attend the *veche* – even when it was discussing church matters, such as the election of a bishop.

The *veche* was the highest legislative and judicial authority in the land. It was responsible for all laws and all foreign and domestic affairs, including war and peace. It was the court for all crimes carrying the death sentence, exile or confiscation of property. The *veche* elected, judged and dismissed all officials. It resolved all disputes between the various branches of executive power (including the prince) and heard all complaints against unfair rulings, abuses of power and corruption.

The *veche* was not a permanent institution which sat regularly for fixed periods of time, like a modern parliament. It was summoned whenever it was required by the ringing of the *veche* bell. This bell became the symbol of not just the *veche*, but of Novgorod's freedom and democratic traditions. Only four people had the right to summon a *veche* – the prince, *posadnik*, *tysyatsky* and archbishop. A *veche* might be wrongly called during a riot, but such assemblies did not have constitutional power and their decisions were not legally binding.

The *veche* usually met on a square called the Yaroslav Court (*Yaroslavovo dvorische*), which had once been the compound of Yaroslav the Wise. This was on the eastern side of the River Volkhov, known as the Trading Side. Judging by the size of the square, a typical assembly attracted around 300 or 400 participants. The *veche* sometimes also met outside the Cathedral of Holy Wisdom (*Sofiiskii sobor*) on the western side of the river, which was known as the St Sophia Side. This mostly occurred when they were electing an archbishop or discussing religious matters, although these sittings were usually preceded by a preliminary assembly on the Yaroslav Court.

The *posadnik* opened the *veche* by ringing the bell and everyone sat down to discuss the business of the day – legislation, a specific debate, or urgent questions. Officials addressed the *veche* from a special platform built on the square. As all *veche* decisions required a unanimous vote, fights often broke out. Whenever two sides could not agree on a matter, the *veche* split into two assemblies – one on each side of the river. The two groups then advanced towards each other on the bridge and decided everything in a pitched battle – unless the archbishop managed to intervene and restore peace.

When the *veche* did come to a decision, the secretary (*dyak*) compiled a charter in a set form in the name of the *posadnik*, *tysyatsky*, boyars, merchants, common people and 'all Novgorod the Great' (the document sometimes began with a blessing from the archbishop). All charters were authenticated with the official seal of the *veche*, to which were added the seals of the *posadnik*, *tysyatsky* and the five administrative districts (one document dating from 1317 bears eleven different seals). They were stored in the *veche* archives on the Yaroslav Court.

Like modern parliaments, the *veche* had political 'parties', only they were not ideological or class groupings, but were based on the five municipal units. The three districts on the St Sophia Side – the Nerevsky, Zagorodsky ('behind the kremlin') and Lyudin ('guildsmen') or Goncharny ('potters') quarters – tended to express the interests of the aristocrats and ruling class. The two on the Trading Side – the Slavensky (Slavno) and Plotnitsky ('carpenters') quarters – represented craftsmen and merchants.

Each district was called an 'end' (*konets*) as it had a major road running through it which ended at the city centre. Every 'end' had its own *veche*, rather like a district council, which operated in the same way as the central *veche* by electing officials, voting on local issues and publishing its rulings in charters stamped with its own seal. Each 'end' was further subdivided into 'streets', which also had their own *veches* and officials.

This meant that local government was run along the same democratic lines as the 'national' or 'federal' *veche* on the Yaroslav Court. The five district *veches* sent delegates to the city *veche*, where they sat together as one bloc, representing the specific interests and inhabitants of each municipal unit. This was the basis for the five 'parties' at the *veche*.

Although each party represented a mixture of all classes of Novgorod society, the wealthier groups – the boyars and merchants – tended to form the ruling elite. But they still competed with each other in elections, each side being supported by representatives of the lower classes. In medieval Europe, the common people tended to be a voiceless mass. But in Novgorod, they took an active part in elections, political debates and even foreign negotiations. In 1370, for example, a treaty between Novgorod and Dmitry Donskoy of Moscow lists the individual names of the representatives of the 'black' or common people alongside the prince and archbishop.

The five parties competed in general elections to appoint the most important officials. There were 147 elections of a *posadnik* in the 352 years between 1126 and 1478 and the victories were spread among all five parties, although the richer St Sophia Side clearly dominated over the poorer Trading Side – Zagorodsky (43), Nerevsky (35), Lyudin (20), Slavensky (17), Zagorodsky-Plotnitsky (9), Plotnitsky (15) and unknown (8). As each *posadnik* was supported by a particular party, his position was secure only as long as the party – or alliance of parties – commanded a majority at the *veche*. As soon as it lost popularity, he suffered the consequences and was overthrown.

This happened in 1209, when a Nerevsky *posadnik* introduced new taxes solely for the benefit of his own party elite. The *veche* rebelled against the decision, ordered the ransacking of the Nerevsky estates and elected a new *posadnik* from the Zagorodsky party: 'The men of Novgorod held a *veche* over *posadnik* Dmitry and his brethren, because they had ordered the levying of silver on the people of Novgorod... And they went to plunder their houses, and set fire to... Dmitry's... That same year they brought back Dmitry dead... and buried him... The people of Novgorod wanted to throw his body from the bridge, but the archbishop forbade them.'[9]

Besides the *veche*, there was an upper chamber called the 'council of lords' (*sovyet gospod*). Like the House of Lords in the UK parliament, it grew out of the consultative assembly which had originally advised the early princes. The council of lords was headed by the archbishop and included the serving *posadnik* and *tysyatsky*, their predecessors, and the elected heads of the five districts and smaller subunits. The result was something like the Roman Senate. The council of lords developed projects for new laws, which were submitted to the *veche* to vote upon. Although the *veche* was theoretically absolute, it eventually fell under the influence of the council of lords, particularly towards the end of Novgorodian independence.

Between Athens and Westminster

This system of checks and balances, parties and elections, democratic institutions and popular representation existed for almost four centuries. While Novgorod was not perfect – prominent clans played a disproportionate role in the parties and in government – it was still ahead of the rest of medieval Europe in its broad extension of the suffrage and the control of the legislature over the executive. Russia's earliest republic can rightfully be called 'a Slavonic counterpart of the city-states of Italy or of Flanders'.[10]

But the roots of the Novgorod system reach back to even earlier times, lying 'in the basic structure of all states run by the people, from Athens and Sparta to Unterwalden or Glarus'.[11] As historian Nikolai Karamzin wrote, the *veche* 'reigned supreme like the assembly of the people of Athens or the Franks at the *champ de mars*'.[12] Because no royal dynasty was ever allowed to establish itself, Novgorod was able to continue many of the ideas and institutions of the ancient democracies. The *veche* was comparable in power and representation to the *ecclesia* of Athens, while anticipating many of the forms and rituals of the modern British parliament.

Novgorod was not the only republic in medieval Russia. After a period as a separate principality, Pskov became part of Novgorod in 1136 but would regain its independence in 1348. Pskov adopted many of the traits of the Novgorod Republic and was also divided into 'ends' with similar rules of governance. In some ways, 'Lord Pskov' was even more democratic than Novgorod. Because it was much smaller in size and wealth, the *veche* was less subject to the influence of powerful clans or political rivalries. The Pskov *veche* met near the Krom (Kremlin), while the *veche* bell hung from a tower next to the Trinity Cathedral. Pskov remained independent until 1510, when Basil III of Moscow conquered the republic and dissolved the *veche*.

Kievan Rus

'The political life of the Russian federation of the Kievan period was
based on freedom.'

George Vernadsky

The main difference between Novgorod and the rest of Rus was the presence of hereditary rulers in Kievan Rus. While the power of the prince diminished over time in Novgorod, the opposite happened in the other Russian lands, where the prince gradually increased his authority. But this was not a continuous process and democracy ebbed and flowed in Kievan Rus.

Initially, there was a tendency towards autocratic rule, from the arrival of Oleg in 882 until the death of Yaroslav the Wise in 1054. Grand Prince Vladimir's adoption of Christianity in 988 added a further source of absolute power – the Orthodox clergy. This also brought the introduction of such Byzantine legal ideas as *caesaropapism* – the concept that the monarch had both secular and spiritual authority.

However, the *veche* still retained its power and sometimes even acted independently of the prince. In 997, for example, the besieged citizens of Belgorod themselves voted to surrender to the Pechenegs. The *veche* had its own militia, which fought under a separate commander and followed the orders and decisions of the *veche*, such as the contingent led by Vyshata in the attack on Constantinople in 1043.

Vladimir's successor, Yaroslav the Wise, transformed Kievan Rus into a rich and influential state closely integrated with the rest of Europe. Larger than Paris and twice the size of London, Kiev attracted scholars from both Rome and Constantinople – as well as the exiled sons of Edmund Ironside after England was invaded by Canute in 1016. Yaroslav married the daughter of King Olof of Sweden and three of his own daughters became European queens.[13] His granddaughter Eupraxia was the wife of the Holy Roman emperor Henry IV, while his grandson, Vladimir Monomachus, married Gytha, the daughter of King Harold II of England.

Before his death in 1054, Yaroslav divided the country up between his five sons. The various principalities constantly engaged in internecine warfare, weakening Kievan Rus in the eleventh and twelfth centuries. One consequence of the civil wars was that the individual rulers grew increasingly dependent on the local population. Each prince was more heavily invested in defeating his rivals than controlling his subjects, who were now his main source of power and support. From the mid-twelfth century to the Mongol invasion almost a hundred years later, no prince could sit securely on his throne without the backing of the people.

The result was a flourishing of democracy in Kievan Rus. The *veche* chose whether or not to support the prince in his wars. In 1147, the people rejected the plans of Izyaslav of Kiev to march against his uncle, Yury Dolgoruky. Alternatively, when Mstislav of Rostov wanted to sign peace with Vsevolod of Vladimir in 1177, the *veche* told him: 'You might give him peace, but we shall not!' The *veche* even interfered in the prince's private life. In 1173, when Yaroslav Osmosmysl of Halych replaced his wife, Princess Olga of Suzdal, with his lover, Anastasia Charg, the *veche* ordered him to take Olga back – and burnt Anastasia at the stake.[14]

This situation lasted until 1223, when the Chronicle of Novgorod reports: 'The same year, for our sins, unknown tribes came, whom no one exactly knows who they are, nor whence they came... but they call them Tartars.'[15] The Mongols launched a full-scale invasion in 1237–40, occupying most of Rus and completely destroying all the old centres of civilisation, including Kiev. Only a few parts in the less accessible west and north escaped – Novgorod, Pskov, Smolensk and Polotsk – although even Novgorod was forced to become a vassal of the Mongols.

While the Mongol occupation had a major impact on many aspects of Russian life, it did not greatly affect the country's internal affairs. The Mongols did not care about the relationship between the prince and the populace. They only dealt with the princes, who acted as their tax collectors and law enforcers. All the Mongols wanted were submission and the payment of tribute – nothing more. However, the invasion did alter the balance of power between the prince and the people. Now wholly dependent on the khan, the princes were less dependent on the local population. The conquered lands could no longer choose their own prince; they had to accept the one appointed by the Mongols. If they did not, the prince could – and did – ask the khan for troops to quell any discontent.

Although the Mongol yoke lasted over two centuries, from approximately 1240 to 1480, it was only oppressive in the first hundred years and weakened after the death of Öz Beg Khan in 1341. The *veches* continued to meet, elect officials and act independently of the princes. In 1262, the north-east of the country rose up against the collection of tribute, massacring officials and expelling tax collectors. The revolt was masterminded in secret by the *veches* without the involvement of the princes (only a few subsequently joined the uprising).

In the fourteenth century, as the Golden Horde declined, a new Russian principality rose in prominence – Moscow. Founded in 1147 by Prince Yury Dolgoruky, the city's remote location in forestland meant that it suffered less damage during the Mongol occupation. The main sources of its power and wealth were the characters and policies of its princes. Ivan I Kalita ('Moneybag') won the khan's favour by crushing a rebellion in Tver in 1327 and was given responsibility for collecting and delivering all the taxes and tribute paid to the Mongols. His grandson, Dmitry Donskoy, became a national hero for leading Russia to her first military victory over the Mongols at the Battle of Kulikovo in 1380.

In just over a century, Moscow grew from a young and relatively weak state into the leading power in north-eastern Rus. But while keeping the Mongols at bay through a combination of sword and diplomacy, the grand princes themselves adopted many of the oppressive institutions and practices of their overlords. Over time, as Moscow extended its control over all the other principalities, this gradually developed into the Russian autocracy. By the mid-fifteenth century, the only independent structure pursuing an alternative form of government was Novgorod.

The Fall of Novgorod

'The boyars stood not for the *veche* bell or for the *posadnik*, but for their own private estates.'

Nikolai Karamzin

Political life in Novgorod had also undergone great changes in the intervening years. The frequent expulsions of the princes by the people

23

ended and the republic increasingly became a battleground between economic classes. In the two centuries between the death of Yaroslav the Wise and the Mongol invasion, ten of the twelve cases of serious unrest had been between the people and the prince. But in the following two centuries, the causes of sixteen of the twenty major disturbances were clashes between social groups.

The style of government moved from democracy to oligarchy. In 1354, the post of *posadnik* was reformed to accommodate the interests of the leading boyar clans, allowing each family to share power without having to compete against each other in elections. Instead of one *posadnik*, there would now be six – one from each of the five parties and one principal or 'sitting' governor (*stepennyi posadnik*). This number was subsequently increased to twelve in the 1410s, twenty-four in the 1420s, thirty-six in the 1460s and over fifty in the 1470s. The same reform was applied to the post of *tysyatsky*. By the early 1420s, there were six of them – and they were now elected from among the boyars and not the common people.

The supreme power of the *veche* was undermined by the growing role of the council of lords. By the fifteenth century, the upper chamber was taking virtually all decisions for the *veche*. Although the council could only submit legislative projects and not vote on them, it was able to use its power and wealth to lobby, bribe and influence the final outcome in the *veche*. All these changes detached the lower classes from the democratic process and weakened their desire to defend the republic – just when a threat was appearing on the horizon in the form of the encroaching power of Moscow.

In 1456, Grand Prince Basil II forced Novgorod to sign the Treaty of Yazhelbitsy, which seriously undermined its sovereignty. A group of anti-Muscovite boyars responded by entering into negotiations with the grand duke of Lithuania. In 1470, a Lithuanian prince was offered the throne of Novgorod. Basil's son, Ivan III, accused Novgorod of breaking the terms of the treaty and planning to convert to Roman Catholicism. He sent an army which defeated the poorly organised Novgorodians at the Battle of Shelon in 1471. Twelve thousand Novgorodians were killed, while the sitting *posadnik*, Dmitry Boretsky, was captured and beheaded for 'treason'.

Although another *posadnik* was elected in Dmitry's place, real power lay in the hands of Dmitry's mother, Martha. She was the widow of an earlier *posadnik*, Isaac (or Simon) Boretsky, and is known in Russian history as *Marfa-posadnitsa*. A rich and formidable woman, once described as 'a

Russian parallel to Elizabeth of England, Catherine de' Medici and the rest of the female offspring of the classical Renaissance',[16] Martha led the doomed cause of Novgorod's independence.

Undaunted by the crushing defeat at the River Shelon, Martha continued to negotiate with Lithuania. This inspired a fresh attack in 1477 by the army of Ivan III, who surrounded Novgorod and entered the city on 29 January 1478. On 7 February, Martha was arrested and extradited to Moscow. Her subsequent fate is unknown, although the Chronicle of Novgorod states that, like her son, 'the charming Martha... was also to lose her life by decapitation.'[17]

The following day, on 8 February, 'the grand prince ordered the *veche* bell to be taken down and destroyed.'[18] Ivan III abolished the *veche* and all elected posts, declaring: 'There will be neither *veche* bell, nor *posadnik* in Novgorod; there will be the one power of the sovereign, as in Muscovy.'[19] And so the curtain fell on a millennium of *veche* rule and what had been, to date, the largest democracy in world history.

Ivan deported thousands of the city's boyars and merchants, awarding their property and estates to Muscovites and turning the enormous republic into a province of Moscow. Many citizens fled from Novgorod to the furthest reaches of the fallen empire. One of them was a man called Yelizarko Yelets. In 1495, he ended up in the northern Urals, where he had a family and his surname became 'Yeltsyn'. This was the ancestor of a man called Boris Yeltsin.

2

The Sixteenth Century – Muscovy

The Autocrats

Ivan III titled himself the 'grand prince of all Rus' and became known as the 'gatherer of the Russian lands' for his role in reuniting the country. But this was no longer Kievan Rus – it was now Muscovite Rus.

The grand princes of Moscow were more like the Asian khans than the Old Russian princes. Their adoption of the Mongol legacy saw the introduction of such practices as the seclusion of women, capital punishment, torture and forced labour. All social classes were now bound to the service of the state, while the old practice of democratically electing officials on merit was replaced by an elaborate system of precedence, based on genealogy and known as *mestnichestvo* ('place position').

A second foreign influence was the Byzantine Empire, which had fallen to the Ottoman Turks in 1453. In 1472, Ivan III married Zoe (Sophia) Palaiologina, the niece of the last Byzantine emperor. Arriving in Moscow with a large entourage of Greeks, she began introducing Byzantine rites and customs into Kremlin court etiquette. The concept of Moscow as the 'Third Rome' – the successor to the Roman and Byzantine empires – was formulated around this time.

Although an autocrat, Ivan III still consulted with his advisory council of noblemen, the Boyars' Duma, which was described as 'a house of lords and a permanent cabinet all rolled into one'.[1] The Boyars' Duma usually met daily and its members could freely argue and disagree with the grand prince, who encouraged contrary opinions and enjoyed a good debate.

Ivan's son and heir, Basil III, was more like his Byzantine mother. He took decisions without consulting his boyars and did not like anyone answering him back. When Ivan Bersen-Beklemishev once argued with him in council, he shouted angrily: 'Get out of my sight, you lowly peasant, I don't need you anymore!' Bersen later grumbled to Maximus the Greek: 'As soon as the mother of the grand prince, Grand Princess Sophia, came here with her Greeks, our land fell into confusion and great disorder, just like in Constantinople.'[2] He paid dearly for such words and was executed in 1525.

After the death of Basil III in 1533, the throne passed to his three-year-old son, Ivan IV – who later became known as Ivan the Terrible. Ivan's mother, Elena Glinska, was appointed regent, but died suddenly (probably by poisoning) when he was only seven. For almost a decade, from 1538 to 1547, power passed into the hands of the boyars. But instead of using this opportunity to legislate and permanently limit the autocracy, they engaged in an orgy of killings, seizing power from one another and abusing it for as long as they could hold onto it.

Ivan was himself abused by the boyars. He was denied food and only dressed properly when he had to meet ambassadors. Surrounded by intrigues, murders and reprisals, he grew up suspicious, vengeful and sadistic. The young tsar participated in rapes, tortured animals and, at the age of thirteen, had a man thrown to a pack of starved hunting dogs. In a letter to Andrei Kurbsky in 1564, he looked back on his childhood as a time of great deprivation and humiliation: 'I will prove in the greatest detail what evil I have suffered from my youth... my brother and I... remained as orphans, [having lost] our parents and receiving no human care from any quarter; and hoping only for the mercy of God... What sufferings did I endure through [no] clothing and through hunger!'[3]

So there was bound to be a terrible reckoning when, at the age of sixteen, Ivan suddenly announced his intention to assume his rights. On 16 January 1547, he had himself crowned in the Dormition Cathedral under the new title of 'tsar of all Russia'.

The Assembly of Reconciliation

Shortly after Ivan's coronation, Moscow was swept by a series of devastating fires. Much of the wooden city was destroyed and thousands of people were killed (the metropolitan was only saved by being lowered from a rope into the river). The Muscovites had also suffered under the boyars and this latest event triggered an outburst of violence against their former oppressors. The tsar's maternal grandmother was accused of using black magic to start the fires and a mob marched to his palace to demand that he hand her over. Her son, Yury Glinski, was chased into the Dormition Cathedral, dragged out and stoned to death.

Ivan was frightened by the violence and saw the infernos as divine punishment for his sins. The riots also showed the need for urgent change in the way the country was governed. Ivan knew that he had to rule over a vast territory and deal with many domestic and foreign problems – yet he had no way of ensuring that the boyars would implement his decrees or truthfully report back to him on the state of the land. He needed to strengthen the autocracy, centralise power and find an alternative source of support. Above all, he thirsted for revenge against the boyars.

In 1549, Ivan IV took the momentous step of creating a rival consultative organ to the Boyars' Duma. He summoned representatives of the whole land to a grand meeting in Moscow, which evolved into the country's first ever national parliament. This institution was known by contemporaries as a *sobor* ('assembly'). Later, from the 1850s onwards, historians used the term *Zemsky sobor* ('land assembly') to distinguish it from the church or 'sanctified' assembly (*Osvyaschyonny sobor*). In sixteenth-century Russia, the word 'land' referred to the state or anything public or secular.

The first Zemsky Sobor was composed of the Boyars' Duma, the metropolitan, the senior clergy and members of every class in Russian society – except tradesmen and peasants (who did take part in later assemblies). While the Sobor was not elected, it still resembled the other European parliaments of that time, in which representatives of the three estates sat in a single chamber. Foreigners sometimes employed their own equivalent terms when referring to the Zemsky Sobor, such as *Sejm*, *Riksdag*, *Landtag* or even 'parliament'.

At the grand opening ceremony on Red Square on 27 February 1549, Ivan IV did something which none of his contemporary European monarchs ever did. Addressing the delegates from a stone platform known as 'Golgotha' (*Lobnoye mesto*), he bowed down before his subjects and apologised for all the wrongs committed during his minority by the boyars. Turning to the boyars, he then declared: 'O unrighteous extortioners, predators and iniquitous judges! What answer will you give us now? How many tears, how much blood has been spilled by you? I am pure of this blood, but you must await the judgement of heaven.' Drawing to a conclusion, the tsar called for national conciliation: 'I beg you, abandon hatred and enmity towards each other... From now on, I am your judge and protector.'[4]

Over the course of the next two days, the 'Assembly of Reconciliation' addressed the problems of corruption and the abuses of power committed by the boyars. There were hearings of all the iniquities suffered by the people, such as illegal taxes and unfair trials. Several important decisions were then made on the basis of the collected evidence. Anyone suffering from an injustice could submit a petition to the tsar, who established a special department to deal with these matters called the Petitions Office (*Chelobitnaya izba*).

The work of the Zemsky Sobor inspired a great creative response and the Petitions Office was soon flooded with further complaints and suggestions for political reforms. Petitions were submitted by the country's leading writers and thinkers, including Maximus the Greek, Hermolaus-Erasmus and Ivan Peresvetov (the author of Russia's first utopia). Peresvetov's proposals contained details suggesting that they may actually have been written by the tsar himself, particularly the advice that 'there cannot a sovereign be without wrath.'

When it was concluded that one of the sources of the abuses was the hopelessly entangled legal system, a second Zemsky Sobor was convened in 1550 to undertake a new codification of the laws. Like the first Sobor, this assembly was not elected and only consisted of those whom the tsar chose to consult. This included the Boyars' Duma and the heads of the *prikazy* (departments or ministries), the Russian Orthodox Church and trade guilds. The result was the *Sudebnik*, a new code of laws which abolished the boyars' judicial privileges and increased the role of the state courts. Although the *Sudebnik* centralised tsarist power, it introduced a requirement for elected representatives of the population to participate in provincial court hearings. The peasant communes were also awarded a degree of self-government and control over local policing and the expenditure of tax receipts. The *Sudebnik* was approved at the Stoglav Sobor in 1551, which was summoned to regulate religious and moral life, publishing its decisions in the form of a book with a hundred chapters (*sto glav* in Russian).[5]

The Parliaments of Ivan the Terrible

There appear to have been as many as ten Zemsky Sobors convened during the reign of Ivan the Terrible. An assembly was held in 1564, when the tsar suddenly abandoned Moscow and set up an alternative 'state within a state' known as the *Oprichnina*. A further Sobor was held in 1565 to 'conduct negotiations' with the absent tsar, who was awarded dictatorial powers on its territory. He subsequently instigated a reign of terror, mainly directed against the boyars, which culminated in the massacre of almost half the population of Novgorod in 1570.

The first Sobor from which the original documents survive was the assembly called in June 1566 to discuss a Lithuanian peace offer to end the Livonian War. Although mainly composed of boyars, noblemen and merchants from Moscow and the western lands affected by the war, the documents record representatives of the people, including the middle classes, debating important matters of state and determining the course of Russian foreign policy.[6]

A group of Lithuanian diplomats visited Moscow in May 1566 and proposed splitting the contested territory between the two countries. Ivan put these terms to the Zemsky Sobor, which concluded that there was more advantage to be gained from continuing the war. The delegates eagerly assured the tsar of their willingness to sacrifice not only their 'stomachs' (meaning their belongings), but also their 'heads' (half of the boyars at the Sobor did indeed later lose their heads).

Of course, it is highly likely that the Zemsky Sobor simply gave Ivan the exact answer he wanted to hear. The tsar was no different from contemporary English monarchs, who also used parliament for their own purposes. King Henry VIII, who died in 1547, built up a strong House of Commons to help push through radical changes, such as divorcing Catherine of Aragon – a very popular queen – and the break with Rome in the 1530s. The Tudors understood the political benefits of allying themselves with parliament – and so did Ivan the Terrible.

This did not stop the tsar from rebuking Elizabeth I for allowing merchants to sit in the House of Commons and place limitations on the English monarchy. In a letter to the queen on 24 October 1570, he writes:

> We had hoped that you were ruler in your Kingdom and that you yourself ruled, and that you yourself looked after your Kingdom's honour and your Kingdom's advantages and that is why we wanted to deal such matters with you. But it appears that other people rule for you. They are not just people, they are trading peasants... And you are in your virginal state like some old unmarried female.[7]

The final jibe possibly betrays the fury of a rejected suitor. Ivan was three years older than Elizabeth and is believed to have made her an offer of marriage in 1567 (the 'matters' he mentions in his letter). Elizabeth

30

ignored this remark and told her ambassador to reply that 'no merchants govern Our State and affairs but We Ourselves take care of Our affairs as is appropriate for a virgin and a Queen.'

In 1575, Ivan pretended to abdicate and named Simeon Bekbulatovich – the baptised ruler of a Tatar vassal state, the Qasim khanate – as tsar in his place. His reasons are unclear, although he possibly wanted to avoid responsibility for a decree confiscating land from the monasteries. A Zemsky Sobor consisting of boyars, military commanders and noblemen met to discuss and approve this move at the end of 1575. Ivan returned to the throne shortly afterwards, in 1576, when another Sobor was held. The final Sobors of his reign were called in 1579 and 1580 to discuss the latest setbacks in the Livonian War.

The last years of Ivan's life were highly dramatic. In 1580, he broke his own laws by taking an eighth wife, Maria Nagaya. The following year, he murdered his eldest son and heir, Ivan, by striking him on the head with his iron staff. The tsar continued to seek an English marriage and his choice now fell on Lady Mary Hastings, sister of the Earl of Huntingdon and a distant relative of Queen Elizabeth. He sent an ambassador to England in 1582 to inspect Mary and negotiate the rights of any children to the Russian throne. After she rejected the fifty-two-year-old tsar, he declared that he would simply go to England and find a bride himself. But before he could carry out this plan, he died in March 1584, in the middle of a game of chess with one of his cronies, Bogdan Belsky.

A month later, a Zemsky Sobor – described by the English ambassador, Sir Jerome Horsey, as 'a sort of parliament composed of the upper hierarchy and nobility' – met to confirm the legitimate succession of Ivan's second son as Fyodor I.[8] The tsar had previously nominated his eldest son as his heir in 1572 but had not changed his will after Ivan's death in 1581. The Zemsky Sobor was now growing from a purely consultative organ into an elective body – and even adding legislative powers, as it gave Fyodor the title of 'tsar' after his father had failed to award him the rank of 'tsarevich'.

The new tsar was a weak and sickly man whose chief pleasure in life was ringing church bells. Knowing that Fyodor would be unable to rule by himself, his father had created a four-member regency council consisting of Ivan Mstislavsky, Ivan Shuisky, Nikita Zakharin-Yuriev and Bogdan Belsky. Belsky immediately tried to seize power in a military coup but was defeated and his place on the council was given to Boris Godunov.

Boris Godunov had risen to power as an *oprichnik*.[9] He married the daughter of Ivan the Terrible's chief henchman, Malyuta Skuratov, while his sister, Irina Godunova, was now the tsaritsa as the wife of Fyodor I. Boris quickly established himself as the *de facto* ruler of Russia by retiring or banishing the other members of the regency council. He personally signed decrees, received foreign ambassadors and conducted all correspondence with European monarchs. Toasts were drunk at royal banquets to the health of both Tsar Fyodor and Boris Godunov.

Fyodor and Irina did not have any children, so the next in line to the throne was the tsar's half-brother, Tsarevich Dmitry, who was the son of Maria Nagaya. Because Fyodor considered Dmitry to be illegitimate, the young prince was banished to the town of Uglich, where he died in mysterious circumstances in 1591. The investigation headed by Vasily Shuisky found that the tsarevich had suffered an epileptic fit while playing with a knife and stabbed himself to death. Many believed that he had been murdered by order of Boris Godunov to clear his own path to the throne, but the patriarch declared it an act of God and the matter was closed.

3

Interregnum

'Spinning Boris'

'Men almost ruptured themselves with frantic wailing and went blue in
the face with the strain. The noise was ear-splitting.'

Vasily Klyuchevsky

Fyodor I died on 7 January 1598, bringing the 736-year Rurikid dynasty
to an end. In his will, he had extracted a promise from his wife to become
a nun after his death. But Irina Godunova claimed that he had in fact
bequeathed the throne to her and declared her intention to 'take power
for a short time, so as to protect the tsardom from tumult'.[1] Although no
woman had ever ruled Russia before in her own right – only as regent –
Patriarch Job and the Boyars' Duma pledged their loyalty to her. The
Piskaryov Chronicle even goes so far as to suggest that she was elected by
a Zemsky Sobor, stating that 'the whole Russian land' swore allegiance to
the tsaritsa, who accepted the throne at the request of 'all ranks and all
Orthodox Christians'.[2]

For nine days, Irina Godunova ruled as 'Great Sovereign'. However, the
people of Moscow called her 'shameless' and rioted. Wishing 'to prevent
great revolt,' Irina hastily relinquished power to the Boyars' Duma on
15 January. In theory, as an autocrat, she had the right to appoint her
own heir. But the tsaritsa said that the Russian people should themselves
elect a new tsar and retired to the Novodevichy Convent, accompanied by
her brother, Boris Godunov. This was a deliberate ploy to pretend that the
Godunov family was not interested in the vacant Russian throne.

The government of the country automatically passed to Patriarch Job,
who summoned a Zemsky Sobor. As the interim head of state, he played

the main role in holding the election. On 16 January, charters were sent to all the towns, informing the people that Irina had abdicated and that a Zemsky Sobor was being called to elect a new tsar. This was the first time that a Russian tsar had ever been chosen by the people and set a precedent for the next hundred years.

Job was indebted to Boris Godunov for his promotion to the rank of Russia's first ever patriarch in 1589 and supported his candidacy. But he was not confident of his success in a nationwide vote, so instead of convening a full Zemsky Sobor, he only summoned representatives from Moscow. The Sobor assembled at the Patriarch's Palace in early February 1598 and consisted of approximately 475 delegates, mainly from the upper classes. The middle classes made up a fifth of the delegates and there was no representation of the lower classes.

The patriarch did all he could to influence the election. He pointed out that Boris Godunov was the closest relative of the tsaritsa and had been the regent for Fyodor. He had a son and heir, experience in the role and was already known to foreign rulers. Job even wrote a pamphlet called *The Story of the Honest Life of the Tsar and Grand Prince Fyodor Ivanovich of All Russia*, which implied that the entire reign of the pious and saintly Fyodor had been spent in prayer, while the running of the country was left to the 'invincible warrior' Boris Godunov. The text was sent to all Russian churches and excerpts were read out at services – and to the delegates at the Zemsky Sobor.

The boyars knew that this was a deliberate distortion of the truth but were happy to support Boris as a continuation of the *status quo*. They also hoped to be rewarded for electing him. There were several other potential candidates for the throne, including Fyodor Romanov – son of Nikita Zakharin-Yuriev, later Patriarch Philaret and father of Tsar Michael – and the former proxy tsar, Simeon Bekbulatovich, who were both backed by Boris's enemies.[3] But the patriarch quickly wrapped up proceedings and, on 17 February, the Zemsky Sobor unanimously elected Boris Godunov as tsar.

That same day, Patriarch Job led a delegation from the Zemsky Sobor to the Novodevichy Convent to offer the crown to Boris Godunov. Wanting to ensure that he had broad public support, Boris now demonstratively refused the crown, telling the delegates: 'It never even entered my mind to think about the tsardom! How can I even contemplate such a height – the throne of such a great sovereign?'

Every day, Job led enormous processions of people to the convent. At a signal from the patriarch, everyone fell to the ground and begged Boris to take the crown. A contemporary recorded: 'The people were driven there by force, and bailiffs were ordered to beat without mercy those who did not want to go. These same bailiffs forced them to shriek out loud and shed tears.' Russian historian Vasily Klyuchevsky wrote:

> Numerous policemen saw to it that this communal petition was offered with 'tears and great wailing' and many people who had no tears at their command smeared their eyes with saliva so as to escape blows from the police... at a given signal they all had to bow down to the ground, and the slow or reluctant were prodded in the neck by the police; and on getting up, they all howled like wolves.[4]

But every day, Boris Godunov said that the idea of sitting 'on the most highest of royal thrones as sovereign' was simply unthinkable. Finally, on 21 February, the miracle-working icon of Our Lady of Vladimir was brought from the Dormition Cathedral. When Boris saw the famous image, he gasped: 'Why, o queen, hast thou performed such an act, coming to me?' The patriarch replied: 'She has come to carry out the will of her son, which no one has the right to resist.' The delegates then went to the cell of his sister, who exclaimed: 'Who can withstand the will of God?' She summoned Boris and finally 'convinced' him to accept the throne.

Of course, as tsaritsa, Irina could simply have named Boris as her heir before abdicating. But he needed to legitimise his position as the first member of a new dynasty in over seven centuries – and he did so by using the Zemsky Sobor. This also allowed him to safely reject any attempts by the other boyars to set limitations on his power. By initially refusing the crown, he ensured that he was unconditionally elected tsar 'by the whole land'. The only problem was that, in the sixteenth century, Russians were unaccustomed to being asked who should rule over them and regarded an elected tsar as a violation of the laws of nature. As Klyuchevsky wrote: 'To elect a tsar was, to their minds, as incongruous as to elect one's father or mother.'[5]

Boris Godunov did not even sound like a 'real' Muscovite tsar when he proclaimed upon ascending the throne: 'I swear that in my kingdom there will be no poor and no beggars! I will share my last shirt with everyone!' So when pretenders appeared – even ones with only a very shaky claim – the people inevitably sided with them. Had Godunov transformed the Zemsky Sobor into a permanent institution, instead of using it merely as an instrument in his election, he might have averted the disasters that shortly thereafter befell his person, his family and his country.

The Time of Troubles

'One woe doth tread upon another's heel, so fast they follow.'

Boris Godunov was crowned in the Dormition Cathedral on 1 September 1598 (Russia followed the Byzantine version of the Julian calendar and this was New Year's Day – the start of the 7,106th year since the Creation). The country now had a stable dynasty, as the new tsar had a son to succeed him and a daughter whom he planned to marry to a European prince. But the coronation was immediately followed by a series of disastrous events which plunged Russia into fifteen years of national calamity known as the Time of Troubles (*Smutnoye vremya*).

Between 1601 and 1603, the harvests failed and famine swept the land. Muscovites were reduced to eating grass, tree bark, dogs, cats and, when there was nothing else, the corpses of relatives and friends.[6] This was followed by a wave of epidemics, which killed a third of the population. In 1603, a number of popular revolts broke out and Irina Godunova died – poisoned, it was said, by her brother. In 1604, there was an invasion by Crimean Tatars – a Zemsky Sobor was called to deal with the matter – and a man claiming to be Tsarevich Dmitry invaded Russia with a Polish army.

Many Russians believed that all these cataclysms were a punishment from God for daring to elect a tsar. In a further sign of divine wrath, Boris Godunov died with blood pouring from his mouth, nose and eyes in April 1605. He was succeeded by his sixteen-year-old son, who was elected as Tsar Fyodor II by a hastily convened Zemsky Sobor. He only reigned for fifty days and did not live long enough to be crowned.

While Muscovites were taking their oath to the new tsar, the 'False Dmitry' was already approaching the capital with his army. The pretender was actually a renegade monk, Grishka Otrepiev, who had fled to Poland in 1602 and attracted the interest of King Sigismund III. Otrepiev had earlier been a bondsman of the Romanovs and it is highly likely that he was part of an intrigue hatched by the boyars opposed to Boris Godunov. As Klyuchevsky wrote of the False Dmitry, 'although he was baked in a Polish oven, the dough was mixed in Moscow.'[7]

'Tsar Dmitry' sent out proclamations, promising to reward those who recognised him as the rightful ruler and to kill those who did not. Town after town fell to his army, abandoning the elected tsar for the 'natural' tsar. On 1 June 1605, a large crowd broke into the Kremlin and arrested Fyodor II and his mother. Nine days later, the two of them were murdered by assassins hired by boyars – although Fyodor was strong and it took four men to kill him by grabbing his testicles and smashing his skull. Their bodies were dumped near the Lubyanka in a common grave for paupers (Boris Godunov's coffin was removed from the Archangel Cathedral and thrown alongside them). Thus ended the seven-year reign of the Godunov family.

The False Dmitry entered Moscow on 20 June 1605 and was recognised as the lawful ruler by the Boyars' Duma and the people. A month later, he was anointed as tsar in the Dormition Cathedral. He summoned his Polish wife, Maryna Mniszech, to Moscow and she was crowned the first ever 'empress of Russia' in May 1606. The couple shocked courtiers by dancing together and eating with forks – which Russians had only ever seen in pictures of the devil. Dmitry had a clean-shaven face and slicked-back reddish hair, while Maryna looked more like an Elizabethan queen than a Muscovite tsaritsa with her frizzed hair and enormous ruffs.

In 1605, the Shuisky family spread rumours that Dmitry was not really the son of Ivan the Terrible. The new tsar promptly summoned a Zemsky Sobor and handed the whole matter over to the assembly to decide. This was the first truly representative Sobor, as it contained delegates elected from all classes, including the lower ranks. Dmitry was particularly popular among the common people, who had benefited from his reforms. He had passed a law stopping peasants from becoming serfs, planned to allow foreign travel and championed religious tolerance – instantly putting Russia far ahead of the rest of Europe in the early seventeenth century.

A trial was held and the Shuiskys were sentenced to death – although Dmitry commuted the punishment to exile and later restored them to Moscow. This was a grave mistake, as Vasily Shuisky wanted the throne for himself. He promised the other boyars a share in collective government and won over the common people by appealing to popular nationalism and warning that Dmitry's Polish bodyguards were planning to kill 'the Russian tsar'.

Shortly afterwards, on the morning of 17 May 1606, Dmitry and his wife were awoken in the Kremlin by the ringing of bells, shouts and gunfire. A mob stormed into their bedroom, murdered the tsar and raped Maryna. After burning Dmitry's corpse, the boyars placed the ashes in a cannon and fired them in the direction of Poland. The deposed empress was arrested and marched with all her relatives to the Polish border.

Two days later, a paid crowd gathered on Red Square and demanded that Vasily Shuisky be crowned tsar. He was duly elected after coming to an agreement with his fellow conspirators. Shuisky's first act was to issue a decree stating that he had been elected by an expanded sitting of the Boyars' Duma which included representatives of the three estates. The Boyars' Duma promised to summon a full Zemsky Sobor 'to choose, by agreement, a tsar who would be acceptable to all.'[8] But Shuisky did not trust the provincial electors and this never happened.

Vasily Shuisky was crowned as Basil IV in the Dormition Cathedral in June 1606. After being proclaimed tsar, he announced: 'I kiss the cross and swear to the whole country not to do any hurt to anyone without the Sobor's consent.'[9] The boyars and men of other ranks advised him that 'he must not take such an oath, for that was not the custom in Muscovy; but he would not listen to anyone.'[10] Like Ivan the Terrible, Shuisky planned to rule alone by using the Zemsky Sobor as a counterbalance against the Boyars' Duma.

In theory, the tsar was now a constitutional sovereign governing in accordance with the law, based on the reverse principle that 'the master of the house does not swear loyalty to his servants and tenants.'[11] Shuisky sent an ambassador to Warsaw to justify the overthrow and murder of Dmitry, explaining that the people of Muscovy had the right to pass judgement on a tsar if he engaged in 'evil sacrilegious deeds'. A Zemsky Sobor was subsequently held in 1607 to cancel the oath to the False Dmitry.[12]

No sooner had Shuisky been crowned tsar than a second pretender appeared, also claiming to be Tsarevich Dmitry. He became known as False Dmitry II and set up camp in the summer of 1608 in the village of Tushino near Moscow, where he established an alternative capital with 100,000 inhabitants. Tushino had its own tsar (False Dmitry II), patriarch (Philaret Romanov) and a Boyars' Duma (including an ancestor of the first Soviet foreign minister, Georgy Chicherin). This second pretender also had a tsaritsa after his forces intercepted the deposed Maryna Mniszech on her way back to Poland. She agreed to recognise him as her husband in exchange for being restored to the throne as empress.

Seeking foreign assistance against the army of False Dmitry II, Shuisky signed an alliance with Sweden in return for territorial concessions. In spring 1609, Swedish troops entered Russia and occupied Novgorod and Pskov. As Sweden had been fighting Poland since 1600, this led Poland to invade Russia from the west in September 1609. After False Dmitry II fled Tushino in a dung-cart dressed as a peasant, his abandoned supporters sought an agreement with the Polish king. Led by Mikhail Saltykov, they offered to recognise the king's fourteen-year-old son Władysław as tsar, presenting their conditions in a document which was 'a complete draft of a constitutional monarchy'.[13]

The proposed agreement established the basic rights of all Russian subjects, going even further than the protections against tyranny adopted by Vasily Shuisky. These included the right to a fair trial, freedom to travel and study abroad, freedom of conscience and the promotion of men of humble rank based on merit. The tsar would share power with the Boyars' Duma and the Zemsky Sobor, which would have the authority to write and change laws, including the constitution. The Polish king agreed and the document was signed in Smolensk on 4 February 1610.

Meanwhile, revolution was breaking out in Moscow. In July 1610, after a Polish army crushed a much larger Russo-Swedish force led by Shuisky's younger brother at the Battle of Klushino, an angry crowd gathered outside the Kremlin. Declaring themselves to be a Zemsky Sobor, they shouted: 'You are no longer our tsar!' When the eighty-year-old patriarch tried to calm them down, he was pelted with earth and rubbish. After holding a hastily arranged Sobor with the people at the Serpukhov Gates, the Boyars' Duma forced Shuisky to abdicate and become a monk (he was later sent as a prisoner to Poland, where he died in 1612).

The Boyars' Duma assumed power themselves, forming a provisional government headed by Prince Fyodor Mstislavsky, which became known as the 'seven boyars' (*semiboyarschina*). The people of Moscow swore allegiance to them 'until God gives us a tsar'. But the new government was unable to convene a Zemsky Sobor to elect a new ruler, as their power did not extend beyond the gates of Moscow. Prince Mstislavsky announced that he did not wish to be tsar himself and, as he did not want any other boyar to rule either, he proposed that they elect a member of a royal family as sovereign. In August 1610, they also offered the throne to Prince Władysław of Poland, who preferred their conditions, which were less onerous than the ones he had signed back in February (he was now only obliged to delegate some of his powers to the Boyars' Duma and to call a Zemsky Sobor for very important matters).

The seven boyars assembled whomever they could find in Moscow to create the semblance of a Zemsky Sobor and duly 'elected' Władysław as tsar. They then allowed a Polish army to enter the Kremlin in September 1610. But after they had done so, Władysław's father suddenly changed his mind and said that he wanted to be tsar himself. He planned to come to Moscow and convert Russia to Roman Catholicism. Although Sigismund was recognised as tsar by the Boyars' Duma – who were now the hostages of the Poles in the Kremlin – the rest of the country regarded this as high treason. The Swedes tore up their military alliance with Russia and launched the Ingrian War to put their own pretender (False Dmitry III) on the throne.

At this point, when the Russian state had basically ceased to exist, the hitherto voiceless people suddenly stirred and re-established the country by themselves – and did so as a democracy. In October 1611, responding to proclamations issued by the imprisoned patriarch and other religious leaders, the citizens of Nizhny Novgorod rallied around their elected elder, Kuzma Minin. Over the winter, they assembled a volunteer army under the command of Prince Dmitry Pozharsky, which set off to restore and unite the rest of the country on 23 February 1612.

The liberation forces stopped for four months in Yaroslavl, where they held a 'council of the whole land' (*Sovyet vseya zemli*). This was composed of two or three 'elected representatives of every class', who came from all cities with instructions from the local citizens. Besides the delegates from the land, there was also a Church Assembly headed by Metropolitan Kirill of Rostov and Yaroslavl – now the senior religious figure after the death of the patriarch in February – and the nucleus of a new Boyars' Duma. All this constituted a fully functioning Zemsky Sobor, which was acknowledged as the supreme government not only by other Russian cities, but also by foreign powers, including Sweden and England.

The Council of the Land reopened the old administrative departments, including the foreign ministry. It appointed ambassadors and town governors, resolved legal disputes, collected taxes and minted coins bearing the name of 'the true-born tsar' Fyodor I. The result was a fully functioning, democratic executive under the general leadership of Minin and Pozharsky. However, this was not an alternative or permanent administration, but a provisional government created with the ultimate aim of electing a new monarch.

The most important task was to prevent the Polish king from reaching Moscow and being crowned tsar. The people's militia set off in July and in August arrived at the outskirts of the capital, where they joined forces with the Cossack armies of Prince Dmitry Trubetskoi already encamped there. This was the remnants of an earlier initiative by a similar 'council of the whole land' in 1611, which had collapsed due to infighting. Concluding that there were no victors in a civil war, the two sides formed a coalition government in September and, together, laid siege to the Kremlin. The Poles fended off starvation by eating their own dead, but finally surrendered on 24 October 1612.[14]

1613

'There is no true sovereign except the nation; there can be no true legislator except the people.'

Denis Diderot

All that was left to do now was to elect a new tsar – and this was also to be done by 'the whole land' through an indirect election. The final act of the provisional government, prior to dissolving itself, was to send out notices on 15 November 1612, in the names of Prince Pozharsky and Prince Trubetskoi, summoning 'ten representatives of every rank from all cities' to Moscow for 'matters of the state and land'.

The Zemsky Sobor was scheduled to start work on 6 December but had to be postponed for a month to allow the participants to arrive from all over the ruined country in the middle of winter. When it finally assembled in the Kremlin on the feast of the Epiphany, 6 January 1613, it was the largest and most representative Sobor ever held in Russia, with delegates from all classes including priests, townsfolk and even state ('black-plough') peasants. Over 800 electors arrived from at least fifty-eight towns. As Moscow lay in ruins, the only building that could accommodate so many people was the Dormition Cathedral.

The first three days were spent in fasting and prayer. On the fourth day, the Sobor passed a motion prohibiting foreign candidates – or, rather, those belonging to other faiths. This ruled out several of the contestants, including Prince Władysław of Poland, Prince Charles Philip of Sweden and even King James I of England. The Sobor also rejected the candidacy of one of the more exotic claimants – 'Tsarevich Ivan', the one-year-old son of False Dmitry II and Maryna Mniszech.[15]

The thirty remaining candidates engaged in a fierce campaign to win the election. Prince Pozharsky was said to have spent 20,000 roubles on canvassing. Prince Trubetskoi targeted the Cossack vote and 'held many feasts for all the Cossacks, forty thousand of them, inviting them to his mansion every day for a month and a half... giving them food and drink and begging them to make him tsar'. The Cossacks accepted his hospitality, 'eating and drinking and flattering him – before returning to their regiments to curse him and laugh at his madness'.[16]

The Cossacks were the most powerful group in Moscow and they wanted to see a Russian on the throne. Their chosen candidate was a frail sixteen-year-old boy, Michael Romanov, whose main advantage was being related to the last Rurikid tsar, Fyodor I. Michael's father – who had been suggested as a candidate against Boris Godunov in 1598 – was the nephew of Anastasia Zakharina-Yurieva, Fyodor's mother and the first wife of Ivan the Terrible.

The second most influential group were the boyars, who wanted a candidate of royal blood and still held out hope for the Swedish prince. One of the 'seven boyars', Fyodor Sheremetev, was related to Michael Romanov and secretly supported his candidacy. He used negative campaigning to try and persuade the other boyars to vote for Michael, smearing his inexperienced relative as a simpleton and an imbecile, who would be easy to manipulate: 'Misha Romanov is young, his reason is immature and he will suit us.'[17]

When the boyars were still not persuaded, the Cossacks resorted to fake news to support Michael's cause. Their ataman claimed that before Tsar Fyodor I had died, 'he bequeathed his tsar's staff and the rule of Russia to Prince Fyodor Nikitich Romanov.' This was Philaret Romanov, Michael's father, who had been the patriarch of Tushino and was now a captive in Poland. But, as the Cossack leader explained, 'there is his root and branch' and so 'it is befitting, according to God's will, for the tsar, sovereign and grand prince Michael to reign over the city of Moscow and all of Russia.'[18]

In a preliminary ballot held on 7 February, Michael failed to secure enough votes. The delegates decided to adjourn for two weeks and dispatch envoys to consult with the rest of the country. The Cossacks accused them of deliberately delaying the election in order to rule by themselves and incited a mob to invade the Kremlin. A Russian captured by the Swedes in 1614 testified: 'The Cossacks and common people came running with great noise and broke into the Kremlin, violently scolding the boyars and the Duma members.'[19]

The Cossacks demanded that the Zemsky Sobor swear allegiance to Michael Romanov: 'By God's will, in the reigning city of Moscow and all of Russia, let there be the tsar, sovereign and grand prince Michael Romanov!' This cry was taken up by the large crowd on the square outside, who shouted: 'Michael Romanov is to be our sovereign and we want no other!' A ballot was held and every rank duly voted for Michael, who was proclaimed tsar on 21 February 1613, following a procession round the Kremlin and a service of thanksgiving in the Dormition Cathedral.

What had started out as a democratic election ended in a military coup and a rigged vote. Ironically, the winning candidate was a minor who had not even stood for election himself – in fact, no one even knew where he was. While he may not have been the obvious choice for the tsardom, Michael won because he offered the best compromise. This was a bitter pill to swallow for many of the losing candidates, such as Prince Pozharsky, who had headed the liberation movement and was himself a direct descendant of Rurik. As for Prince Trubetskoi, 'his face turned black with grief and he fell ill and lay for three months without leaving his house.'[20]

Letters announcing the election of Michael Romanov were sent to every town in Russia and abroad – leading to fresh attempts at foreign interference. A French mercenary in Polish service, Jacques Margeret, wrote to King James I, urging him to send an army to Russia. He explained that the Cossacks had chosen 'this child' solely to manipulate him and rule themselves – and that most Russians would prefer an English invasion. When the Poles learnt that Michael had been elected tsar, they sent troops to find and kill him. They had heard that he was living on his mother's estate in the village of Domnino near Kostroma but did not know the way. A local peasant, Ivan Susanin, saved Michael's life by leading them into a swamp, where they all perished.

The Zemsky Sobor assembled a large delegation of clergymen, boyars and public officials, headed by the archbishop of Ryazan, with the instructions to 'travel to His Majesty, Tsar and Grand Prince Michael of All Russia, in Yaroslavl or wherever he might be'. They eventually tracked Michael down to the Ipatiev Monastery in Kostroma, where he and his mother had taken refuge. Arriving on 14 March, the delegates asked him to accept the throne. But his mother replied that she would not let her son become tsar, as the Muscovite people had either killed or been disloyal to their previous rulers. They admitted that this was true, but 'we have now been punished and have come to an agreement in all the towns.' After pleading, arguing and finally threatening Michael's mother, the envoys eventually secured her blessing on 19 March. Michael returned with them to Moscow and was crowned tsar on 11 July 1613 on the eve of his seventeenth birthday.

During the first years of his reign, Michael was controlled by his domineering mother, who was known as 'the great nun Martha'. This lasted until her husband, Philaret Romanov, returned from Polish captivity in 1619. He was canonically enthroned as patriarch, becoming co-tsar in a diarchy with the title of 'great sovereign'. Philaret had previously written that he would rather die in prison than see a return to the absolute power of the old tsars. But he changed his mind following the election of his own son and actively rolled back democracy after being made co-ruler in 1619.

4

The Seventeenth Century –
The Age of the Zemsky Sobor

Tsar Michael

'Formerly, it seemed easier to imagine a tsar without the people than a state without a tsar. Now experience had shown that a state could, at least, for a time, exist without a sovereign, but neither a sovereign nor a state could exist without the people.'

Vasily Klyuchevsky

In May 1613, the Zemsky Sobor issued a statutory act called *The Certified Charter Confirming the Election of Michael Fyodorovich Romanov as Tsar of the Muscovite State*. This lengthy document did not contain any 'constitutional points' and restored the autocracy to the way it had been before the Time of Troubles. The Sobor swore allegiance not only to Michael, but also to his heirs, indicating that the new dynasty would not face re-election after his death.

Contemporary reports suggest that there was an attempt to introduce a 'managed autocracy' by making Michael promise always to consult with the Boyars' Duma and not pass the death sentence on any member of the nobility. A Swedish prisoner-of-war in Russia later reported second-hand that Michael had sworn an oath not to make laws or declare war by himself and to always adhere to the rule of law on important matters.[1] But there are no traces of any limitations on the tsar's power in the official documents.

The Zemsky Sobor still held a lot of sway during Michael's first decade on the throne, when it sat practically incessantly as a permanent institution and sometimes acted as the government. The dynasty was still weak and the treasury was empty, so the tsar was unable to take any important foreign or domestic decisions without first consulting the Sobor. His decrees began with the words, 'We, the Great Sovereign, have held a Sobor and resolved...' or 'According to Our decree as Great Sovereign and by resolution of the Whole Russian Land...' The Sobor convened in 1613 to elect a new tsar appears to have remained in Moscow until 1615, before being immediately replaced by a new assembly following fresh elections.

In 1613, the Zemsky Sobor sent a charter to King Sigismund III of Poland on the termination of hostilities and the exchange of prisoners. In 1614, it also sent notices to the Don and Volga Cossacks and dispatched a deputation to deal with rebel Cossacks operating north of Moscow, furnished with written instructions: 'At the Sobor... all ranks of the people have decided...' Other measures taken to restore order were a law of 1614 confiscating the estates of any landowner deserting from the army and an emergency capital-gains tax of 20% ('fifth money') on all townsfolk to finance the militia. Tax collectors were given copies of the Sobor's resolution as confirmation of their powers – although the text was poorly worded and some of the agents misinterpreted it as a property or income tax, leading to arguments and even riots.

A new Zemsky Sobor was summoned in January 1616. Every city was requested to elect and send three delegates to Moscow, representing the merchants, the artisans and the state peasantry. Notices were sent to towns as far away as Arkhangelsk and Perm. In April 1616, the delegates gathered in Moscow and presented themselves to the duma secretary, Pyotr Tretyakov, at the Ambassadorial Prikaz. The main aim of this assembly was to approve a new emergency tax, which raised an additional 190,000 roubles for the budget.

In September 1616, the Sobor discussed the ongoing peace negotiations with Sweden – although rather than debate the terms themselves, they appear to have consulted with the government. In June 1617, they considered the request of the English ambassador, Sir John Meyrick, to allow English merchants to transport goods duty-free through Russia to Persia (permission was denied after consultations with Russian traders). Other business included planning the defence of Moscow against a fresh attack by Prince Władysław in 1618, confirming Philaret Romanov as patriarch and updating the country's tax records in 1619. One of the final acts of this Sobor was to summon new representatives from every town in 1619 to 'tell of their grievances, molestations and plunder', so that the tsar could learn of 'their needs and hardships and all their deficiencies' and 'might try to arrange everything for the best'.[2]

When Poland broke the terms of the Truce of Deulino in 1621, the Zemsky Sobor approved the tsar's proposal to raise an army and called for a declaration of war in alliance with Sweden, Turkey and the Crimean khanate. The clergy promised to pray for victory, the boyars and servicemen pledged to fight 'not sparing our lives' and the tradesmen vowed to donate as much money as they could afford. This Sobor finished work in 1622 and no further assemblies were held until 1631. By this time, Michael felt more secure on the throne and only summoned the Sobor as a last resort – just like his contemporary, Charles I of England, who did not call any parliaments at all from 1629 to 1640.

After King Sigismund died in April 1632, the tsar held a Zemsky Sobor, which voted unanimously to declare war on Poland to try and win back the lands lost in 1618. Sitting in the Kremlin in the Banqueting Chamber (*Stolovaya palata*), the assembly raised money for the war by setting taxes and a voluntary subscription called appeal money. The clergy contributed from their private funds, while the boyars and servicemen promised to give what they could. The Sobor also elected the military commanders – Mikhail Shein and Artemy Izmailov.

The Zemsky Sobor met again in 1633 to collect further 'voluntary contributions' for assisting the armed forces in 1634 and to levy another round of 'fifth money' – without which the treasury 'could not carry on'. All the ranks represented replied that 'they would give money according to their means, as much as they could spare.'[3] The tsar thanked the Sobor and assured the delegates that he 'would always remember the people's coming to his assistance and would show favours to them in the future in every possible way'.[4]

In 1637, Russia was drawn into a dispute with the Ottoman Empire after Don Cossacks seized the Turkish fortress of Azov. The matter was initially discussed at two Sobors in 1637 and 1639. In 1641, the Turks raised an army of a quarter of a million men to recapture the stronghold, but were repulsed by the 6,000 Cossack defenders, who offered the fortress to Tsar Michael. In January 1642, the Zemsky Sobor met to discuss the dilemma. The tsar put two questions to the assembly: 'Are we to go to war with the Turks over Azov? And, if so, where is the money to come from?'

Fearing a serious entanglement with Turkey, the Sobor decided not to support the Cossacks. But opinions were sharply divided, based mainly on narrow class and financial interests. The clergy said that this was a military matter and that their role was simply to pray for victory and contribute whatever money they could afford. The Moscow nobility left the decision to the tsar but suggested sending volunteers – although two noblemen vigorously dissented and issued a statement in favour of accepting Azov and sharing the burdens of any war among all social ranks. The middle and lower classes were in favour of war but complained bitterly about ruinous taxation and begged the sovereign 'to consider their poverty'.

Although the provincial gentry were prepared to 'lay down their heads' against the enemy, they asked that the recruits be assembled from all classes of society and added: 'We are despoiled worse than by the infidel Turks and Crimeans by Moscow lawyers, unjust courts of law, and all the wrongs they inflict on us.'[5] Two of their submissions were more like radical political pamphlets, sharply criticising the state of Russia and presenting a full programme of reforms. They were particularly critical of the Moscow bureaucrats, who had grown rich 'through bribery and corruption' and 'built themselves splendid mansions such as in the old days even men of noble lineage had not dwelt in'.[6]

These mutual incriminations reflected the fundamental disunity of the Zemsky Sobor. The representatives of each class attacked one another, unable to find any common cause, just a conflict of interests. The segregation of the Sobor into different ranks sitting in different rooms prevented the assembly from working as one to extract concessions from the tsar and limit royal power – just as their parliamentary colleagues were doing over in England. In January 1642, while the Zemsky Sobor

COMPARISON OF THE ENGLISH & RUSSIAN PARLIAMENTS (17th CENTURY)

	House of Commons	Zemsky Sobor
Limited power of monarch	✓	✗
Increased power of monarch	✗	✓
Elected monarch	✗	✓
Executed monarch	✓	✗
Initiated legislation	✓	✗
Amended legislation	✓	✓
Elected members	✓	✓
Salary	✗	✗
Expenses	✗	✓
Representation of population	2%	4%
Property qualification	✓	✗
Upper classes	✓	✓
Middle classes	✓	✓
Lower classes	✗	✓
Tax-raising powers	✓	✓
Foreign & defence policy	✗	✓
Divisions	political parties	social classes

was wrangling over the Azov question, the House of Commons rose up against Charles I after he entered the chamber and tried to arrest five MPs – an event which led to the king's overthrow and the establishment of a republic until 1660.

Tsar Alexis

After the death of Tsar Michael in 1645, two delegates were sent from each town to 'elect' a new tsar. This was the sixteen-year-old tsarevich Alexis, son of the dead monarch. He had been prepared for the role from birth and there were no other candidates, but the precedent had been set for the Zemsky Sobor to technically elect the tsar, adding a democratic veneer to his absolute power.

Grigory Kotoshikhin, a Russian diplomat who later emigrated to Sweden, wrote that Alexis 'was elected tsar and did not sign any conditions that the previous tsars gave and was not required to'.[7] By this time, the tsar generally felt strong enough to govern without consulting the people, although the practice of holding Sobors did not end completely. Under Alexis, the Zemsky Sobor met five times – half the number which his father had summoned and only in the first eight years of his reign.

Tsar Alexis faced an early challenge to his authority when the Salt Riot erupted in Moscow in 1648. Angry crowds lynched every corrupt official they could find (plus some who probably were not) and 2,000 people were killed in the violence. One of the demands of the protestors was the calling of a Zemsky Sobor to compile a new code of laws. An assembly was convened in September 1648 and duly issued the 'Sobor Code' (*Sobornoye ulozheniye*) in January 1649.

This Zemsky Sobor was more like a rubber-stamp parliament and the delegates were not even asked for their advice or agreement. Their role was mainly reduced to listening to the draft of the new codex, which was read out to the elected delegates in the Ambassadors' Reception Chamber (*Otvetnaya palata*) in the Kremlin, while the clergy and boyars sat elsewhere in the presence of the tsar. They could only petition the tsar to change various articles, but not compose any amendments themselves. Ironically, the representatives ended up institutionalising serfdom by insisting on more extreme restrictions on movement than the tsar himself desired, effectively turning four-fifths of the population into slaves.[8]

A Zemsky Sobor was called in 1650 following major uprisings in Pskov and Novgorod, where the local citizens had set up their own regional governments. A delegation was sent from Moscow to pacify the rebels using the high moral authority of the Sobor. In 1651, the Zemsky Sobor voiced its support for the Cossack uprising against Polish rule in Ukraine, but it did not provide any concrete assistance.

After the Cossack leader, Bogdan Khmelnitsky, offered sovereignty over Ukraine to the tsar, a Zemsky Sobor was convened in 1653. This assembly took the historical decision to reunite Ukraine with Russia and declare war on Poland. However, many delegates opposed the motion – some feared an international backlash and foreign sanctions, while others thought that the freedom-loving Ukrainians might infect Russians with dangerous ideas.

This was the last Sobor summoned by Tsar Alexis. For the next twenty-three years, he governed alone, only consulting with the Boyars' Duma and the Church Assembly. The Russian people now had no voice at all and any murmurs of dissent were actively suppressed. As Samuel Collins, formerly personal physician to Tsar Alexis, wrote in 1671: 'He has his spies in every corner, and nothing is done or said at any feast, public meeting, burial, or wedding but he knows it.'[9]

The stifling of democracy contributed to further and greater waves of public disorder. There was the Copper Riot in Moscow in 1662, an uprising at the Solovki Monastery in the White Sea from 1668 to 1676 and the revolt of Stepan Razin in southern Russia from 1670 to 1671, which developed into a mass political movement and the largest jacquerie in Europe in the seventeenth century. Razin's rebellion was the most dangerous, because his 'Cossack republic' on the Don represented a democratic alternative to 'the increasingly centralised and bureaucratic despotism of Muscovy'.[10]

Fyodor III

Tsar Alexis died in 1676 and was succeeded by his son, Fyodor III.[11] There was no Zemsky Sobor, as Alexis had already removed the formal process of electing a new tsar by holding a ceremony on Red Square in 1674, in the presence of the senior clergy, Boyars' Duma and foreign ambassadors, in which he formally designated his eldest son as his heir. This single act was enough to lend legitimacy to the accession of Fyodor, although the attempt to simply bequeath power in the presence of the people, with their tacit consent, did not take root.

Fyodor III might not have been elected by a Zemsky Sobor, but he immediately showed his willingness to consult with the people. One month after becoming tsar, he met with elected representatives of the merchantry to discuss ways of improving trade with Holland and Persia. The result was the signing of a new trading agreement with the Dutch. In 1678, he held a council with the upper clergy and boyars to debate the Russo-Turkish War of 1676–81. In 1681, he summoned elected representatives from the towns to discuss taxes and municipal services. Finally, in 1682, he consulted with servicemen on the subject of military reforms.

The young tsar undertook many other reforms, mostly under the influence of his first wife, Agafia Gruszecka, who advocated the shaving of beards and the opening of Polish and Latin schools in Moscow. In 1676, he abolished the hated secret police department, the Bureau of Secret Affairs. The practice of mutilation was banned in 1679. After the Zemsky Sobor of 1681–82 recommended the abolition of the system of precedence (*mestnichestvo*), the tsar symbolically burned the ancient books of rank in January 1682. Unfortunately, Fyodor was disabled from birth – his legs were so swollen that he had to be carried to his coronation – and he died in May 1682 after only six years on the throne.

Peter the Great

'In Russia, there was a pretender in almost every reign to the end of the eighteenth century – and for lack of one in Peter the Great's time, popular rumour declared the tsar himself to be a pretender.'

Vasily Klyuchevsky

Fyodor III had no children and did not designate any heir. He had two younger brothers – the fifteen-year-old Ivan (son of Maria Miloslavskaya) and the nine-year-old Peter (son of Natalia Naryshkina). Normally, the choice would have fallen on Ivan, but he was physically and mentally deficient, whereas Peter was strong, healthy and big for his age.

Peter was technically elected tsar by a Zemsky Sobor on the day of Fyodor's death. After filing past the dead tsar's body and stopping to kiss his hand, Patriarch Joachim and his archbishops met with the boyars to discuss which of the two boys should be crowned. They concluded that they had to ask 'the people' – which at that moment meant the crowd gathered outside the palace windows. When the question was put to them, the majority shouted for Peter. When consulted, the bishops and boyars gave the same reply, so the patriarch gave Peter his blessing.

But they had not reckoned with Ivan's six elder sisters, who saw power slipping into the hands of the rival Naryshkin clan. They incited the Streltsy guards to revolt and march on the Kremlin, where they murdered several members of Peter's family and demanded a change to the occupancy of the throne. So a second Zemsky Sobor was held and this time, in the interests of 'popular reconciliation', both brothers were ordained as co-tsars with Ivan's sister Sophia as regent.

This was the last time that a tsar was ever chosen by a Zemsky Sobor. Peter I later decreed that every ruler would appoint his own successor – and the people would have no say in the matter. In 1689, Peter overthrew Sophia and incarcerated her in the Novodevichy Convent. Ivan V died in 1696, leaving Peter as the sole ruler. In 1697, he set off on a European tour, spending nearly a year in Holland and England.

During his time in London, Peter was invited to the Houses of Parliament. He went incognito and watched from an upper gallery as King William III gave his assent to several bills, causing a fellow observer to remark: 'Today, I have seen the rarest thing in the world – one monarch on the throne and another on the roof.' Peter listened to the debate with an interpreter and declared that, while he would never accept parliamentary limitations on royal power, 'it is good to hear subjects speaking truthfully and openly to their king. This is what we must learn from the English!'[12]

Peter was forced to hurry back to Russia to deal with another Streltsy uprising. The last Zemsky Sobor was summoned in 1698 to put Sophia on trial for conspiring with the Streltsy guards, although no incriminating evidence was found. No further Sobors were held during Peter's reign or ever again. After his recent experiences with the Streltsy revolts, he regarded any form of dissent as a disorder requiring instant suppression, and the absolute power of the tsar – emperor from 1721 – increased during his reign. In any case, the transformations which Peter pushed through were so radical that it would not have been possible to hold any parliamentary discussions on the matter. After visiting the West, he resolved to create a whole new type of state – and had no intention of asking the people whether they agreed or not.[13]

Although Peter's sweeping reforms were based on what he had seen in Europe, he had no intention of importing Western-style democracy. His sole aim was to make the Russian state stronger and more efficient, especially as a military power. The tsar wanted Western science, technology and culture – but not its parliamentary democracy. Peter was democratic only in the way that he forced every class to toil equally for the benefit of the state. As Mikhail Khodorkovsky said in 2003, 'everyone thinks that he pushed Russia closer to the West, but in reality he, much like Ivan the Terrible, pushed it towards the East, by devaluing human life.'[14]

The Zemsky Sobor represented the old Muscovite past and was swept away, along with all the other medieval symbols, customs and ways. The Boyars' Duma was abolished and replaced by a Senate in 1711. The Senate was originally created to act as a temporary administrative commission while Peter was away fighting wars, but it became a permanent body mainly charged with enforcing his decrees. The old state offices (*prikazy*) were replaced in 1718 by 'colleges' based on the Swedish system. Regional government was also reorganised along Swedish lines – although the hasty introduction of Western institutions proved incompatible with the realities of Russian life, requiring further changes in 1722.[15]

5

Imperial Russia

The Eighteenth Century: Female Power

'...mon âme a toujours été singulièrement républicaine.'
Catherine II to Johann Georg Zimmermann

Peter the Great died in 1725 and was succeeded by his fun-loving second wife, Catherine I. In 1726, she founded the Supreme Privy Council, which displaced the Senate as 'a sort of permanent super-cabinet under the presidency of the ruler'.[1] After Catherine's death in 1727, the country was briefly ruled by Peter the Great's grandson, Peter II, who died unexpectedly on 19 January 1730 without appointing an heir.

The Supreme Privy Council had been secretly aspiring to share sovereignty by limiting the autocracy and met that same day to choose a new ruler. Believing that it would be easier to manipulate an unmarried woman, Prince Dmitry Golitsyn proposed Anna Ioannovna, a daughter of Ivan V and widowed countess of Courland. She was offered the throne in return for signing a series of 'conditions' which would have transformed Russia into a constitutional monarchy. The empress could only rule with the agreement of the Privy Council and was not allowed independently to declare war, make peace, sign treaties, raise taxes, marry or appoint an heir. But this was still better than being a widow in a provincial capital, so Anna happily signed the conditions on 25 January.

Arriving in Moscow in February 1730, the empress quickly established close ties with the imperial guards and the minor nobility. They secretly pledged their support to Anna, who publicly tore up the signed conditions on 25 February. The Supreme Privy Council was abolished three days later and absolute rule was restored. Had the plan succeeded, Russia would have become only the second country in recent history – after England in 1689 – to constitutionally limit the power of its sovereign. Dmitry Golitsyn had drafted plans for a senate of thirty-six members and elected chambers of the nobility and urban classes. Looking back on his unsuccessful attempt to become the author of Russia's first constitution, the prince sadly said: 'The banquet was ready, but the invited guests proved unworthy.'[2] Anna Ioannovna never forgave him and he was later sentenced to life imprisonment in Schlüsselburg fortress, where he died in 1737.

The following two empresses, Elizabeth Petrovna and Catherine the Great, came to the throne in palace coups with the help of the imperial guards. Empress Elizabeth was the younger daughter of Peter the Great and announced that she would reign in the spirit of her late father. However, on the eve of her own seizure of power from the infant Ivan VI, she vowed that, if successful, she would not sign a single death sentence as empress. Elizabeth kept that promise and there were no executions in Russia between 1741 and 1761 – a time when, in Great Britain, even members of the House of Lords were beheaded in public in the aftermath of the Jacobite rebellion of 1745.

Elizabeth left the throne to her German-born nephew, Peter III, who immediately freed the nobility from compulsory state service. He passed a law secularising church property which his predecessor had refused to sign, reduced the salt tax and proclaimed religious freedom – once again putting Russia far ahead of Western Europe. But he made so many enemies at court and among the guards – particularly after withdrawing Russia from the Seven Years' War when she was on the point of victory over Prussia – that the private coup of his wife, Catherine the Great, was more like a popular movement.

After overthrowing her husband in June 1762, Catherine allowed her chief ministerial adviser, Count Nikita Panin, to draft a project limiting the autocracy. For twelve years, Panin had been Russia's ambassador to Sweden, where he had become a firm advocate of constitutional monarchy. He proposed creating a supreme legislative body called the Imperial Council. The empress would appoint its half-dozen members, including four secretaries of state for the army, navy, foreign affairs and the interior. Any decree or regulation in these areas would require both the monarch's signature and the agreement of the appropriate minister. There would also be a supreme executive organ called the Senate, which had the right to reject any legislation which infringed upon the 'state laws or the common welfare'.

Catherine signed a decree establishing the Imperial Council in December 1762, but then changed her mind and removed her signature from the document.[3] Although she made a great display of her liberal values – she invited Denis Diderot to St Petersburg and corresponded with Voltaire for fifteen years – the empress was staunchly convinced of the need for absolute rule in Russia. She readily agreed with Voltaire that monarchy was the only rational form of government – provided that the monarch was enlightened, of course. Voltaire himself openly despised democracy, which he called 'government by the rabble'.[4]

Although Catherine firmly believed in autocracy, she still had to consider public opinion. She once discussed this with Vasily Popov, the aide of her long-term lover, Prince Grigory Potemkin:

> It is not as easy as you think... In the first place, my orders would not be carried out unless they were the kind of orders which *could* be carried out... I examine the circumstances, I take advice, I consult the enlightened part of the people, and in this way I find out what sort of effect my laws will have. And when I am already convinced in advance of good approval, then I issue my orders, and have the pleasure of observing what you call blind obedience. That is the foundation of unlimited power. But, believe me, they will not obey blindly when orders are not adapted to the opinion of the people.[5]

Public hopes were raised in 1766, when Catherine announced a measure long forgotten in Russia. This was the nationwide election of deputies – only not for a parliament, but to compile a new code of laws. Every town or district was to send one delegate to Moscow, creating an assembly representing all classes and nationalities in the Russian Empire. The 564 members of the commission arrived with detailed instructions from the local inhabitants on their various needs and problems – and how best to solve them.

When the deputies gathered in Moscow in July 1767, Catherine presented them with her 'Instructions for the Guidance of the Assembly' (*Nakaz*). This was a statement of legal principles, based on the works of Montesquieu and Beccaria, proclaiming the equality of all men before the law and condemning the death penalty, torture and serfdom. Predating the American Declaration of Independence by nine years, the document was so radical that it was banned in France – even after Catherine's ministers had insisted on removing at least half of the original text.

Over a period of eighteen months, the commission held 203 sittings, but ultimately achieved nothing. Every conceivable topic was discussed and all sections of the population submitted their various grievances. But when some of the delegates suggested abolishing serfdom, the nobility urged the empress to curb such dangerous ideas. Fortunately, the outbreak of war with the Ottoman Empire gave Catherine an excuse to send the deputies home in December 1768.

As hopes of reform turned to disappointment, discontent mounted, and the empress faced the largest uprising in Europe prior to the French Revolution. Like the earlier insurrection of Stepan Razin, it started among a band of Cossacks, who were led by Yemelian Pugachev. Claiming to be Catherine's overthrown husband, Peter III, Pugachev issued decrees abolishing serfdom and granting land, civil rights, religious freedom and liberty 'from taxes, levies, recruitment, evil landowners and corrupt judges'.[6] The movement attracted over a million disgruntled peasants and ethnic minorities, turning into a full-blown revolution and civil war in 1773. The rebels captured several major cities until they were defeated by the regular army in 1774. Pugachev stood trial in Moscow and was executed in 1775.

The outbreak of the French Revolution in 1789 frightened the empress, who became increasingly intolerant and reactionary. When Alexander Radischev published a critical report on the state of the nation in 1790, she had him exiled to Siberia. Catherine died in 1796 and was succeeded by her son Paul, who quickly earned a reputation for petty tyranny. As a young man, he had dreamt of justice and the rule of law. But the 'Russian Hamlet' hated his mother for the murder of his father and he reversed her reforms – such as her charters of 1785 granting a limited degree of self-government to the nobility and the towns. The upper classes chafed under Paul's despotism and he even persecuted his own family. In March 1801, the emperor was murdered in his bedchamber in a palace coup and replaced by his eldest son, Alexander I.

The Nineteenth Century: Male Power

'"Everything is strained to such a degree that it will certainly break," said Pierre – as those who examine the actions of any government have always said since governments began.'

Leo Tolstoy, *War and Peace*

Ascending the throne in 1801, Alexander I immediately published a manifesto promising to rule according to the laws and spirit of his grandmother, Catherine the Great. She had personally supervised his education and had chosen a Swiss republican and revolutionary, Frédéric-César de La Harpe, as his tutor. In his early letters, Alexander even toyed with the idea of introducing representative government to relieve him of his duties as an autocrat, so that he could retire abroad. He was influenced at the start of his reign by four young friends, who were known collectively as the 'private committee'. They drew up endless plans for reforms, but little was done beyond reorganising the State Council and the Senate. As Alexander gained experience, he abandoned their ideas and was then sidetracked by the Napoleonic Wars.

After signing the Treaty of Tilsit with Napoleon in 1807, Russia was drawn into the Continental System and war with Sweden. Victory in 1809 brought Russia the Grand Duchy of Finland, which was allowed to retain its ancient liberties and constitution as an autonomous part of the Russian Empire. Although the Finnish Diet was not called until 1863, elections were then held on a regular basis and it met every three years. In 1906, the Grand Duchy of Finland would become the first territory in Europe to grant women the right to vote and run for office. They first exercised these rights in March 1907, when sixty-two women stood for election and nineteen were elected to the Diet.[7]

In 1808, Alexander returned to the idea of political reforms and asked Mikhail Speransky to draw up plans for a complete reorganisation of the way the country was governed. As Sergei Shakhrai, one of the authors of the 1993 Russian constitution, observed: 'Speransky solved an extremely challenging task – how to combine a monarchy, parliament and responsible government in a federatively structured state... the emperor would have become an arbiter standing outside the branches of power.'[8] Speransky's draft project divided the country into administrative units, each with its own parliament, headed by an Imperial Duma meeting annually in St Petersburg. But Alexander could not bring himself to sign such a radical document and dismissed Speransky from office in March 1812.

The following years were taken up with the Patriotic War against Napoleon, who invaded Russia in June 1812. The final victory in 1815 resulted in Russia acquiring the Kingdom of Poland, which was granted one of the most liberal constitutions in Europe. The legislative assembly (Sejm) consisted of a senate nominated by the tsar and a chamber of deputies elected by the propertied and professional classes. The Sejm controlled taxation and the government was responsible to parliament.

Poland was also granted freedom of the press and religion. However, the Sejm was rarely summoned. On one of the rare occasions when it met, Alexander's viceroy, his brother Constantine, publicly declared that he prayed to God for deafness – or, better still, to cut off the tongues of the Polish parliamentarians.

Alexander retrieved Speransky's plans from the archives in 1818 and hinted, at the opening of the Polish parliament, that he was preparing a surprise for his own people. But nothing came of it. While he readily granted constitutions to Finland and Poland, he did not seem to think that Russians were worthy of the same. The emperor once told the French ambassador, Comte de La Ferronnays: 'I like constitutional institutions and think that any orderly person must like them. But can they be introduced equally for all nations? Are all nations ready to accept them to an equal degree? I do not know.'[9] Many Russian rulers shared Alexander's view – forgetting that it was the Russian people who had, in national emergencies, come to their rescue and saved the country. Alexander abolished serfdom in Estland in 1816, Courland in 1817 and Livonia in 1819 – but not in Russia, whose serfs had defeated Napoleon's army in 1812.

Alexander I could be very democratic in his personal behaviour. Every year on 1 January he threw open the doors of his palace to everyone in St Petersburg, including

> ...simple bearded peasants and serfs, if they were decently dressed... the Winter Palace was sometimes invaded by up to 30,000 people. Foreigners never ceased to marvel at the order and decorum of the crowd and the trust of the sovereign in his subjects, who crowded around him for five or six hours... Absolutely no etiquette was observed, yet no one abused their proximity to the emperor.[10]

The Napoleonic Wars took many young and educated officers all across Europe to Paris, where their minds were opened to the latest political ideas. Returning to Russia, they formed several secret societies. Pavel Pestel headed a group in the south that wanted a republic, although most joined the more moderate 'northern' society led by Nikita Muravyov, which preferred a constitutional monarchy. A chance to realise these plans came on 1 December 1825, when Alexander I suddenly died and there was confusion over who would succeed him. Constantine was the next in line, but he had renounced his rights to the throne after marrying a

Polish woman and not told anyone – not even the next brother, Nicholas. Both proclaimed the other as emperor and the Russian crown was passed around 'like a cup of tea which nobody wanted'.[11]

The conspirators – who became known as the 'Decembrists' – planned to exploit the temporary interregnum by replacing the monarchy with a provisional government, which would issue a constitution and hold free and democratic elections to a popular assembly. On 14 December 1825, they led 3,000 men onto Senate Square in the centre of St Petersburg, aiming to prevent the Senate and the army from taking their oaths to the new tsar. But Nicholas surrounded the rebels with 12,000 loyal troops and, after a stand-off lasting several hours, he gave the order to open fire. Over 1,000 men were killed and five of the ringleaders were put on trial and executed (120 others were exiled to Siberia or sentenced to hard labour).

Passing sentence on the Decembrists in July 1826, the new emperor vowed that conditions in Russia would be improved through gradual reforms and 'perfection of the national institutions'. He held an inquiry into the reasons for the uprising and compiled a digest of the testimony and opinions of some of those brought to trial. But although he often consulted this document, he never implemented any of its points. A secret committee presided over by Count Victor Kochubei spent six years trying to draw up a scheme of reforms, but ultimately achieved nothing.

Nicholas had been tutored by a French-Swiss émigré, Baron du Puget, who taught him to hate liberal ideas. As the third son, he was never expected to rule and had been destined for a military career. He was a harsh disciplinarian who introduced rigid censorship and ran the whole state like an army unit under the official ideology of 'Orthodoxy, autocracy, nationalism'. He crushed the Polish uprising of November 1830 and abolished the Polish constitution and parliament in 1832. On the other hand, he was personally capable of 'democratic' behaviour. A pupil of the Gatchina Orphans Institute remembered the day they were visited by the tsar: 'When it was time to depart, he let the noisy crowd of laughing children carry him outside in their arms. When he was getting in his sledge, one of the boys even pinched the emperor on the backside, but Nicholas only wagged a finger at him.'[12]

Nicholas I died in 1855 during the Crimean War, which exposed the failings of his reactionary system. Facing military defeat at home and diplomatic isolation abroad, Nicholas's son and heir, Alexander II, realised that fundamental changes were required. Public opinion fell behind the young emperor, who was advised and supported by an enthusiastic team of like-minded liberals, including his brother, Grand Duke Constantine Nikolaevich, and his aunt, Princess Charlotte of Württemberg (Grand Duchess Elena Pavlovna).[13]

Alexander's most famous accomplishment was the emancipation of the serfs in 1861, for which he became known as the 'tsar-liberator'. The abolition of serfdom was followed by reforms of the judiciary, army, finances and education. In 1864, a new form of local government was introduced in the countryside known as the *zemstvo*. This was an elected assembly with extensive powers to raise money through taxation, which was then spent on hospitals, schools, welfare and roads.

The Zemstvo law of 1864 was extremely important, because it finally signalled the return of representative government in Russia. While this was only at the provincial level, many observers supposed that it was only a matter of time before it would be extended to the national level. This logical sequence of events was known in Russia as 'crowning the building' – the zemstvos were the foundations and the city dumas were the walls, but the building still lacked a 'roof', meaning a parliament and a constitution.

In January 1865, the Moscow gentry petitioned the emperor 'to gather elected people from the Russian land to discuss the common needs of the state'. But Alexander II rejected this proposal, emphasising his own exclusive right of initiative, and the parliamentary issue was laid to rest for over a decade. In the meantime, Russia started falling behind Asian countries, as Japan debated which constitution to adopt following the Meiji Restoration in 1868 and the Ottoman Empire established a parliament in 1876.

Alexander II ran in an election himself in 1862, when Greece held a plebiscite to choose a new head of state. There was no official list of candidates and Greeks were free to select their own choice of ruler or preferred form of government. When the results were published in February 1863, Alexander II came fourth with 1,841 votes. The plebiscite was won by Queen Victoria's second son – and Alexander's future son-in-law – Prince Alfred, who got 230,016 votes. However, the London Conference of 1832 barred members of the British and Russian ruling houses from occupying the Greek throne. The crown was eventually offered to Prince William of Denmark (who had only received six votes).

Throughout the 1870s, large sections of Russian society continued to press for representative government. Liberals favoured a Western-style parliament, while Slavophiles proposed resurrecting the Zemsky Sobor. All this occurred against a background of political assassinations carried out by a revolutionary organisation called the People's Will (*Narodnaya volya*). One of their members gained employment at the Winter Palace and placed a time-bomb beneath the imperial dining room on 5 February 1880. By chance, the whole family happened to be dining half an hour later that day and so escaped the blast, although a dozen palace guards were killed.

A week later, Alexander appointed a Supreme Executive Commission with special powers to deal with the terrorist threat. The chairman, Count Mikhail Loris-Melikov, convinced the emperor that the best countermeasure would be to start implementing plans for an elected parliament. On 1 March 1881, Alexander II approved Loris-Melikov's project for a consultative legislative body, announcing that he had taken 'the first step towards a constitution'. But just two hours later, he was murdered by terrorists as he drove along the Catherine Canal in St Petersburg.

The assassinated 'tsar-liberator' was succeeded by his more authoritarian son, Alexander III. He immediately issued the Manifesto of Unshakable Autocracy, asserting his 'faith in the strength and rightness of autocratic power' and his firm intention to 'preserve it from any encroachment'.[14] Count Loris-Melikov and other liberal ministers were replaced by conservatives. The new minister of the interior, Count Nikolai Ignatiev, was also dismissed after he suggested holding a Zemsky Sobor at Alexander's coronation in Moscow.

Alexander III was heavily influenced by his former law tutor, Konstantin Pobedonostsev, an extreme reactionary known as the 'high priest of social stagnation'.[15] Pobedonostsev believed that constitutions were 'a fundamental evil' and that parliamentary government was 'one of the greatest illustrations of human delusion'. He wrote to Alexander III in March 1883: 'The blood freezes in the veins of a Russian at the very thought of what would have happened if the project of Count Loris-Melikov and his friends had been implemented.'[16]

Alexander III abandoned the 'criminal and hasty step towards a constitution' and restricted the electoral rights of the peasants in his Zemstvo law of 1890. On the other hand, he claimed to have been impressed by the British parliamentary system when attending a debate in the House of Commons in 1873. He signed a military and political alliance with republican France and was the only Russian ruler to marry the daughter of a constitutional monarch, Princess Dagmar of Denmark.

Gently but persistently urged on by her father, King Christian IX, she tried to steer her husband in a more democratic direction, but had more success with her weaker son, Nicholas II.[17]

Nicholas II gave an early indication of his own attitude towards democracy after becoming tsar in 1894. He was sent a traditional message of congratulations by the Tver Zemstvo, a stronghold of liberalism, which hoped that 'the voice of the people's need would be heard from the heights of the throne.' The new tsar responded by expressing his 'extreme astonishment and dissatisfaction' in a speech on 17 January 1895:

> I know that recently in some rural assemblies the voices have been heard of people carried away by senseless daydreams of the representatives of the zemstvos participating in the business of domestic administration. Let all be appraised that I... shall preserve the principle of autocracy as firmly and steadfastly, as it was preserved by my unforgettable late father.[18]

But the emperor was unable to stifle the demands from every section of Russian society for a share in power. The growing calls of middle-class liberals for a democratic constitution combined with the revolutionary activities of the underground parties operating among the rural peasants (Socialist Revolutionaries or SRs) and the urban workers (Social Democrats).[19] The start of the twentieth century witnessed 'endless agrarian outbreaks, national insurrections, industrial disputes and revolutionary political activity, bloodily suppressed, but ever renewed.'[20] Events came to a head on Sunday 9 January 1905, when striking workers marched to the Winter Palace with a petition for the tsar, demanding limitations on the autocracy and the election of a constituent assembly. Troops opened fire on the crowd, killing several hundred people.

'Bloody Sunday' unleashed a wave of even more strikes, riots and rebellions across the empire. There were peasant uprisings in half of all Russia's provinces. The tsar's uncle, Grand Duke Sergei, was assassinated as he drove out of the Kremlin in February 1905. In June, the crew of the battleship *Potemkin* mutinied and killed their officers. By autumn, the whole country was paralysed by a general strike. Nicholas II had two options – either use force to crush the revolution or offer concessions. He chose the latter and, on 17 October 1905, signed the 'Imperial Manifesto on the Improvement of the State Order', which granted broad civil rights and an elected parliament or duma. Russia was now – at least, on paper – a constitutional monarchy.

6

'Dress Rehearsal' – 1902–1906

Soviets

'All power to the soviets!'

Vladimir Lenin, April 1917

In the course of the 1905 revolution, the industrial workers of large cities brought a new weapon into play – the soviet of workers' deputies. A soviet was a council of elected delegates from all the factories in one city. There were also soldiers' deputies and elected peasant committees in rural areas. The soviets appeared spontaneously – first in Alapayevsk in March 1905 and then as mass committees of striking textile workers in Ivanovo-Voznesensk in May. The St Petersburg Soviet was chaired by Leon Trotsky and largely dominated by Mensheviks, while the Moscow Soviet was led by Bolsheviks and attempted an armed uprising in December 1905.

The soviets were not a feature of Marxist ideology, which had developed in industrialised Western Europe. They arose completely unplanned in Russia, an agricultural country, where peasants had traditionally met to discuss important matters at the village assembly. Historically, their roots stretched back to the medieval *veche* and the 'councils of the whole land' created in 1611–12. Lenin and other exiled Marxists did not initially understand them and tried to associate them with the Paris Commune of 1871. Besides acting as strike committees, the soviets sometimes also assumed executive functions, which led Lenin to later envisage them as 'the embryo of a new organ of power'.[1]

But even before 1905, the inhabitants of one part of the Russian Empire had already taken power into their own hands – without the need for soviets or the help of professional revolutionaries. This was in the Georgian region of Guria, which lies on the Black Sea near the Turkish border and was an independent principality from 1491 until 1810. The region was incorporated into Kutaisi Province in 1828 but was never completely pacified and experienced at least three armed rebellions in the nineteenth century.

The Gurian Republic

'The Gurians... curtailed the power of the tsarist state and the church. They instituted a kind of direct democracy in the villages, with their weekly meetings. They established a system of justice which, while primitive, was nevertheless an improvement over the previous regime. They created a public space for women to air their views, help set the agenda and vote. These were no small accomplishments... at a time when the tsarist regime was still strong, long before the 1905 revolution.'

Eric Lee

The history of the Gurian Republic began in the village of Nigoiti in May 1902. Led by the schoolteacher, Grigol Uratadze, 700 disgruntled peasants took a common oath not to pay taxes or work for the landowners. Uratadze sought help from the local Social Democrats in Batumi, but they refused to support the peasants. Karlo Chkheidze – who later headed the Menshevik faction in the Duma and chaired the Petrograd Soviet in 1917 – explained to the schoolmaster: 'We are Marxists. Marxism is the philosophy of the proletariat. The peasant, as a small proprietor, is incapable of perceiving the ideology of Marxism. As a petit bourgeoisie, he is closer to the bourgeoisie than to the proletariat. Therefore, we cannot have a peasant movement under our banner.'[2]

But the protest movement grew and news of it spread across the whole country. Leo Tolstoy first heard about it in April 1903 and closely followed events, writing in his diary on 29 January 1905: 'In the morning a fine fellow... related wonderful things about what is happening in the Caucasus – in Guria, Imereti, Mingrelia, Kakheti. The people have decided to be free of government and rule themselves.'[3] Tolstoy's own ideas were a mixture of Christian anarchism and pacifism and he wrote in 1900: 'The anarchists are right in everything... They are mistaken only in thinking that anarchy can be instituted by a violent revolution.'[4]

By 1904, the government had lost control of the district and 'Guria had become an island of democracy in the autocratic Russian empire.'[5]

The village assembly passed laws, administered justice and decided all important matters, from the setting of rents to grazing rights on confiscated land. These gatherings became a weekly tradition, attracting up to 5,000 participants and contributing to a high level of political engagement in the region: 'Meeting follows meeting, and you would be surprised how the peasants, burdened by their work in the fields, hurrying everywhere, take active part in the debates, sitting for long hours, sometimes days, at meetings.'[6]

Luigi Villari, an Italian writer, visited Guria in September 1905 and reported:

> What is peculiarly remarkable about the movement is the unanimity with which it has been carried out, all classes agreeing in the necessity for getting rid of the Russian authorities. The various parties were quarrelling among themselves as to the future form of government to be established... but that the Gurians must administer their own country was unanimously recognised. Even most of the landlords, who have lost income by the new arrangement, acquiesce in it fully.[7]

Guria became the first place in Europe to grant women the same political rights as men after a motion of equality was passed in 1905. The village assembly also adopted a law that marriage should be for love and not financial gain. Any man who had received a dowry was invited to return it to the bride's parents; parents could still offer dowries to their daughter, but it was up to her to accept it or not. Expensive weddings and funerals were banned and in some villages religious ceremonies were replaced by secular services.

The administration of justice was an interesting mixture of ancient practices and modern psychology. The death sentence and imprisonment were abolished. The most common form of punishment was ostracism – a practice developed by the Athenians, who also applied it after voting at their democratic assemblies. A man and a woman who had pleaded guilty to adultery were made 'to ride through the village stark-naked on the back of a donkey; during their progress they proclaimed their sin before all the assembled villagers, declared their contrition and vowed to lead a pure life in future.'[8]

Luigi Villari described a legal case heard by an assembly of 200 villagers: 'The court is composed in a very simple way. There are no judges, no jury, no public prosecutor, no counsel; but every person present, whether man, woman or child, native or foreign, has the right to act in any or all of these capacities, and verdict and sentence are decided by the vote of the majority. One man is elected chairman, but merely for the sake of convenience, and he has no official authority.' The writer witnessed an appeal from a merchant who had committed adultery and been condemned to ostracism:

> I admit my sin and the justice of your punishment; but I am deeply penitent, and swear in future to lead a reformed and virtuous life. The sufferings I have undergone since you boycotted me have been so great, so unbearable, that it would have been better if you had killed me outright. I am lost, ruined beyond hope, unless you relent, and I have come to ask you to forgive me and withdraw the boycott.[9]

There then followed a lively discussion, as the peasants took turns to express their opinions on the matter. The speakers referred to 'the latest results of science' and quoted a range of 'obscure German philosophers' and modern socialist writers.

> For over an hour the speeches followed each other, illustrated by more or less appropriate arguments, until finally the chairman moved a resolution that the boycott should be withdrawn. On a show of hands those in favour of it were obviously in a majority; but the opposition demanded a formal counting of votes. After some discussion as to ways and means, it was decided to use the church as a 'polling station'. One of the peasants recorded the votes, while a priest stood by to give a religious sanction to the proceedings... The counting of the votes confirmed the result of the show of hands, the boycott was withdrawn, and the penitent was forgiven and admitted once more into the community.

At the end, one of the peasants asked the Italian visitor: 'Is it not better to be tried in this way than by three scoundrels in black robes?'[10]

When a crime was committed, the whole community felt obliged to help catch the wrongdoer. A Georgian newspaper reported in 1905: 'While theft and other crimes have not been completely eradicated, they have almost disappeared.'[11] The Gurians elected their own policemen and managed to capture one of Georgia's most wanted criminals, Datiko Shevardnadze – the uncle of Eduard Shevardnadze, who was born in Guria and later served as Soviet foreign minister (1985–90, 1991) and the president of Georgia (1995–2003). The Russian government even sent a university professor from St Petersburg to study their methods of justice and communistic administration.

Events in Guria took a radical turn after Bloody Sunday in January 1905. Portraits of the tsar were destroyed, while government representatives were driven out and sometimes killed. Self-defence police units called 'Red Hundreds' were formed to defend Guria and a two-rouble tax was introduced to purchase arms. Luigi Villari writes: 'I was told of frequent gatherings of thousands of armed Gurians who practised military manoeuvres, shooting and other warlike exercises, including ambulance service.'[12] The Red Hundreds studied how to build barricades and rob trains. In December 1905, they dispatched a mission in support of a workers' uprising in Tiflis and sent ten bombs to assist the Novorossiisk Republic.

In February 1905, the tsar appointed a liberal politician, Count Illarion Vorontsov-Dashkov, as viceroy of the Caucasus. He sent his assistant, Nikolai Sultan-Krym-Girei,[13] to meet the Gurians and learnt that they wanted 'the same rights and privileges as the citizens of European Russia' – although he later confessed that their demands were too extreme to seriously consider and that 'the Constitution of France would not have been enough to satisfy them.'[14] By this time, the whole province was in the hands of revolutionaries and Count Vorontsov-Dashkov believed that the only way to pacify Guria was to grant wide concessions. He drew up plans for land reform and even to legalise their court system, 'which administers justice far more honestly and efficiently than do the state tribunals'.[15]

In July 1905, Count Vorontsov-Dashkov appointed his friend, Vladimir Staroselsky, as the governor of Kutaisi Province. Staroselsky became known as the 'red governor' after he visited the Gurian Republic in an escort of Red Hundreds. When soft tactics failed to work, Staroselsky was dismissed by the tsar – who called him 'a real revolutionary'[16] – and a hundred Cossacks were dispatched to restore order. But the Cossacks were defeated by an army of several thousand Gurians at the bloody Battle of Nasakirali on 20 October 1905. The Red Hundreds then captured the district centre – the town of Ozurgeti – and elected Benjamin Chkhikvishvili as president of an enlarged Gurian Republic in November 1905.

After the government gradually regained control over the rest of the country in December 1905, twenty battalions of soldiers and a squadron of Cossacks with twenty-six cannons were sent to retake Guria. Completely outnumbered and overwhelmed, the republic fell on 10 January 1906. Hundreds of houses and shops were burnt down, an unknown number of people were killed and several hundred villagers were exiled to Siberia.

But the Gurian Republic had a sequel when the Democratic Republic of Georgia was established after the revolution. Many of its leaders originated from Guria and had participated in the movement, including the prime minister Noe Zhordania. In 1918, they applied the lessons of the Gurian Republic across the whole country, creating a democratic alternative to the Bolshevik regime – until the Red Army invaded in 1921 and popular representation disappeared in Georgia for another seventy years.[17]

1905 Republics

'Our people's republic lasted only thirteen days. For thirteen days, the sun shone upon us, but then it disappeared again behind the impenetrable clouds of the autocratic regime.'

Ivan Arsentiev from Stary Buyan

The events of the 1905 revolution fuelled the establishment of other short-lived 'independent republics' all over the country. Some of these pockets of self-government were peasant statelets, while others were led by workers' soviets or had ethnic foundations. But they were all democratic and, like the Gurian Republic, several of them came to international attention.

Markovo Republic

An independent republic of over 6,000 peasants existed for eight months in Markovo district – less than a hundred miles from Moscow. On 30 October 1905, an invitation was sent round all the villages to meet in Markovo the next day to discuss the tsar's recent manifesto. A thousand peasants arrived at the teahouse, where a worker from St Petersburg (Timofeyev) explained the difference between a monarchy and a republic and the benefits of republicanism. Upon hearing this, the peasants decided to declare a republic and elected the village elder, Pyotr Burshin, as their president.

The 'government' consisted of the local schoolteacher as 'prime minister', an agronomist as 'foreign minister' and a district elder as 'security minister'. They published a programme of twelve points known as the 'Peasant Manifesto'. Besides demands for land and the abolition of redemption payments, they called for the abolition of the autocracy and the holding of a constituent assembly. The manifesto was not only published in Russian newspapers, but also found its way into the American and French press.

The peasants confiscated the local landlords' estates and distributed the land fairly among themselves. They used the wood from the trees to repair bridges and build a public barn, where they held parliamentary assemblies. Rents were controlled, church schools were nationalised, a health service was opened and free fuel was distributed. The revolutionary movement spread to the surrounding provinces. When textile workers in Volokolamsk went on strike at the end of November, the village assembly sent them humanitarian aid in the form of two hundred sacks of potatoes, rye and cabbage.

The Markovo Republic existed until 18 July 1906 – six months after the revolution had been suppressed in the cities – when Cossacks arrived and restored order. Three hundred peasants were arrested and the ringleaders were exiled to Siberia. By this time, news of the republic had spread around the world. On 30 July 1906, Markovo was visited by an American delegation, headed by a professor from the University of Chicago and the prominent journalist Arthur Bullard, who interviewed the local peasants. There was an international scandal when the Americans were arrested by the local police, questioned and only released after the intervention of the US consul in Moscow, Samuel Smith.

Stary Buyan Republic

On 12 November 1905, a peasant rebellion overthrew the local authorities in the village of Stary Buyan near the city of Samara and established a direct democracy known as the Stary Buyan Republic. The village assembly adopted a five-article constitution known as the 'Provisional Law on Stary Buyan People's Self-Government'. This detailed document was compiled with the help of a constitutional lawyer who had spent nine years in the Peter and Paul Fortress in St Petersburg for revolutionary activities. Because the Provisional Law refused to recognise any government except one 'elected by all the people on the basis of a universal, equal, direct and secret ballot without regard to sex, nationality and religion', the peasants decided to govern themselves until the calling of a national constituent assembly.

The government was headed by a professional revolutionary called Antip Knyazev. The deputy president was a landowner who announced his intention to donate all his estates to the republic. All other public officials were directly elected by the people. Freedom of speech, press, assembly and religion was guaranteed. The legislative organ was known as the People's Congress and had a quorum of 120 adults.

All land, forests, meadows, rivers and minerals were nationalised. Confiscated land was divided equally among the peasants, according to the size of their families. The purchase and sale of land, the unauthorised felling of trees and the burning down of mansions were banned. Primary and secondary education was declared 'secular and free in all schools.' Each school was run by a council of teachers and peasants elected by the citizens. There were plans to open a public bank and a university with a council elected by the People's Congress. All government taxes were abolished and all medical services were free. Legal disputes were resolved at the general assembly. Envoys were sent to other villages to encourage them to join the Stary Buyan Republic.

A militia of a hundred men armed with hunting rifles, pistols, axes and pitchforks kept order and defended the borders of the republic. The schoolmistress taught girls to make bandages and dress wounds. No crimes were committed in the short history of the republic. The government introduced prohibition and closed the taverns 'forever more as a green serpent poisoning the human mind'. The republic was supported by the local priest, who explained to worshippers: 'There is no sin in taking land and bread from the landowners, because the land and bread are God's creation. All the fruits of the earth and the bread of the landlords are the products of your labour and only those who work should enjoy them.'

The government sent a police unit from Samara to crush the rebellion, but it was defeated by the peasant militia. When a much larger Cossack force was dispatched, the revolutionary council met to discuss the republic's response. Opinions were split over whether to resist or to flee to the forest and neighbouring villages. The last to speak was Sergei Antipov: 'Citizens of the Stary Buyan Free Republic! We can give our lives for the republic and perish, but we cannot save the republic… We are alone now in the struggle, but in the near future all towns and villages will rise up… We shall retreat now – but return later!' The republic voted to dissolve itself on 26 November 1905. The ringleaders were arrested in January 1906 and exiled to Arkhangelsk Province in 1909.[18]

Ruzayevka Republic

Ruzayevka is hard to find on any map, but it achieved a great deal over the ten days when it was an independent state. As Afanasy Baikuzov, the president, said on 20 December 1905: 'We should be proud that Ruzayevka – for many an unknown station – has shocked tsarist Petersburg... Ruzayevka has, in a way, become a tiny republic.'[19]

On 10 December 1905, inspired by the uprising in Moscow, a strike broke out at a junction of the Moscow-Kazan Railway in Mordovia, seventy miles north of Penza. The railway workers formed a government of nineteen 'ministers' headed by engine-driver Afanasy Baikuzov and a militia of 150 men led by Lev Wietzmann, a Bolshevik student. The government met every day so that it was accountable to the people. There was a freeze on food prices and a free canteen was opened for unemployed workers. The sale of vodka in the station buffet was banned and the taverns and wineshops were shut down. The passage of all trains through Ruzayevka was halted, except for food and humanitarian supplies.

The local merchants were forced to pay a 'contribution' of 1,500 roubles or face arrest and the confiscation of all their property. As the workers had not received any wages since the start of the strike and were refused credit in the shops, the Ruzayevka Republic issued 'bonds' with a face value of one or three roubles, which were printed on a jellygraph with the president's signature and the stamp of the railway trade union. The idea of the bonds was copied by a member of the Moscow Soviet, who later told the story to Vladimir Lenin: 'He grew particularly merry when I told him how I had sent the shopkeepers notes with a demand to give out food. "And what happened?" Vladimir Ilich asked. "Did they take them?" "They did," I replied. And when I related that, at Ruzayevka station, the engine-driver deputy Baikuzov had printed bonds and given them out to the workers, who used them to buy food from the shopkeepers, Vladimir Ilich completely cracked up and even called his wife to tell her about it.'[20]

The militia was divided into five groups of thirty workers who took it in turns to patrol the station. On 11 December, they caught three thieves and marched them handcuffed through the whole town, before handing them over to the tsarist police in Insar. At first, the militia only had eight pistols and four hunting rifles. They forged their own daggers and iron lances and purchased more weapons in Penza with the money appropriated from the local merchants. The railway workers also managed to stop two trains carrying 1,627 rifles.

On 13 December, the committee sent a telegram to the soldiers of the Manchurian army in Harbin, calling on them to support the Ruzayevka uprising 'for freedom and land'. But help did not come and on

21 December, following the defeat of the Moscow uprising, the executive committee decided to end the strike. Sixteen workers later stood trial and received prison sentences ranging from one to eighteen months, although five were acquitted.

Chita Republic

In November 1905, revolutionary soldiers and armed workers took control of a major city in eastern Siberia and established the Chita Republic. On 16 November, the soldiers and Cossacks of the Chita garrison passed a resolution demanding 'a constituent assembly elected on the basis of a universal, direct, equal and secret ballot and the establishment of a democratic republic'.[21] On 22 November, they elected a soviet and issued a further programme of seven points, including the full implementation of the October Manifesto in the army. That same day, the local workers formed a 4,000-strong militia, headed by a twenty-nine-year-old revolutionary, Anton Kościuszko-Valyuzhanich.

On 24 November, a demonstration of 5,000 workers forced the military governor, General Ivan Kholschevnikov, to free three political prisoners. The general submitted to their demands to avoid any escalation of violence, leading to accusations that he secretly supported the revolution (he was sentenced to sixteen months in the Peter and Paul Fortress in January 1906 and later joined the Red Army). The following day, the soldiers presented their own requests to the governor. While many of them were aimed at improving military life – compulsory education for illiterate conscripts, the opening of soldier's libraries and reading rooms, the right to freely attend theatres, meetings, rallies, lectures and read books without an officer's permission – half of them were political. These included the abolition of the death sentence, universal suffrage, the calling of a constituent assembly, the transfer of all land to the people and a general amnesty for political prisoners. Their demands were accompanied by a declaration that 'we reject the State Duma, which will not have our true representatives, and will strive for a constituent assembly, elected by all people without distinction of class, nationality and sex – rich and poor, educated and uneducated – casting equal votes by direct and secret ballot.'[22]

By the end of November, power in Chita was more or less in the hands of the soviet – although the city council and town duma continued to function. The workers took over the railways on 11 December and the postal and telegraph services on 22 December, while the militia seized rifles and munitions from stockpiles and trains supplying the Russian army in Manchuria.

On 22 January 1906, superior government forces commanded by General Paul von Rennenkampf surrounded the city and overthrew the Chita Republic. Four hundred people were arrested and seventy-seven were sentenced to death, including Anton Kościuszko-Valyuzhanich. However, as prime minister Sergei Witte observed, most of the accused were simple workers who had been 'suddenly seized by a sense of freedom' and that 'no repressions can destroy this feeling.' The introduction of martial law throughout the region meant that the spring Duma elections were not held there.

Krasnoyarsk Republic

After the declaration of a nationwide strike in October 1905, the workers of another Siberian city, Krasnoyarsk, introduced an eight-hour working day and formed a soviet of 120 Bolsheviks, Mensheviks, SRs and independent socialists on 6 December. Three days later, they took power in the city and established a provisional revolutionary government. The workers passed laws on freedom of the press and assembly, assumed control of the railway and factories, created a people's court and organised military patrols to maintain order in the town. They appointed a president and prepared to hold elections to a new city duma. But the Omsk Regiment entered the city on 27 December and overthrew the Krasnoyarsk Republic on 3 January 1906.

Shulyavka Republic

The Shulyavka Republic officially existed for only four days, from 12 to 16 December 1905. The events happened in the Shulyavka district of Kiev, where a mechanic at the Grether and Krivanek Factory, Fyodor Alexeyev, proposed forming a soviet as an alternative to the city duma. Nine factories elected representatives on the basis of one delegate for every hundred workers and held the first sitting of the soviet at the Polytechnic Institute on 30 October. Fyodor Alexeyev was elected chairman, while a provisional bureau was created as its executive organ with one representative from each factory.

The soviet raised funds to support the families of striking workers. A free canteen served food donated by the nearby villages and a library of revolutionary literature was opened. The soviet formed a militia to defend itself, while the students of the Polytechnic Institute made bombs and other explosives. By the middle of November 1905, Shulyavka was an autonomous unit with its own government and armed forces.

The authorities tried to cause trouble in Shulyavka by paying local criminals to rob houses and attack people on the streets. But the militia ran round-the-clock patrols and apprehended the hooligans, who were sentenced to perform community work (although one of them was executed). The militia successfully repulsed a police attack and several spying missions launched by agents of the tsarist secret police (Okhrana).

On 12 December, in solidarity with the uprising in Moscow, a proletarian republic was declared in Shulyavka with the Polytechnic Institute as the capital and seat of government. The workers issued a manifesto: 'The citizens of the Shulyavka Republic advocate the overthrow of monarchist absolutism, freedom of assembly and speech, social liberation, an amnesty for political prisoners, the national emancipation of the Ukrainian, Polish, Jewish and other peoples of the Russian Empire and the immediate cessation of pogroms, which shame our people.' The republic issued an appeal to Western nations not to provide loans to the Russian government, which would only be used to suppress democracy.

Four days later, on the night of 16/17 December, Shulyavka was surrounded by 2,000 policemen accompanied by cavalry units, Cossacks and dragoons. They began house-to-house arrests and by five in the morning the republic had fallen. Seventy-eight revolutionaries were arrested. Fyodor Alexeyev escaped but was apprehended in Saratov and sentenced to four years in prison (he emigrated in 1912, but returned to Kiev in 1928).

Chechelyovka Republic

Chechelyovka is a district in the Ukrainian city of Dnipro, which was known as Ekaterinoslav until 1926. On 17 October 1905, a soviet of 400 workers' deputies was elected there on the basis of one delegate for every hundred workers. An executive committee was appointed and headed by Grigory Petrovsky, a famous Ukrainian revolutionary in whose honour the city was named Dnipropetrovsk from 1926 to 2016.

On 8 December, the city soviet called a general strike in the factories, which spread the next day to all government institutions. The strike committee formed an autonomous zone that became known as the Chechelyovka Republic. They kept the railways, bakeries and hospitals running, operated free canteens and opened a medical station. The payment of rents and taxes was abolished, food prices were frozen and publishers were only allowed to print revolutionary literature and the bulletin of the strike committee.

Once again, the fate of democracy was decided by the force of arms. Government infantry and artillery units entered Dnipro on 18 December and, after two weeks of self-government, the soviet voted to end the strike. The Chechelyovka Republic ended its existence after only two weeks on 22 December.

Lyubotin Republic

The Ukrainian town of Lyubotin was founded by runaway Cossacks in 1650 and is located near the city of Kharkiv. On 8 December 1905, a group of striking railway workers occupied the train station and telegraph office and declared a provisional government. They were led by a local student, Konstantin Kirsta, who paraphrased Louis XIV by declaring: 'Lyubotin *c'est moi!*'

The workers disarmed the police and imprisoned them in the blacksmith's cellar, along with the owner of the local wineshop. They were all released the following day after signing a written pledge of loyalty to the republic. However, in the absence of Kirsta – who was captured while trying to persuade soldiers to join the rebellion – the policemen were rearrested by his deputy. They were put on trial, sentenced to death and burnt alive in the chimney of the steam-locomotive plant.

On 17 December, regular army and Cossack units arrived with a cannon and retook control of Lyubotin after nine days of independence. Kirsta was sentenced to two years in prison. Six others received one-year terms, although forty-eight were acquitted thanks to their lawyer, Alexander Alexandrov, who was later elected to the Fourth Duma. Kirsta distinguished himself in the First World War and was awarded the St George's Cross in 1916.

Republica de la Comrat

The town of Comrat in south-west Moldova is mainly inhabited by the Gagauz – a Turkic people who are Orthodox Christians. In January 1906, a peasant uprising led to the proclamation of the Comrat Republic. Events started with the night-time arrest of a local revolutionary, Andrei Galaţan, after he called for the overthrow of the autocracy. The following day, on 6 January 1906, an angry crowd of 1,000 people demonstrated outside the police station. Armed with blunderbusses and pitchforks, they arrested the local judge, policemen and other officials and liberated Andrei. They then proclaimed a republic and elected a government headed by Galațan.

The Comrat Republic abolished all taxes, nationalised the land and declared an end to redemption payments. A Russian newspaper reported on 10 January 1906: 'Comrat, a town of 10,000 inhabitants, is in the hands of rebels. Autonomy has been declared. The authorities have been overthrown and arrested. The dragoons are powerless.'[23] The following day, the governor sent reinforcements to smash the barricades built by the citizens and put an end to the republic. Dozens were killed and many more were arrested. Galațan spent one and a half years in prison, while others were sentenced to hard labour in Siberia. The local authorities were also severely punished for letting events spin out of control in the first place.

Although the Comrat Republic only lasted five days, it set the tone for further rebellions in Bessarabia, including the uprisings in Khotin (January 1919), Bender (May 1919) and Tatarbunary (September 1924). A later echo of these events was the formation of the Gagauz Autonomous SSR in November 1989 and an independent Gagauz Republic in August 1990. One of the streets in Comrat is now called Strada Galațana.

Novorossiisk Republic

In December 1905, Nicholas II received a telegram from the commander of the Black Sea Fleet, reporting alarming events in the port city of Novorossiisk: 'Complete anarchy, revolutionaries have seized power.' The tsar was meanwhile informed from other sources that 'a provisional government headed by a presidium has been declared in Novorossiisk'.

On 8 December, following the declaration of a general strike in Novorossiisk, the soviet of workers' deputies voted for an armed uprising. The governor hid in a railway car at the station while the rest of his administration fled the city, handing control to the workers in a 'velvet revolution' on 12 December. The soviet assumed power and elected a schoolteacher, Sinyukhov, as the 'revolutionary governor'.

The Novorossiisk Republic passed laws to improve the lives of the poorer sections of society. An eight-hour day was introduced in all factories and shops, which were run by workers' committees. Unemployment benefit was paid and a progressive income tax was introduced. The owners of local businesses were forced to increase wages and rehire sacked workers. Food prices were frozen and the sale of vodka was banned. The banks, post office, telephones and even the city duma all continued to function.

Telegraphs sent by the new government to the nearby stations ended with the words: 'Long live the republic!'

The republic's armed forces initially consisted of 300 workers. Employing the slogan 'use weapons to get weapons', they disarmed the city police and collected guns and bullets from the local peasants. Further ammunition was supplied by two other breakaway republics – a thousand guns from Gagra and ten bombs from Guria. The republic also manufactured its own lances, sabres and daggers. By 20 December, the army had grown into a force of 3,000 men.

On 24 December, two Russian battleships entered the harbour and a Cossack detachment arrived at the railway station. The revolutionaries voted 'in view of the hopelessness of resistance' to surrender and dissolve the soviet. The Novorossiisk Republic ended after only two weeks on 25 December. Seven of the leaders were sentenced to death (later commuted to life in prison), while thirteen others were condemned to hard labour.

Sochi Republic

After the collapse of the Novorossiisk Republic, some of the revolutionaries fled down the coast to Sochi, where they helped to set up an independent state which lasted four days.

The day after the publication of the October Manifesto, a group of revolutionaries met in a Sochi cafe and voted to create a militia to defend their new freedoms. One of their leaders was Avxenty Gvatua, an impoverished Georgian nobleman, who supplied them with sixty Swiss rifles donated by an Abkhazian aristocrat. Fully armed, the militia took to the streets of Sochi on 27 December. They defeated the tsarist police and the local infantry battalion by shelling their barracks from a nine-foot cannon dating from 1705. The revolutionaries did not have proper ammunition, so they used dumbbells until some old cannonballs were retrieved from a sunken ship. After a bombardment lasting all morning, the rebels accepted the 'honourable surrender' of the government forces on the afternoon of 1 January 1906.

Nikifor Poyarko, a worker who had deserted from the army during the Russo-Japanese War, was appointed president of the Sochi Republic. The new government released all prisoners and destroyed the police files. But independence only lasted for as long as there was a storm on the Black Sea. When the weather improved, the government landed Cossacks from a warship and restored order on 5 January. Nevertheless, for almost one month, alternative regimes had been established in two major cities bordering the Black Sea.

Gagra Republic

The 1905 revolution led to the temporary establishment of democratic republics in several parts of Abkhazia. Besides the Gudauta Republic, which existed for almost two months, a group of Bolsheviks set up the Gagra Republic in November 1905. The government introduced a property tax to raise proceeds for the revolution and opened a tribunal which handled all criminal and civil cases. The Gagra Republic lasted until tsarist power was re-established in January 1906.

Samurzakano Republic

The Samurzakano Republic was founded by Platon Emukhvari, an impoverished Abkhazian prince who now worked as a schoolmaster and was a member of the Social Democratic Party. On 15 December 1905, armed with a bomb, he went to the local police station and threatened to blow everyone up unless they surrendered all their weapons to him. He then used the captured guns and rifles to set up the Samurzakano Republic.

On 1 January, singing the *Marseillaise*, the socialist prince marched with a group of Red Hundreds to the church in Gali, where he interrupted the service, planted a red banner inscribed 'Down with Nicholas II' at the altar and demanded that the priest hold a memorial service for victims of the revolution. The Samurzakano Republic was crushed just eight days later. Emukhvari was arrested and sentenced to four years of hard labour in 1908. He was imprisoned again in 1914, released after the February revolution of 1917 and died in 1922.

In a lecture on the 1905 revolution, Lenin positively appraised the many attempts to establish independent republics: 'For a time, several cities in Russia became something in the nature of small local "republics". The government authorities were deposed and the soviet of workers' deputies actually functioned as the new government. Unfortunately, these periods were all too brief, the "victories" were too weak, too isolated.'[24] While all the short-lived democratic states were eventually overthrown by the tsarist government, they made a positive contribution by turning the revolutionary events of 1905 into what Lenin described as the 'dress rehearsal' for 1917.

7

The Imperial Duma

'Papa, the Duma is yours, do what you want.'

Grigory Rasputin to Nicholas II

'Russia, thank God, is not a constitutional country.'

Alexandra Fyodorovna to Nicholas II

When the Fundamental Laws of the Russian Empire were amended in April 1906 to take account of the October Manifesto, Russia was still described as an 'autocracy' – just no longer an 'unlimited autocracy'. While the manifesto promised that 'no law may go into force without the consent of the State Duma,' the tsar still retained most political powers. The Duma could initiate legislation and controlled the budget, but the emperor remained in supreme command of the armed forces, foreign policy, declaring war and peace and had the sole right to appoint and dismiss ministers. He could dissolve or prorogue parliament at any time and, under Article 87, issue special decrees when it was not in session – although such laws had to be later approved by the Duma.

Nicholas II diluted the Duma's powers before it even met by issuing a decree in February 1906 which transformed the State Council into an upper chamber with equal legislative rights. This second house would have 196 members, half appointed by the tsar and half elected by professional organisations – fifty-six from the provincial zemstvos and congresses of landowners, eighteen from the assemblies of nobility, twelve from financial, trade and business associations, six from the Academy of Sciences and universities, and six from the Russian Orthodox Church. The Finnish Diet was allocated two seats but declined to participate.

Nevertheless, in a short period of time, Russia had passed over difficult terrain which had taken several centuries in the West. In several areas, Russia leapfrogged countries like Great Britain and the United States. The State Council was more democratically constituted than the House of Lords and no worse than the US Senate, which was not directly elected until 1913. Duma deputies were paid an annual salary of 4,200 roubles – the equivalent of £450 – while it took another five years for British MPs to receive the slightly smaller remuneration of £400 (about £50,000 today) under the terms of the Parliament Act of 1911.[1]

The electoral law published in December 1905 gave the vote to almost all men over the age of twenty-five who met certain land or property qualifications. However, the elections were not direct or equal. There was a system of curiae, which decided how many seats were elected by each social class. Each curia chose electors, who then formed a college to elect the Duma deputies. A system of weighted voting determined the correlations of voting power between the four curiae – rural landowners, urban dwellers, peasants, workers – which was initially set at 1:3:15:45.

The First Duma

Russia held its first ever general election campaign in spring 1906. Because everything was so new, no one knew how to behave. Election meetings were often banned or broken up by the police. Rumours spread that civil servants who took part in voting would be sacked. The only parties which had existed before October 1905 were the Socialist Revolutionaries and the Social Democrats and they boycotted the elections. So did the nationalists, monarchists and the far right, who were vehemently opposed to any limitations on the autocracy. As a result, the turnout was much lower than expected, ranging from a high of 50.2% in Samara Province to a low of 0.7% in Vologda Province.

Despite the government attempts to manipulate the outcome through the electoral law, the First Duma was far more revolutionary than anyone had imagined. A new party of radical liberals called the Cadets (Constitutional Democrats) won a relative majority of 176 of the 524 seats. Led by historian Pavel Milyukov, they advocated a full constitutional monarchy, workers' rights, the expropriation of landed estates for redistribution to the peasantry and autonomy for non-Russian nationalities.

The second largest party was the Trudoviki (Labourites) with 107 seats. They mainly represented the peasants and included many socialists who had ignored the boycott (ten members later set up a separate Social

Democratic faction). The following blocs were the Autonomists (70 seats) and the Progressives (60 seats). The smallest party was the Octobrists, a group of moderates who supported the October Manifesto (13 seats). A hundred Mensheviks and Socialist Revolutionaries were elected as independents, creating a solidly left-wing parliament which became known as 'the duma of public anger'.

The opening ceremony was held in the Winter Palace in St Petersburg on 27 April 1906 – a date now celebrated as 'Russian Parliamentarianism Day'. The newly elected deputies assembled in St George's Hall alongside the members of the State Council, the Holy Synod, the imperial family and the court. The tsar's cousin, Grand Duchess Maria Pavlovna the Younger, recalled that 'the Winter Palace looked more like a fortress, so greatly did they fear an attack or hostile demonstrations,' while 'even the emperor, ordinarily able to hide his feelings, was sad and nervous' following a sleepless night.[2]

The event was planned by the court master of ceremonies, Baron Paul von Korff, with help from Empress Alexandra Fyodorovna, who wanted something 'which agreed with Russian customs and did not imitate Western examples'.[3] The emperor was dressed in the uniform of the Preobrazhensky Guards, while the ladies of the imperial family wore 'nearly all their jewels' and 'were literally covered with pearls and diamonds'. As Vladimir Gurko, the assistant minister of the interior, observed: 'This oriental method of impressing upon spectators a reverence for the bearers of supreme power was quite unsuited to the occasion. What it did achieve was to set in juxtaposition the boundless imperial luxury and the poverty of the people.'[4]

Nicholas II read out his address from the throne: 'I welcome you, those best people whom I commanded my beloved subjects to choose from among themselves, with an ardent faith in Russia's brilliant future.'[5] The emperor went on to remind the deputies that 'for spiritual greatness and prosperity of the state we need not freedom alone, but order based on law.' Nicholas ended with the words: 'May the Lord help me and you!' and was answered with a resounding cheer of 'Hurrah!' – although one parliamentarian found the speech 'insipid and lacklustre', while another simply stood and brazenly cracked sunflower seeds as the tsar spoke.

The deputies then trooped across the city to take up their seats in the Tauride Palace, where they elected Sergei Muromtsev of the Cadet Party as chairman and immediately set themselves at loggerheads with the government. On 18 May, they compiled an aggressive 'Address to the Throne', demanding a responsible government, full legislative rights, the abolition of capital punishment, an amnesty for political prisoners, equal rights for all citizens and a fully elected State Council. When their demands were rejected by the government, Vladimir Nabokov – a Cadet deputy and father of the famous novelist – leapt onto the rostrum and shouted to deafening applause: 'Let the executive power bow before the legislative power!'[6]

After the Duma compiled a motion of no confidence in the government, which was passed almost unanimously, Nicholas decided to get rid of it. On 8 July, he replaced the elderly premier, Ivan Goremykin, with the more energetic and forceful Pyotr Stolypin and asked him to immediately prorogue parliament. When the deputies turned up for work the next morning, they found the doors of the Tauride Palace locked and a decree dissolving the Duma posted nearby.

Two hundred members got on a train and travelled across the border to Vyborg in Finland, where they assembled in a forest and declared that 'the sessions of the Duma are hereby resumed.' They issued the Vyborg Manifesto, calling for citizens not to pay taxes or send recruits to the army until the Duma was restored. But the country was now tired of revolutions and ignored the appeal. All the deputies who signed the Vyborg Manifesto were arrested on their return to Russia and 167 of them were later sentenced to three months in prison.[7]

The Second Duma

Although elected for five years, the First Duma had lasted just seventy-two days and only passed one law. One of the founders of the Octobrist Party, Count Peter van Heiden, commented: 'Dissolving the Duma is endless stupidity. Any new Duma will end up being more left-wing and radical and even harder to work with.'[8] This was exactly what happened when new elections were held for the Second Duma, despite government attempts to again influence the outcome. Officials were encouraged to disqualify whole classes of voters and remove names from the electoral registers. Opposition parties had their meetings broken up and their newspapers were confiscated. Jews were threatened with banishment if they voted. But the results of the second elections were even less favourable to the government than the first.

Only thirty-two members of the First Duma were re-elected, as all those who had signed the Vyborg Manifesto were served with a lifetime ban on standing for office. The top two parties now changed places and the largest bloc was the Trudoviki (104 seats), followed by the Cadets (98 seats). Lenin announced that the boycott of the First Duma had been a mistake and that the Social Democrats would take part this time. He ran for election under the name of 'Karpov' in the Moscow district of St Petersburg but failed to get elected, although his party still secured sixty-five seats and finished third overall. When added to the Socialist Revolutionaries (37) and the Popular Socialists (16), this gave the revolutionaries a third of the 518 seats, while a total of 222 places went to left-wing parties. Thirty monarchists and nationalists were also elected, including the infamous far-right rabble-rouser Vladimir Purishkevich.

Shortly after the Second Duma opened on 20 February 1907, the ceiling of the chamber caved in. This happened early in the morning, when no one was present, but it was an appropriate metaphor for a parliament which was, for the tsar, even worse than the first. While the Cadets tried to make the Duma a real political force, the revolutionary parties used it to attack the regime in every possible way. The right wing exploited the conflict between the liberal and radical wings for their own purposes, creating disorderly scenes with the aim of discrediting the Duma and, hopefully, getting it abolished once and for all. Purishkevich courted controversy with a series of outrageous actions, such as wearing a red carnation in the fly of his trousers on May Day or writing an insulting letter to feminist Anna Filosofova, comparing the First All-Russian Congress of Women to a brothel (she successfully brought charges against him and he was sentenced to a month in prison, later commuted to one week by the tsar).

Extremists on both sides of the house submitted impossible bills and gave flamboyant speeches simply to get their names in the papers, which were now flourishing thanks to freedom of the press. Together, they turned the Duma into 'a madhouse of shouts, insults and brawls'. As the tsar's mother wrote in a letter to her sister, Queen Alexandra of England, in May 1907: 'The majority of those who sit in the Duma are revolutionaries and anarchists, which they do not even attempt to conceal. On the contrary, they boast loudly about this. I do not understand how it is possible to stand for all this, why not throw them straight out of there?'[9] Nicholas II himself explained his strategy in a letter to his mother: 'I am getting telegrams from everywhere, petitioning me to order a dissolution, but it is too early for that. One must let them do something manifestly stupid or mean, and then – slap! And they are gone!'[10]

The chance came a month later, when the tsar found an excuse to dissolve the Second Duma with the help of a police provocation.

A compromising document was planted on a Social Democrat deputy, which allowed Stolypin to accuse the faction of planning an armed uprising. He went to the Tauride Palace on 1 June with a warrant for the arrest of sixteen members. The Duma immediately set up a commission of investigation, but was itself dissolved two days later, before it could come to any decision. The second parliament had lasted not much longer than the first – 103 days – and only passed three bills.

A total of thirty-seven Social Democrat deputies were arrested on the night of 2/3 June, the minute the decree of dissolution came into effect. Some of them had just returned from their Fifth Party Congress in Hackney in London and had no idea what was going on. Two escaped to America, but the rest stood trial and sixteen were sentenced to hard labour. Three of the former deputies died in prison, where another, Gerasim Makharadze, went insane (he was later shot by order of Stalin in 1937).

A Socialist Revolutionary deputy, Alexei Kuznetsov, also spent time in jail. He was first arrested in May 1907 for drunkenly relieving himself in front of two policemen (he was released without charge after showing his parliamentary credentials). He was then expelled from his Duma faction for smashing a portrait of the tsar over a man's head while fighting in a tavern. Kuznetsov resigned his seat and returned to his home village, where he was arrested for brawling and imprisoned for two years.

While in jail, he met a famous cracksman, Jan Peters ('Vaska Strauss'), and helped him carry out several daring heists after his release in 1912 (his nickname in the criminal underworld was 'The Deputy'). The two men burgled the American confectionary store of Joseph Blickhen and Max Robinson in St Petersburg, then stole securities and cash worth 26,000 roubles from the Stroganov Palace. Kuznetsov was caught by the police in October 1912 and sentenced to a further six years in prison in April 1914.

The Third Duma

Nicholas II did not abolish the Duma altogether. Instead, he changed the voting laws to the detriment of the peasants and workers and the even greater advantage of the landowners and wealthy city-dwellers. The total size of the Duma was reduced to 442 seats with the main losses occurring in four regional strongholds of the opposition – Poland (14 seats), Caucasus (19 seats), Siberia (6 seats) and Central Asia (all seats). Changing the electoral system without the approval of the Duma or State

Council was a direct violation of Article 87 of the Fundamental Laws, but the 'coup of 3 June 1907' aroused even less protest than the dissolution of the First Duma. The revolution of 1905–07 was now well and truly over.

Elections for the Third Duma were held in autumn 1907 and the majority of seats were won by centrists and conservatives. The membership even included forty-five Orthodox priests. The liberal-left opposition was greatly reduced as the Social Democrats dropped from sixty-five to nineteen, the Trudoviki fell from 103 to ten and the Cadets went from ninety-eight to fifty-three. The Socialist Revolutionaries and Popular Socialists boycotted the elections. The moderate right jumped from twenty-four to sixty-nine, the far right grew from ten to forty-nine and nationalists won twenty-six seats.

The largest party was now the Octobrists, who increased their membership from twenty to 148 seats. Led by Alexander Guchkov, who was elected chairman in March 1910, they formed a solid bloc in the centre with which the government could finally cooperate. On the other hand, because the Duma no longer represented the wider population, public interest in parliamentary politics gave way to apathy and indifference.

The Third Duma started work on 1 November 1907 and served its full term of five years, passing 2,197 bills. The deputies voted large sums of money for a fifteen-year expansion of education and passed laws providing workers with state insurance. They supported Stolypin's agrarian programme and frequently recommended military expenditures even higher than the sums proposed by the war ministry. Ironically, the government increasingly found that its reform measures were being passed by the Duma but blocked by the State Council.

A constitutional crisis arose in March 1911 after the State Council amended a law already passed by the Duma, creating zemstvos in the western provinces. Stolypin used Article 87 of the Fundamental Laws to promulgate the legislation by proroguing both chambers for four days. This raised a storm of protest in the Duma, which pronounced Stolypin's action to be illegal. The deputies passed a motion of censure on the government and the chairman, Alexander Guchkov, resigned in protest. This dispute destroyed the nascent trust and goodwill which had been slowly developing between the Duma and Stolypin – who was assassinated six months later in Kiev.

Guchkov had previously resigned as chairman in June 1910 after he fought a duel with a member of his own faction, Count Alexei Uvarov, and was sentenced to four months in the Peter and Paul Fortress (he was freed by the tsar after only two weeks and subsequently re-elected speaker). Guchkov was a colourful character who had fought against the British in the Boer War, where he had been taken prisoner. He challenged Pavel Milyukov to a duel in 1908 and fought another duel in 1912 with a colonel whom he had publicly accused of being a German spy: 'The duel was fought in the island suburbs. Guchkov coolly awaited his opponent's shot, and then discharged his revolver in the air and walked off without shaking hands, to show he did not regard his opponent as worthy to take part in a combat of honour.'[11]

In 1910, Guchkov made a famous speech in which he spoke for the first time about a subject which had, up until then, 'only been whispered about in corners' – the presence of 'dark forces' close to the throne.[12] This was the only subject in Russia on which both the government ministers and all the Duma deputies, from left to right, were in complete agreement – the figure of Grigory Rasputin. He was a Siberian peasant who had become an intimate friend of the tsar and his wife, mainly due to his gift for semi-religious soothsaying and apparent ability to heal their haemophiliac son, Tsarevich Alexis. To the rest of the country, however, he was better known for his debauched and outrageous behaviour in restaurants and in female company.

The 'Rasputin question' soon began to dominate the political scene. In 1911, Guchkov obtained copies of letters written by the empress and her daughters to Rasputin, which he had copied and circulated. People began to speak openly and even write about the scandal in the newspapers, some of which were fined or closed down. This brought the whole affair into the public arena, as Guchkov proposed submitting an official question to the government on the legality of censoring the press. The motion was passed in January 1912 by an overwhelming majority with only one vote against.

The new Duma chairman, Mikhail Rodzianko, was granted an audience with the tsar in February. Nicholas agreed to a new investigation of Rasputin's character, which would be conducted by Rodzianko himself. Resisting a direct attempt at interference by the empress, who tried to confiscate part of his evidence, Rodzianko wrote and submitted his report the following month. Time passed and he heard nothing from the tsar. When he finally asked for another audience, his request was denied with the words: 'I do not wish to receive Rodzianko... The conduct of the Duma is deeply revolting.'[13]

Parliament had now crossed a line by daring to touch on matters concerning the personal life of the imperial family.[14] For Nicholas, this was the final straw in his relations with the Duma and he never again received its chairman. As Octobrist deputy Nikandor Savich wrote in his memoirs: 'From now on, not only Guchkov, but the entire Duma would have an irreconcilable foe in the empress and every last hope of improving relations between the tsar and the representative government was lost.'[15]

One of the last acts of the Third Duma was to investigate a massacre of striking miners at the Lena Goldfields in Siberia in April 1912. A peaceful march of over 2,000 workers was fired upon by soldiers commanded by a drunken police captain, killing several hundred people. Fearing a whitewash by the government commission – the tsar's mother was a major shareholder in the mining company – the Duma set up its own public enquiry, headed by an unknown lawyer called Alexander Kerensky. Kerensky's report condemned the police actions and the minister of the interior, Alexander Makarov, was forced to resign.

The Fourth Duma

The elections for the Fourth Duma were held in autumn 1912 amid the hysteria surrounding the Beilis affair – Russia's equivalent of the Dreyfus affair. Menahem Mendel Beilis was a Hasidic Jew wrongly accused of the ritual murder of a Russian boy in Kiev (he was acquitted in 1913). Although the Octobrists remained the largest party in the Duma, their representation dropped to ninety-eight seats. The nationalists and other right-wing deputies now held a combined 153 seats. The other parties were the Cadets (59), Progressives (48), Centrists (32), Social Democrats (14) and Trudoviki (10). The Socialist Revolutionaries and Popular Socialists again boycotted the elections. The Fourth Duma opened on 15 November 1912 and re-elected Mikhail Rodzianko as its chairman. (See plate section.)

Rodzianko stood up for the rights of the deputies at a special service marking the tercentenary of the House of Romanov in St Petersburg on 21 February 1913. Learning that the places reserved for the Duma in the Kazan Cathedral were 'not in accordance with the dignity of that institution' and far behind the seats for members of the State Council and the Senate, Rodzianko pointed out that, 'in 1613, it was an assembly of the people and not a group of officials that elected Michael Romanov as tsar of Russia.' As a result, the Duma members were given the places reserved for the Senate, who were relegated to the back of the cathedral.[16]

In November 1913, the Octobrists accused the government of acting in direct contradiction to the October Manifesto and moved into opposition.

They increasingly joined forces with the Cadets to pass laws on freedom of the press, assembly and association – although these acts were then blocked by the State Council. In March 1914, the government attempted to prosecute the Menshevik leader, Karlo Chkheidze, after he made a speech advocating the establishment of a republic, but the case was dropped after all the other factions supported him. The deputies passed a vote of no confidence in the minister of the interior, Nikolai Maklakov, who later urged the tsar to abolish the Duma and assume dictatorial powers.

All this was forgotten when Germany declared war on Russia on 19 July/1 August 1914. The Duma was recalled from its summer recess for an extraordinary one-day session exactly a week later. After an audience with the tsar in the Winter Palace, every group except the Bolsheviks voted to pass the government's military budget (the five Bolshevik members were arrested on treason charges in November and exiled to Siberia). The Duma was prorogued until January 1915, when it met for two days to pass the next budget and was dismissed again by the emperor until the following year. But military setbacks in May and failings in the supply of food and equipment for the army led to demands that parliament be given a greater role in organising the war effort. The government was forced to dismiss the minister of war, Vladimir Sukhomlinov, and recall the Duma in July 1915.

A broad centrist alliance of 236 deputies, ranging from the Cadets to conservatives like Vasily Shulgin, formed a Progressive Bloc in August 1915 to push for a 'government of confidence' with ministers drawn from the legislative chambers. Their programme was supported by almost half of the State Council and eight ministers. The response of the emperor was to announce that he was taking personal command of the army and moving to the *Stavka* (general headquarters) in Mogilyov, where he remained for the rest of the war. During the next few months, he dismissed all eight members of his cabinet who had supported the Progressive Bloc. Ministers were now appointed under the influence of Rasputin and the empress, who were implacably hostile to the Duma.

During his time at *Stavka*, in January 1916, Nicholas II revealed his thoughts on the transfer of powers to the Duma in a conversation with Sir John Hanbury-Williams, chief of the British military mission to Russia: 'His own ideas as a young man were that he had, of course, a great responsibility, and felt that the people over whom he ruled were so numerous and so varying in blood and temperament, different altogether from our Western Europeans, that an emperor was a vital necessity to them.' The tsar said that the specific problems, religious feelings, habits and customs in Russia 'generally made a crown necessary, and he believed this must be so for a very long time, that a certain amount of decentralisation of authority was, of course, necessary, but that the great and decisive power must rest with the crown. The powers of the Duma must go slowly.'[17]

When the Duma reconvened on 1 November 1916 for what would be its last session, the Progressive Bloc openly criticised Rasputin and Alexandra Fyodorovna. Pavel Milyukov, the group's leader, made a famous speech which referred to the widespread – though entirely false – rumours of their treachery on behalf of Germany: 'The name of the empress is increasingly heard alongside the names of the opportunists who surround her... What is this – stupidity or treason?' Even the ultra-monarchist Vladimir Purishkevich joined in the attacks on their 'evil' influence: 'The tsar's ministers... have been turned into marionettes, marionettes whose threads are firmly guided by the hands of Rasputin and Empress Alexandra Fyodorovna – the evil genius of Russia and the tsaritsa who has remained German on the Russian throne and alien to the country and its people.'[18]

Purishkevich spoke for two hours and concluded by shouting at the ministers sitting in the government box: 'Be off to headquarters, throw yourself at the feet of the tsar and beg his leave to open his eyes to the awful reality... beg him to deliver Russia from Rasputin and his followers.' When they failed to do so, the patriotic deputy took matters into his own hands, following up on his emotional words to Rodzianko four years earlier: 'Oh, my God! I want to sacrifice myself and kill this vermin!'[19] He hatched a plot with two of the tsar's relatives, Prince Felix Yusupov and Grand Duke Dmitry Pavlovich, to physically eliminate Rasputin. On 17 December 1916, they lured the peasant to the Yusupov Palace, where they shot him in the basement.

Almost all of Nicholas's Russian relatives supported their action and begged him to make concessions to the Duma. Meanwhile, the empress urged her husband to dissolve the Duma and banish the deputies to Siberia. She wrote to him in a letter on 14 December: 'Be Peter the Great, [Ivan] the Terrible, Emperor Paul – crush them all under you – now don't you laugh, naughty one – but I long to see you so with all those men who try to govern you... Disperse the Duma at once.'[20]

For a very brief moment, Nicholas II seemed on the point of agreeing to the Duma's demands. Rodzianko's memoirs mention a curious episode with the last prime minister of Imperial Russia, Prince Nikolai Golitsyn, on 22 February 1917: 'I learnt casually that the emperor had summoned several of the ministers, including Golitsyn, and expressed his desire to discuss the question of a responsible ministry. The conference ended in the emperor's decision to go to the Duma the next day and proclaim his will to grant a responsible ministry. Prince Golitsyn was overjoyed and came home in high spirits.' But not long after making this announcement, Nicholas changed his mind – which can only have happened after he shared his decision with his wife. 'That same evening [Golitsyn] was again summoned to the palace, where the emperor announced to him his intention to leave for the *Stavka*. "How is that, your Majesty?" asked Golitsyn, amazed. "What about a responsible ministry? You intended to go to the Duma tomorrow." "I have changed my mind... I am leaving for the *Stavka* tonight."'[21]

The following morning, revolution broke out on the streets of Petrograd.[22]

8

1917

The February Revolution

'In the spring there will be omens, and thereafter extreme changes, reversals of kingdoms and mighty earthquakes. These will be accompanied by the procreation of the new Babylon, miserable daughter enlarged by the abomination of the first holocaust. It will last for only seventy-three years and seven months.'

Nostradamus, *Epistle to Henri II*, 1558

On the morning of 23 February/8 March 1917, factory strikes and discontent in the bread queues sparked mass demonstrations calling for an end to the autocracy. Over the next few days, the Cossacks summoned to disperse the crowds refused to obey orders, while the city garrison mutinied and went over to the insurgents.

On the evening of 26 February, Rodzianko sent an urgent telegram to the tsar:

The situation is serious. The capital is in a state of anarchy. The government is paralysed; the transport service has broken down; the food and fuel supplies are completely disorganised. Discontent is general and on the increase. There is wild shooting in the streets; troops are firing at each other. It is urgent that someone enjoying the confidence of the country be entrusted with the formation of a new government. There must be no delay. Hesitation is fatal.[1]

The emperor showed this telegram to General Alexeyev with the words: 'Some more rubbish from that fat Rodzianko, which I shall not even bother to answer.'[2] He telegraphed Prince Golitsyn to suspend the Duma.

The following day, Rodzianko sent a second telegram:

> The situation is growing worse. Measures should be taken immediately as tomorrow will be too late. The last hour has struck, when the fate of the country and dynasty is being decided. The government is powerless to stop the disorders. The troops of the garrison cannot be relied upon. The reserve battalions of the guard regiments are in the grips of rebellion, their officers are being killed. Having joined the mobs and the revolt of the people, they are marching on the offices of the ministry of the interior and the Imperial Duma.[3]

At eight in the morning of 27 February, the leaders of all the political parties conferred at the Tauride Palace and decided to ignore the emperor's order to disperse. As crowds of workers and soldiers poured into the building, Vasily Shulgin advised Rodzianko: 'Take power... if you don't, others will.' At three in the afternoon, the Duma elected a provisional government of eleven ministers, headed by Prince Georgy Lvov, with representatives from all the major parties, including Pavel Milyukov as foreign minister, Alexander Guchkov as war minister and Alexander Kerensky as justice minister. The first decision of the new government was to promise full civil rights and the summoning of a constituent assembly based on universal suffrage.[4]

As one observer commented, 'in less than a week, the long-awaited revolution, triggered off by disturbances in the bread queues, had come about... The revolutionaries were as much taken by surprise as anyone.'[5] Even members of the Romanov family rushed to join the revolution. Grand Duke Kirill Vladimirovich raised the red flag above his palace in Petrograd, while Grand Duke Nikolai Konstantinovich sent a telegram of congratulations to the Provisional Government from his place of exile in Tashkent. Meanwhile, as the regiments of the garrison declared themselves in favour of the Duma, the workers and soldiers repeated the experience of 1905 by recreating the Petrograd Soviet.

The Petrograd Soviet represented an alternative and rival government and also sat in the Tauride Palace. Kerensky, who joined the SRs in

March 1917, was elected vice-chairman of the Soviet, in addition to his portfolio in the Provisional Government. He later wrote about this uneasy situation of dual power: 'The wing to the left of the entrance remained at the disposal of the Duma; the right was given to the Soviet. Two different Russias settled side by side: the Russia of the ruling classes who had lost (though they did not realise it yet) ... and the Russia of labour, marching towards power, without suspecting it.'[6] The empress described these developments in a letter to her husband on 2 March: 'There are two groups – the Duma and the revolutionaries – two snakes that, I hope, will bite each other's heads off.'[7]

As Alexandra Fyodorovna was writing these words, Guchkov and Shulgin were travelling to Pskov, where they secured the abdication of the emperor. Nicholas initially relinquished the throne in favour of his son, but then changed his mind and abdicated on behalf of them both, in favour of his brother Michael, 'in agreement with the Imperial Duma'. The following day, 3 March 1917, Michael published a manifesto which was the last act of the Romanov dynasty:

I have firmly decided that I will accept power only if that is the will of our great people, who must by universal suffrage elect their representatives to the Constituent Assembly, in order to determine the form of government and draw up new fundamental laws for Russia. Therefore, calling for the blessing of God, I ask all citizens of Russia to obey the Provisional Government, which has arisen and has been endowed with full authority on the initiative of the Imperial Duma, until such time as the Constituent Assembly, called at the earliest possible date and elected on the basis of universal, direct, equal and secret suffrage, shall by its decision as to the form of government give expression to the will of the people.[8]

Nicholas wrote later that day in his diary: 'It transpires that Misha has abdicated. His manifesto ends with a four-tail formula for the election of a constituent assembly within six months. God knows who put it into his head to sign such stuff.'[9]

But Michael was acting strictly in accordance with Russian history. He was returning power to its original owner – the Russian people, who had given the crown to his namesake, Michael Romanov, in 1613. It was now up to the people to decide what to do with this power. Would they give it to a new tsar? Or would they choose to keep it for themselves?

Year Zero

'The 27th February of the year 1917 marked the end of a long and painful trail, from pure absolutism to absolute democracy... The people themselves were in power, the people themselves were the owners of Russia.'

Alexander Kerensky

The first step in deciding what to do next was to elect a constituent assembly. This would not be a permanent institution but an interim body to choose a new system of government and resolve the most pressing issues facing the country – the ownership of land, the continuation of the war and the question of national autonomy. The assembly would then dissolve itself and hand over power to a new, democratically elected parliament and government. Fyodor Kokoshkin, a constitutional expert and former Cadet deputy, compared the situation in 1917 to the biblical story of the Creation, when the earth was still without form: 'A living and creative spirit also moves above the sea of our revolution... We do not yet have a new constitution, but the basic foundation of this constitution already exists, and that is recognition of the supremacy of the people.'[10]

There was already an internationally established precedent for holding a constituent assembly after a revolution. In 1787, the Constitutional Convention met in Philadelphia following the American Revolution, while the National Constituent Assembly sat in France from 1789 to 1791. Similar assemblies were convened in France and Germany after the revolutions of 1848. In Russia, the idea of a constituent assembly had been widely discussed throughout the nineteenth century, from the Decembrists in the 1820s to the People's Will in 1880. Lenin had advocated calling a Zemsky Sobor in the 1890s, while the demand for a constituent assembly was included in the programme of the Social Democrats in 1903. As Russian historian Vasily Klyuchevsky dryly observed in 1905: 'The constituent assembly, which is being demanded by all... is the combination of the Russian monkey-mind: they had it abroad, so we too must have it.'[11]

On 6 March 1917, the Provisional Government issued a list of its main objectives, which included 'immediate preparation for the convocation of a constituent assembly, on the basis of universal, equal, secret and direct voting, which will establish the form of government and constitution of the country'. Even earlier, on 28 February, the Petrograd Soviet had called for 'the complete elimination of the old government and the convocation of a constituent assembly based on universal, equal, direct and secret elections.'[12]

On 25 March, the Provisional Government set up a 'special council' to draft a new electoral law. Chaired by Fyodor Kokoshkin, the council included representatives of all the major political parties, from the Cadets to the Bolsheviks. Several days later, the Petrograd Soviet created its own rival commission with thirteen members headed by Leon Bramson, a Socialist Revolutionary who in 1922 co-founded the American ORT Federation. In the spirit of this period of shared power, the commission cooperated closely with the government council, negotiating and sharing its findings with ministers.

The Provisional Government passed the electoral law in three stages on 20 July, 11 September and 21 September. But the interim leaders kept postponing the date of the elections, fuelling accusations that they were deliberately delaying the vote in a bid to cling onto power. Vladimir Nabokov secretly believed that Russia was not yet ready for universal elections, while Pavel Milyukov opposed 'this stupid idea of a constituent assembly'.[13] However, the main reason for the constant delays was simply the desire to make the vote as free and fair as possible. As Leon Bramson proudly boasted in June 1917: 'The electoral law which will be published in about ten days is the most democratic law... which has ever seen the light of day in any state in Europe – possibly even... the whole world.'[14]

On 14 June, the election date was set for 17 September. Joseph Stalin immediately issued a rallying call to his fellow Bolsheviks from the pages of *Pravda*: 'The Constituent Assembly election campaign has begun. The parties are already mobilising their forces... We are in favour of a people's republic, without a standing army, bureaucracy or police force... We are opposed to the reintroduction of the death penalty. We are in favour of all the nations of Russia being granted the right to freely arrange their lives in their own way and of none of them being subjected to oppression... To work, comrades!'[15]

The first part of Stalin's article was published in *Pravda* on 5 July but was not continued because the paper was suppressed after the 'July Days'. This was several days of street fighting in Petrograd on 3-5 July, largely involving anarchists and revolutionary soldiers – encouraged though not officially endorsed by the Bolshevik leadership. The unrest was put down by Alexander Kerensky, who became prime minister on 7 July as the head of a new coalition government after the resignation of all the Cadet ministers. Kerensky's cabinet was mainly composed of moderate socialists and now sat in the Winter Palace. On 9 August, he postponed the elections yet again, this time until 12 November.

The Bolsheviks initially supported the calling of a constituent assembly, because it would clearly be more radical than the Provisional Government. But their position changed in April 1917 after Lenin returned from exile in Switzerland and the Seventh Party Conference adopted his resolution advocating 'the transfer of all state power into the hands of the soviets of workers' and soldiers' deputies or other organs directly expressing the will of the people'.[16] However, this did not stop the Bolsheviks from attacking the Provisional Government for postponing the elections. Between March and October 1917, Lenin mentioned the Constituent Assembly fifty times in his letters and speeches. As late as 8 October, he was warning that Kerensky's policies 'carry the clear threat of the rigging and falsification of the elections to the Constituent Assembly'.[17]

The Provisional Government set up the electoral commission (*Vsevybory*) on 1 August. All the leading parties were represented, except the Bolsheviks, who had either been arrested or gone into hiding after the July Days. The commission was chaired by Nikolai Avinov (Cadet) with Leon Bramson (SR) and Vladimir Nabokov (Cadet) as deputy chairmen. The commission sat in the Mariinsky Palace in Petrograd and began work on 7 August.

On 25 August, General Lavr Kornilov, the commander-in-chief of the Russian army, launched a revolt against the Provisional Government and started moving troops from the front towards Petrograd. He wanted to establish a more authoritarian regime or even a directorate, ostensibly 'to bring the people to the Constituent Assembly, where they will decide their own fate and choose the style of their new state life.'[18] There is much confusion over Kornilov's exact aims and some sources suggest that he planned to combine a military dictatorship with a representative government in the form of a Zemsky Sobor.[19]

Kerensky dismissed Kornilov and called on 'all democratic forces' – including the Bolsheviks, who were now freed from prison – to halt the approaching battalions, which was done by railway workers outside Petrograd on 30 August. Kornilov was arrested and Kerensky took over as commander-in-chief. Symbolist writer Zinaida Gippius wrote in her diary on 31 August: 'I am almost certain that the celebrated divisions were marching to Petersburg for Kerensky – with his full knowledge or in response to an informal order from him.' Later, in August 1991, many believed that Gorbachev did the exact same thing as Kerensky, issuing a secret command to hardliners to restore order, then taking fright at the last moment and appealing for help to 'democratic forces' – only to let them take power themselves.

The October Revolution

'A republic of soviets is a higher form of democracy than the usual bourgeois republic with a constituent assembly.'

Vladimir Lenin

On 1 September, Kerensky declared Russia a republic and set up a consultative body called the Pre-Parliament as a stop-gap between the Provisional Government and the Constituent Assembly. The Bolsheviks were invited to participate, although Trotsky led their deputies out of the first sitting on 7 October. Three days later, Lenin called for an armed uprising at a meeting of the Central Committee: 'It is senseless to wait for the Constituent Assembly, which will obviously not be with us, for this will only complicate our task.'[20]

On 25 October/7 November 1917, the Bolsheviks seized all the key government buildings in Petrograd. The following morning, the members of the Provisional Government were arrested in the Winter Palace – Kerensky managed to escape – and Lenin proclaimed that all power had passed to the soviets, where the Bolsheviks now had a majority. The Bolsheviks immediately passed two new laws based on their election promises. The Decree on Peace proposed an immediate withdrawal from the war, while the Decree on Land nationalised all property and redistributed the former estates among the peasants. For now, the Bolsheviks claimed that their government – which was called the Council of People's Commissars (*Sovnarkom*) – was also 'provisional' and that these 'interim acts' still required formal ratification by the future Constituent Assembly.

The initial address of the Second All-Russian Congress of Soviets on 25 October 'to the workers, soldiers and peasants on the victory of the revolution' pledged that the elections to the Constituent Assembly would still go ahead as planned. But Trotsky later testified: 'A few days, if not hours, after the October revolution, Lenin raised the question of the Constituent Assembly. "We must postpone the elections," he declared. "We must enlarge the suffrage by giving it to those who are eighteen years old. We must make possible a new arrangement of the electoral lists. Our own lists are worthless..." He shook his head in dissatisfaction and repeated, "It is a mistake, an open mistake, that may cost us very dear! If it only does not cost the revolution its head."'[21]

9

The Constituent Assembly Elections

'We shall advance, and we shall advance more rapidly than the others, because we have come after them, because we have all their experience and all the work of the centuries which precede us.'

Pyotr Chaadayev, 1835

The Constituent Assembly election campaign really only began in September 1917, when the competing parties drew up their lists of candidates. The town dumas and provincial zemstvos were responsible for compiling the electoral roll and sending voting papers to everyone on the register. As zemstvos did not exist in the Caucasus, Siberia and Central Asia, these areas had to vote twice – first to appoint these organs and then for the Constituent Assembly. By now, some Russians were beginning to suffer from voter fatigue. Local elections had been scheduled for thirty-seven provinces between June and September, but only took place in nine. The turnout in the 650 town duma elections was also low – only 38% in Moscow – and the voting was often disrupted by revolutionary soldiers.

The local elections in summer 1917 were the first time that most Russian women went to the polls.[1] All women had been given the vote by the Provisional Government following a mass rally of 40,000 demonstrators in Petrograd on 19 March.[2] But there were still opponents of this move on both left and right wings. The right believed that women were generally ignorant about politics, prone to rash extremism and easily seduced by Bolshevik demagoguery. The left claimed the exact opposite – that women were conservative, sentimental and wanted to restore the monarchy (a delegate from Vologda warned at the All-Russian Conference of Soviets on 2 April that 'our womenfolk are still weeping over Nicholas II').[3] In the village of Novo-Troitskoe in Tauride Province, the local zemstvo annulled the elections because women had voted, and they were not admitted the second time they were held. In the Ukrainian village of Platonivka, women were also forbidden from voting in the summer rural elections.[4]

On 10 September, the Provisional Government allocated six million roubles towards the cost of holding the elections, but that was still not enough. The electoral law had to be published in sixteen languages, while 100 million identity documents and a billion ballot papers had to be printed – so many that orders had to be placed with factories in Finland and Sweden. An additional problem was a shortage of glue and paper after stationery factories went on strike in August and September.

Voting Rules

'Russia is to be one of the most democratic countries and the freest in all
the world.'
Vladimir Nabokov to Pitirim Sorokin, 1 March 1917

As promised by the Provisional Government, voting was universal, equal, direct and secret. There were no property, class, income, literacy, religious, gender or ethnic qualifications. All men and women who had reached the age of twenty on election day could vote.[5] This easily made it the most democratic electoral law in the world. By comparison, only 15% of Russians could vote in the Duma elections, while 30% of Britons had the franchise in 1917.

For the first time in history, the vote was given to all those serving in the armed forces (ten million men and women). The five army fronts, two fleets and the Foreign Expeditionary Corps serving in France and the Balkans elected eighty delegates. The only people not given the vote were prisoners, deserters, lunatics or anyone under criminal investigation (this went against the presumption of innocence and was one of the defects of the law). The suffrage was extended to travellers, tramps, nomads, leper colonies and the thousands of homeless refugees fleeing the advancing German armies.

Voting was based on the system of proportional representation already widely used in European countries, including Finland from 1906. Russia based its system on the Belgian model – parties drew up lists of candidates and the d'Hondt method was used to calculate the number of seats awarded to each party. A simple majority was employed in remote areas with small or nomadic populations and the two electoral districts outside the Russian Empire – the Foreign Expeditionary Corps in Europe and the Chinese-Eastern Railway in Manchuria.

Provision was made for other voters living abroad. The Russian population of Finland was included in Petrograd Province and could cast their ballots at polling stations in Helsinki, Turku, Vyborg and Terijoki. Russian citizens in the Emirate of Bukhara were attached to Samarkand. Uryankhai (Tuva), which was previously part of China, but declared a Russian protectorate in 1914, was joined to Yenisei district. There was also a need to accommodate the requests to vote from Russian prisoners-of-war in Germany, the Danube River Fleet and the Seventh Cavalry Corps stationed in Persia.

Each party submitted lists with the names of its candidates. Voters had to select one list (two in Olonets). Thirteen nationwide and thirty-four local or 'ethnic minority' groups took part. Parties sometimes formed alliances to run as a 'bloc' – though not always with the same party. The Ukrainian SRs joined with the Left SRs in some districts and with the Mensheviks in others. There were all sorts of exotic combinations, such as the 'Siberian Tatars' in Tobolsk or the 'Kyrgyz Socialists' and 'Muslim Democrats' in Omsk. Independent candidates could also run, but only a handful were elected. Over 7,000 candidates stood in total (63% were socialists and 22% were Cadets).

The lists had to be submitted thirty days before the election, so that voters had time to make up their minds. Most parties held conferences to compile their lists in September or early October. Because literacy levels were low, each list was given a number, depending on the order in which they were registered by the local electoral commission.[6] The average number of lists in an electoral district was nine. The lowest was one (Caspian district for the nomads of the Kalmyk Steppe) and the highest was nineteen (Kharkiv). A candidate was not allowed to run in more than five electoral districts. Lenin broke this rule by running in six (Petrograd, Moscow, Petrograd Province, Ufa Province, Northern Front and the Baltic Fleet). He also violated the law by standing when there was still technically a warrant out for his arrest, after he fled to Finland following the July Days.

The voting procedure was very simple. Each voter was previously sent an identity document and copies of all the party lists. Voting had to be done in person at the polling station, where the voter underwent a name check before being given an envelope. The voter entered a booth and placed his or her chosen list unseen into the envelope, which was then sealed and dropped into the ballot box. This had the advantage of not requiring anything to be written on the ballot paper. Alternative voting methods using balls with numbers were allowed in several backward regions, such as Yakutia. There were strict rules on the size of the ballot boxes, which had locks on the lid and a hole for the ballot papers. Portable boxes were not allowed, which meant that many women in the Kazakh steppes were unable to vote, as they stayed in their yurts all winter and did not have any warm clothing. Campaigning was allowed on election day, but not in polling stations.

The country was divided into eighty-one electoral districts, which roughly corresponded to the existing provinces. There were seventy-two on the territory of the former Russian Empire, eight for the armed forces and one for the Chinese-Eastern Railway in Manchuria. The two largest cities of Petrograd and Moscow constituted separate districts. The original plan was to elect 850 deputies, but thirty electoral districts were in the five provinces occupied by the Central Powers, so the number was reduced to 820. This worked out as one delegate for every 219,000 people in Europe and every 140,000 people in Asia. Kamchatka only had 20,000 voters, but still elected one deputy.

All the main political forces took part – with the exception of the monarchists and anarchists. The Romanov family was barred from voting or standing for election. The Special Council initially voted 38-5 to give them full electoral rights, but was overruled by the Provisional Government, who feared accusations of holding pro-monarchist sympathies. Grand Duke Nikolai Mikhailovich – a committed republican known as 'Nicholas Égalité', who had planned to stand for the assembly himself – appealed against this decision, along with several other relatives, but was unsuccessful.[7]

Nationalists did not openly campaign for a restoration of the monarchy, preferring to blame everyone from the Cadets to the Bolsheviks for the general anarchy caused by the revolution. The Union of Monarchists declared that no law passed by the Constituent Assembly was legally binding on the Russian people. The Moscow Federation of Anarchists pointed out that 'no government, parliament or constituent assembly can give the people what they have not already taken themselves.'[8] Some anarchists welcomed the elections, as 'then even the blind will see that no government gives or leads to anything.'[9]

Campaign

'Russia has perished, master, you mark my words, it's perished. We can't have this voting thing... No, master, I ain't going to any elections, I'll die first.'

Ivan Bunin, *Cursed Days: A Diary of the Revolution*

Each major party had its own distinctive programme and style of canvassing. The Bolsheviks attacked both the Provisional Government and the other socialists. They campaigned on a policy of bread, peace and land. The party compiled its lists in September, when Lenin was in hiding in Finland. When he returned to Petrograd, he sharply criticised the lists for lacking 'real' workers and including former Mensheviks. In Stavropol, the local Bolsheviks criticised the decision to give Stalin first place on their list, pointing out that he was unknown to voters, and petitioned to get him moved down to third place.

Because the party was not rich and its electorate tended to be poorly educated, the Bolsheviks reduced their manifesto to several snappy slogans – 'peace to the trenches', 'land to the peasants', 'factories to the workers' and 'power to the soviets'. They did not have so many newspapers as some of the other parties, so they shut down rival presses and used soldiers and sailors for direct verbal agitation, especially in the countryside. The Bolsheviks encouraged peasant soldiers to write letters home and printed special election leaflets for them to slip inside the envelopes. This tactic helped them to win the Cossack settlement of Iletskaya Zaschita, where 'the majority of soldiers' wives, receiving letters from the front, voted for the Bolshevik list.'[10]

The Bolsheviks and the Cadets both used aircraft to canvass voters. *Kavkazskoe slovo* newspaper described the first day of the elections in Tiflis: 'Seven in the morning... The characteristic drone of an engine is heard – an aeroplane is flying. It descends lower and something like a flock of white silvery doves surrounds the cabin of the aeroplane. The pilot is flinging out political leaflets... Those voting for No. 5 are promised peace, bread, land and much more. The aeroplane describes circles, the leaflets fly and fly. On the eve of the elections, another aeroplane was flying about, throwing for No. 2 [Cadets].'[11]

The Cadets promised law and order, civil liberties and a strong Russia. They attacked the general inability of left-wing parties to govern, declaring that 'socialist parties can only issue promises' and that, under a leftist government, all Russian land would effectively belong to Kaiser

Wilhelm II. The Cadets had the experience of fighting four Duma campaigns and no shortage of money. They were supported by people tired of the revolution, but they faced an uphill battle in rural and industrial areas. Their canvassers were physically threatened in workers' districts, while typographers in Poltava and Vladivostok refused to print their brochures.[12] The Cadets commissioned professional artists to design their posters and widely employed female images – usually a Russian housewife or a woman symbolising freedom (a forerunner of the *Motherland Calls!* image in Soviet wartime posters). Green was used in their posters to symbolise growth and rejuvenation.

The Socialist Revolutionaries (SRs) aimed for victory and a majority of the seats. Their programme was written by professional economists and sociologists and targeted the peasants, promising land and an end to the war – although, unlike the Bolsheviks, they wanted a negotiated and not a separate peace. The SRs also advocated a federated democratic republic, autonomy for ethnic minorities and a mixed economy. They had a well-run party network backed up by a million members and a hundred newspapers. The SRs were the only party to focus on personalities, such as the seventy-three-year-old Ekaterina Breshko-Breshkovskaya, who was known as 'the granny of the Russian revolution'. Thanks to her foreign contacts, the SRs secured sizeable donations from the American Red Cross. Combined with their healthy finances in Russia, this allowed them to 'flood the place with all sorts of literature, proclamations, posters, newspapers, etc... dozens of every possible poster were pasted on almost every single house and prominent place.'[13] Like the Cadets, the SRs employed colour psychology in their posters and leaflets – red for the revolutionary struggle and yellow for corn and abundance.

Just before the elections, the SRs split into two separate parties, after the leftists broke away from the centre-right majority. As the Left SRs were usually further down the party lists, this possibly helped the main bloc to pick up additional radical votes – allowing Lenin to argue against the legitimacy of the Constituent Assembly by claiming that 'the people voted for a party which no longer existed.'[14] However, he only said this on 21 November, after voting had already taken place; none of the other parties had any objections going into the elections. The main bloc possibly also lost votes when supporters of the Left SRs crossed out the names of the Right SRs on the lists, rendering the ballot paper invalid. In some electoral districts, such as Voronezh, Yenisei, Tobolsk, Kuban-Black Sea,

Amur and the Baltic Fleet, the Left SRs ran separately from the main SRs. In a few cases, the Right SRs were opposed by a bloc of Centre-Left SRs.

There were also splits in the Menshevik camp between the Internationalists (who opposed the continuation of the war) and the Defencists (who supported a limited defensive war). They ran on separate lists in a dozen districts, including Petrograd and Moscow, while in ten other districts the Internationalists allied with the Bolsheviks. The Mensheviks were not optimistic of success after only polling around 10% in the summer local elections. While the masses wanted rapid changes, the Mensheviks were not convinced that Russia was rich enough, sufficiently industrialised or psychologically ready for socialism. Their electorate mainly consisted of educated workers or soldiers and officers with an intellectual interest in Marxism. The Mensheviks also benefitted from American cash. On 12 September, their central election committee voted to seek help in the campaign from 'American comrades'.[15] By the end of October, their electoral fund stood at 105,000 roubles – ten times the planned amount. By comparison, the Bolsheviks had only raised 7,000 roubles at the end of September.[16]

As a proletarian party, the Mensheviks left the countryside to the SRs and focused on the urban areas, where the moderate socialist vote was split among two other competing parties – the Popular Socialists and 'Unity'

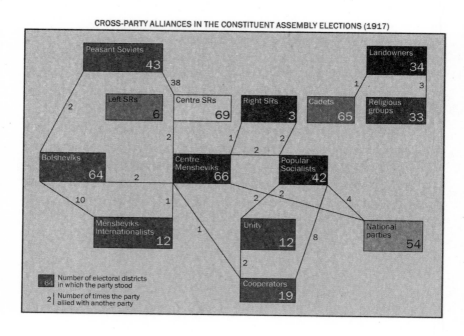

CROSS-PARTY ALLIANCES IN THE CONSTITUENT ASSEMBLY ELECTIONS (1917)

(*Yedinstvo*). Unity was founded by Georgy Plekhanov, 'the father of Russian Marxism', who returned to Russia at the end of March after thirty-seven years in exile (he arrived at the Finland Railway Station just three days before Lenin). Although now sixty, Plekhanov believed that 'an old soldier of the revolution should be at his post,' although he suffered harassment on the street and searches of his home by revolutionary soldiers.[17] Plekhanov supported the continuation of the war and opposed the Bolshevik seizure of power, believing – like the Mensheviks – that 'Russia has not yet ground that flour from which a socialist pie can be baked.'[18]

Election Day

From building to building over
The street a rope skips nimble,
A banner on the rope:
ALL POWER TO THE CONSTITUENT ASSEMBLY.
This old weeping woman is worried to death,
She doesn't know what it's all about:
That banner – for God's sake –
So many yards of cloth!
How many children's leggings it would make
And they without shirts – without boots

Alexander Blok, *The Twelve*, January 1918[19]

The Russian electorate was an estimated eighty-five million people, making the vote the largest ever held in history and the world's greatest exercise of universal suffrage – all in the middle of winter, during the First World War, in a country with limited infrastructure and only a fortnight after the Bolshevik revolution. The electoral commission faced a daunting task. Where could they find election officials for the ninety inhabitants of Novaya Zemlya in the Arctic Ocean? Or entire areas with no literate population at all, thousands of miles from the capital? The elections were held on a territory six times the size of Europe with hundreds of different nationalities, confessions, languages and classes. The majority of people were voting for the first time and Russia had no prior experience of universal, direct, equal or secret ballots.

This enormous display of democracy began on the morning of Sunday 12 November 1917, when polling stations opened their doors across eleven time zones, stretching from the 197 stations in Petrograd in the west to Chukotka next to Alaska.[20] Voting usually lasted for two and

105

a half days – from 9 am to 9 pm in the towns (or 8 am to 8 pm in the countryside) on the first two days and then until 2 pm on the third day. Places with low turnouts, such as Amur Province, were allowed to extend the period of voting. In Tomsk, where there was a combination of revolutionary fighting and voter fatigue, polling stations stayed open until the following Saturday.[21]

The elections had already been held over a single day on 29 October in Kamchatka, as its one deputy had to catch the last ship departing for the mainland on 10 November, before the region was cut off by ice. The results were then sent by telegram to Petrograd.[22] Transport difficulties and printing problems meant that voting was only held in the Kuban on 2-4 February 1918 – a month after the Constituent Assembly had been dissolved. Other parts of the country had already descended into civil war when their elections took place. The results in Orenburg Province, where power repeatedly changed hands, were only announced in July 1918.

The elections were held over seven days in the army, where they were initially scheduled for 8-14 November, but postponed until 22-28 November because of the Bolshevik coup. The navy was given even longer – fourteen days. The elections also took a fortnight on the Caucasian Front (1-14 November), which included parts of modern-day Turkey and Iran. Seventeen thousand soldiers voted in the city of Erzurum, which was captured by the Russians in February 1916.

In Petrograd, the electoral commission covered the whole of Nevsky Prospekt, Palace Bridge and many other streets and crossings with banners urging citizens to 'Save Russia!' 'Go to the polling stations!' and 'Long live the Constituent Assembly!' Theatre audiences were treated to short lectures in the intervals from the actors, who encouraged people to vote – including, sometimes, for which of the parties. Petrograd was a two-way battle between the Bolsheviks and Cadets. Cadet posters with No. 2 were plastered over 'all houses, shop windows and fences'. Their canvassers drove around the city in private cars, throwing out leaflets. The Bolsheviks used public transport and caused confusion when passengers mistook their posters for the No. 4 tram.

The rule on prisoners was broken at the Peter and Paul Fortress, where the arrested ministers of the Provisional Government were led out to vote under armed guard on 14 November. However, the law was applied arbitrarily and the unpopular ex-tsarist minister of justice, Ivan Scheglovitov, was not allowed to vote. When the polling stations closed their doors on the afternoon of 14 November, over 70% of the Petrograd electorate had voted (941,000 people). The chairman of the district electoral commission reported: 'The elections generally passed off calmly and any incidents were so insignificant as to be not worth mentioning.'[23]

The ongoing revolution forced some cities, such as Kiev and Kazan, to postpone the elections. Voting started a week later in Moscow, on 19 November, after the seat of the electoral commission was sacked during street fighting. Many Muscovites fled the city or locked themselves inside their houses, but the local committees performed wonders in getting the vote out and delivering all the necessary papers to voters.

A special service of thanksgiving was held at the Cathedral of Christ the Saviour on the first day of voting in Moscow. Otherwise, as one Menshevik newspaper reported, 'Sunday morning did not suggest in any way that this was the day of elections to the Constituent Assembly, coveted by several generations. The streets are deserted... The polling stations are empty. The voter is in no hurry. Three whole days at his disposal. The streets only gradually came to life towards midday. The voters came in greater numbers with the "tail ends" stretching down the street.'[24]

There were thirty-five recorded violations in Moscow. The most serious was when soldiers fired shots at voters in Presnya, wounding one worker.[25] An SR car was confiscated, a Cadet had his election literature seized near the Alexander (Serpukhov) Barracks and there were reports of soldiers voting multiple times. The turnout in Moscow was slightly lower than in Petrograd – just under 70% (774,000 voters) – but the figure was still much higher than in the recent local elections on 24 September (38%).

Several murders occurred during the campaign. In Oryol Province, the chairman of a rural electoral commission illegally campaigned for the party of landowners and was lynched by a group of peasants. In Pskov Province, Bolshevik soldiers killed a priest who chaired the local electoral commission. One Bolshevik campaigner remembered the time he spent the whole night putting up election posters in Khabarovsk:

When the last poster had been pasted, I turned round to leave and saw a big fat priest behind me, reading the poster. After reading it, he began to 'anathemise' me, calling me an anti-Christ, a German spy, an apostate and so on... but when he reached out to tear the poster from the wall... I was unable to contain myself (youth, impulsiveness, fatigue) and shot him... God rest his soul.

There were cases of domestic violence in the voting booths, such as in Kharkiv, where a man told his wife to vote for the Bolsheviks and slapped her when she refused.[26]

The Bolshevik seizure of power had no real effect on the voting, as the electoral commission established by the Provisional Government delegated ultimate authority on the ground to all its local organisations, which followed the letter of the law and prevented any form of interference.[27] On 13 December, the Ufa electoral body ordered its district commissions 'to open criminal investigations into all violations of the law and hand all cases over to the district prosecutor'.[28] There were no protests lodged by candidates, although the electoral commissions sometimes negated the results in cases of widespread violations. A total of 35,000 votes were annulled in Tambov Province, including over 20,000 for the SRs and over 7,000 for the Bolsheviks, suggesting that the officials worked independently without external pressure.

The turnout was generally higher in the villages (60-80%) than in the towns (58%), mainly due to the urgency of the land question and the traditions of obedience and communal voting in the countryside. In a village in Chelyabinsk Province, one person failed to vote and a special protocol was drawn up with a stern rebuke for the absentee (called a *nyetchik* in Russian).[29] The high turnout in the countryside helped the SRs, as 89% of their votes came from rural areas. Women tended to vote more than men, as they were exercising this right for the first time and had more to gain from the Constituent Assembly. In Tambov Province, for example, the female turnout was 77% in the villages (compared to 70% for men) and 54% in the towns (compared to 47% for men).[30] There were no cases of women breaking the electoral laws. In the end, only ten of the 767 elected delegates were women.

Muslim women were allowed to vote in separate polling stations and generally displayed a high turnout (77% in Baku). Ironically, the reason for this was the traditional submissiveness of women in such societies and their tendency to dutifully follow orders (which, in this case, was an instruction to vote). In the Crimea, a ninety-five-year-old Tatar woman, who had not left her bed for several years, was carried to a polling station to vote.[31] However, in the village of Tikhvinskoe in Tobolsk Province, an assembly of men declared: 'This women's equality seems somewhat strange to us and so we have not allowed women to participate in the elections in any way. We ask the Provisional Government not to reproach us.'[32]

In some parts of Turkestan, the lists were delivered on camels and voting only started on 29 January 1918. In the Mughan plain in south Azerbaijan, the election transport was attacked by Persian tribesmen. Trucks carrying ballot papers were lost in the mountains of Dagestan. Several electoral instructors were swept away by an avalanche in Turkish Armenia. No deliveries could be made to six polling stations in North Sakhalin and one in the Arctic Circle.

In the Steppe electoral district, the voting was twice postponed, first to the end of November and then to the end of December. But word did not reach the electoral commission in Akmola Province, which went ahead with the elections on 12-14 November as originally planned (the results were declared invalid). One million voters in the Sirdaryo district, which included the city of Tashkent, never got a chance to vote at all. Their elections were constantly postponed – first until 3 December, then 15 December, then 17 January – before finally being abandoned altogether.

All the documents for Mogilyov-Podolsky in Ukraine were mistakenly sent to Mogilyov in Belorussia. Copies of the electoral law only arrived in Simbirsk the day after the elections ended. Voters in Grozny, Pyatigorsk and Kutaisi had to write the numbers on sheets of paper stamped by the local electoral commission when the ballot papers failed to arrive. Some people never received their voting papers – 6,000 in Barnaul, 10,000 in Vitebsk and 20,000 in Astrakhan. In the port of Sevastopol, where the turnout was only 47%, a fifth of all voters were excluded from the electoral register.

In Tomsk, Fyodor Semyonov complained to the electoral commission that he had not been included in the list of voters – despite being a candidate himself. The commission discovered that he had been mistakenly registered under his old revolutionary pseudonym (Arseny Lisenko). He was allowed to vote and was duly elected to represent the SRs.[33] In Vyshny Volochyok in Tver Province, 2,000 factory workers went on strike and besieged the council building after they were not included in the electoral register. Fearing a riot, the local authorities decided to hold additional elections. This happened in other places and, although illegal, the central electoral commission usually turned a blind eye.

The Tambov electoral commission found the best solution to all these problems and one very much in the spirit of the times. They simply allowed anyone to vote, regardless of whether or not they were on the electoral roll, because 'under the current freedom, all are equal and free to do whatever they like.'[34]

Results

Immediately after the polling stations closed, the ballot boxes were opened and all the votes were counted in public. This was the procedure in a ward in the Tomsk electoral district: 'At 2 pm on 18 November, the chairman announced that the election was over and all those present were invited to observe the counting of the votes. The boxes were opened and all the glued envelopes were removed (3,820 out of an electorate of 7,469). A member of the commission then opened the envelopes, removed the voting slips and gave them to the chairman, who called out the list numbers. All the lists were arranged in party groups and then placed in separate packages on which the list number, the name of the party and the number of votes were written. Forty-nine were found to be invalid as they had inscriptions or other markings or writing on them. The following day, 19 November, there was a public sitting of the municipal electoral commission, which counted all the votes for the city of Tomsk and the Seventy-Ninth Tomsk Garrison.'[35] The Cadets came first in the city of Tomsk with 28.8% of all votes, but when the army garrison was added, the Bolsheviks pulled ahead on 40.2%. For the whole Tomsk electoral district, however, the Socialist Revolutionaries were the outright winners on 85.2%. As a result, the SRs were awarded nine of the ten seats, while the tenth went to the Bolsheviks.

The exact results will probably never be known, because much of the documentation was either lost or destroyed by the Soviet regime.[36] There was not even a complete list of all the delegates when the Constituent Assembly opened on 5 January 1918. This was mainly due to some candidates switching from one list to another and the associated problems with communications and postage in such an enormous country. A deputy elected in more than one district had to choose which area to represent and reject the others in writing within three days. But there were delays and confusion with this process. For various reasons, the elections were not held in fifty-three districts, so that reduced the total number of delegates from 820 to 767.

What is beyond doubt is that the elections to the Constituent Assembly were won by the Socialist Revolutionaries, who secured 39.5% (19.1 million votes), giving them 347 seats. They dominated in the southern and eastern agricultural areas and on the southern fronts. Their best results were in Stavropol (89%), Altai (87%), Caucasian Front (86%), Tomsk (85%), Kursk (82%), Penza (81%) and Voronezh (80%), while their worst result was in Estonia (1.17%). The SRs benefited from the high turnout among the peasants – there were rumours that those who did not vote would not get any land – and the quirks of the system used to translate votes into seats, which allowed them to pick up a higher proportion of places (45.2%) than their share of the vote (39.5%). They frequently polled in the eighties, which was enough to win all the seats in the district. In Penza, for example, 81% gave every place to the SRs, while the Bolsheviks on 8.6% got nothing.

The Bolsheviks came second with 22.4% (10.9 million votes), giving them 183 seats. They were the clear winners in the urban areas and the north-west of the country. The Bolsheviks won the cities of Petrograd (45%) and Moscow (48%) and were also strong in the Baltic states (72% in Livonia and Estland). However, they failed to capture such industrial centres as the Urals and Donbass. Their worst result was in the Caucasus (3.81%), where they were thrashed by the Mensheviks – but did attract the convict vote. In Tiflis, a group of prisoners held an election meeting and decided: 'The Bolsheviks are our comrades. We will vote for them.' So 432 of the 450 inmates in Baku and Tiflis prisons voted for the party.[37] The Bolsheviks slightly benefited from the d'Hondt system, as their overall 22.4% translated into 23.9% of all seats.

The Bolshevik successes in Petrograd, Moscow and Reval (Tallinn) show that their support was not confined to workers and soldiers. The financial classes often supported them as a source of strong power, while some monarchists liked the Bolsheviks for overthrowing those who had overthrown the tsar. Other right-wingers voted for them in order to hasten their inevitable fall from power and then, in the ensuing anarchy, establish a dictatorship or restore the monarchy. Some Bolsheviks thought that they would win the elections after the ease with which they had seized power in Petrograd. Their defeat came as a great shock and left them deeply traumatised by democracy – with a perpetual fear of free elections. Polling under a quarter of all votes 'was practically a vote of no confidence by the population in their new rulers'.[38] Their second place anticipated the 1990s, when the 'party of power' never won a general election in Russia.

The October revolution probably worked against the Bolsheviks and reduced their overall share of the vote. They had previously benefitted from being in opposition and attacking the government but were now criticised by all the other parties for seizing power. Their opponents were encouraged to turn out and vote for the Constituent Assembly as an alternative to the Bolsheviks, while their supporters regarded the assembly as 'a trap laid by the bourgeoisie' and stayed at home.[39] The Bolsheviks were unable to interfere in the elections, as the district electoral commissions had already been established and they only controlled a tiny part of the country. A telegram sent from Tobolsk to the central commission reported: 'The elections have passed off calmly. The Bolshevik movement in the district has not been observed and its influence has not been felt on the elections.'[40]

The following three parties were also socialists. The Ukrainian Socialist Bloc came third on 12.7% (110 seats) and the Ukrainian SRs were fourth on 7.7% (81 seats). However, they decided on 3 January to send only a few delegates to Petrograd on account of war between Russia and Ukraine. The Left SRs won around forty seats and only defeated their former colleagues in the Baltic Fleet, while in several districts – Voronezh, Yenisei and Tobolsk – they only got 1%.

The Cadets won 4.6% of the overall vote (2.2 million votes), but this only gave them sixteen seats, because they often just failed to reach the required minimum proportion (if the elections had been held using a single-constituency format, they would have won 35 seats). The Cadets performed well in the cities, coming second to the Bolsheviks in Moscow (35%) and Petrograd (27%) and first in eleven provincial capitals. Their best results were in Kursk (62%), Voronezh (58%) and Kaluga (49%), while their worst result was in the Caucasus (1.05%), although they did win 40% in Tiflis. Students, the wealthy and the intelligentsia tended to vote for the Cadets, except in the countryside, where these groups preferred the SRs. The relatively poor performance by the Cadets signalled the rejection of liberalism as a viable alternative to socialism in Russia.

The Mensheviks only scored 3.2% (1.5 million votes), but this translated into more places than the Cadets (18 seats). Their share of the vote was concentrated in Transcaucasia, where they were the leading party (27%) and their 662,000 votes gave them eleven seats – whereas 860,000 votes spread across seventy-four other districts only resulted in four more places. The Mensheviks also scored a rare victory on the Chinese-Eastern Railway. But the overall results were regarded by the party as a disaster. They got less than 1% in eleven districts, only 0.5% in the Altai and did not win any seats in Siberia or the Western and Caucasian Fronts, where they had expected to pick up half a dozen. An article by the Menshevik leaders in one of their newspapers confessed: 'The party stands in the face of a great political defeat.'[41]

The Russian Orthodox Church stood candidates in over thirty districts and managed to get one delegate elected – the future Patriarch Sergius – in

Nizhny Novgorod. They tended to pick up votes from conservatives and monarchists as the only representatives of the old regime running in the elections. Priests were banned from campaigning but tended to support the Cadets and attacked the socialists for their anti-clerical views. In Pskov Province, a deacon was caught red-handed in the act of removing all the Bolshevik lists from the ballot boxes and replacing them with Cadet lists. However, in Kharkiv Province, one priest was banned from a polling station for canvassing for the Bolsheviks. The Old Believers also ran in thirteen districts, including Moscow, Perm, Altai, Volga, Don and the Urals, but failed to win any seats.[42] The total right-wing vote in the elections was just under 300,000.

More than half of the population was non-Russian and national and ethnic parties won around 9% overall (4.7 million votes). The Constituent Assembly promised to be a colourful parliament with sixty-two Muslim delegates and fifteen Cossacks from the Don and Orenburg. Muslim and Jewish groups both got half a million votes, while national parties took 63% of all the votes cast in Transcaucasia. Azerbaijan went to the liberal Müsavat ('Equality') party, which supported national autonomy, social justice and pan-Islamism. They won 25.08% overall in the region and 57% of the Azerbaijani vote outside Baku. The Armenian elections were won by Dashnaktsutyun (Armenian Revolutionary Federation), which campaigned on a mixture of democratic socialism and civic nationalism. They won 22.74% overall in the region and 89% of the votes in Yerivan Province.

In Bessarabia, the elections were won by the Moldovan SRs, who had been expelled from the main party for separatism. They got five seats and their representatives included the president (Ion Inculeț) and prime minister (Pantelimon Erhan) of the short-lived independent Moldavian Democratic Republic (1917–18). Kazakhstan was won by the centre-left Alash party, which ran on a manifesto of national autonomy, civil liberties, workers' rights, free and compulsory education and the return of all unsettled land to the native population. Alash won a total of forty-three seats, taking 75% of the vote in Turgai and 57.5% in Zhetysu. Elsewhere in Central Asia, the vote was completely dominated by Muslim groups.

There was a general tendency for ethnic minorities to vote for their own national parties. The Buryat National Committee took 530 of the 552 votes at the Buddhist monastery of Tsugol datsan – while almost all the votes in the surrounding Russian villages went to the SRs. Yakutia was won by the Yakutia Federalists, who managed to defeat three of the federal parties – the SRs, Mensheviks and Cadets. There were only a few cases of inter-ethnic alliances. In Penza, the Ukrainians, Poles, Lithuanians and Muslims formed a bloc and won 4.69%. The Union of Ukrainian Peasants, Ukrainian Refugees and Tatar SRs got 4.91% and narrowly missed winning a seat in Saratov. In Terek-Dagestan, there was a joint list of Kabardians, Balkars and Russians and a combined Chechen-Ingush list – despite armed conflicts taking place between several of these groups.

On 24 November, Russian army headquarters on the South-Western Front reported that 'the elections have been held with great enthusiasm and without excesses.'[43] The overall turnout was 72% and as high as 93% in the Black Sea Fleet, 80% on the Northern Front and 79% on the Romanian Front. All eighty seats elected by the armed forces were won by socialist parties – thirty-five SRs, thirty-four Bolsheviks, seven Ukrainian SRs, two Ukrainian socialists, one Menshevik and one Ukrainian social democrat.

The Bolsheviks came first on the Western Front (67%), Northern Front (56%) and in the Baltic Fleet (57.4%). The Baltic Fleet used the majority system to elect its two representatives and the Bolsheviks won both seats – although Lenin, technically the head of government, came second to sailor Pavel Dybenko (now promoted to commissar of naval affairs). The Bolsheviks did less well on the South-Western Front (30%) and Romanian Front (15%) and did not submit a list on the Caucasian Front. Only 20.5% voted for the Bolsheviks in the Black Sea Fleet, where the SRs won 42.3% – but they proved popular among the women of Maria Bochkaryova's famous Battalion of Death, who voted overwhelmingly for the Bolsheviks (219 votes), followed by the Ukrainian SRs (41 votes) and SRs (30 votes).[44]

The high levels of support for the Bolsheviks in the armed forces can be explained by their campaign pledge to immediately withdraw from the war. The SRs promised land and the Cadets promised civil liberties, but as one conscript put it: 'What good are land and freedom to me if I am killed?'[45] Of course, this meant that the Bolsheviks were now duty bound to deliver peace at any price. As another soldier explained, 'if Lenin deceives us and does not give us peace, we will hang him from the same rope as Kerensky.'[46] Observing all this, a provincial Menshevik newspaper concluded: 'The Russian revolution of 1917 is a soldiers' revolution.'[47]

Lenin was technically elected in three districts – Petrograd, the Northern Front and the Baltic Fleet – but chose to represent the latter. Trotsky was elected in Novgorod and Stalin was elected in Petrograd. The leaders of the Cadets (Pavel Milyukov) and the Socialist Revolutionaries (Victor Chernov) also represented Petrograd. Other famous names among the delegates to the Constituent Assembly were Alexander Kerensky (SR), Vladimir Nabokov (Cadet) and future Ukrainian president Symon Petliura, who was elected on the Romanian Front.

The estimates of the total turnout vary from just over half to two-thirds of the electorate. Whatever the true figure, at least fifty million people voted in what was, at the time, the world's greatest ever display of democracy. Only 1.58% of all ballot papers were declared invalid (the highest figures were 22.4% in Yalutorovsk in western Siberia and 16.1% in Lodeinoe Polye near Finland). Common reasons were voters mistakenly placing all the lists in the envelope, nationalists crossing out Jewish surnames or people writing remarks on the ballot papers. Several voters, for example, added 'Michael Romanov, president of the Russian Republic' to the Bolshevik lists.[48]

The first truly free elections in Russia demonstrated that the majority of people wanted a socialist republic. Left-wing parties won over 80% of the vote. The SRs and their national allies (Ukrainian and Muslim SRs) scored 59%, followed by the Bolsheviks (22%), Mensheviks (3%) and Popular Socialists (0.9%). On the other hand, 40% voted for the Right SRs and another 16% voted for centrist parties. Even in their main citadel of Petrograd, the Bolsheviks were below 50%. The results showed that Russians largely supported the ideals of the February revolution and the peaceful transition from a monarchy to a republic, but they opposed the October revolution. The country voted in 1917 for political freedoms, democracy and a multi-party system and against Marxism, extremism and civil war.

Unfortunately for Russia, despite the enormous democratic advances and transformations of 1917, all important matters were still ultimately decided not at the ballot box or in the division lobbies, but at the point of a gun.

10

1918

'Great and terrible was the year of Our Lord 1918, of the Revolution the
second.'

Mikhail Bulgakov, *The White Guard*, 1926

'Bloody Friday'

'For nearly a century, the best of Russians have dreamt of this day...
Thousands of the intelligentsia, tens of thousands of workers and
peasants, have died in prison and in exile, have been hanged and shot for
this dream. Rivers of blood have been shed for this sacred idea.'

Maxim Gorky, 9 January 1918

The Provisional Government had scheduled the opening of the Constituent
Assembly for 28 November. However, on 26 November, Lenin signed a
decree that it would only start work once half the elected members had
registered at the Tauride Palace.[1] Two days later, Red Guards arrested
the leaders of the Cadet Party, including Fyodor Kokoshkin and Andrei
Shingaryov, who had both been elected to the assembly. This was a direct
violation of the law on deputies' immunity from prosecution, but the
Bolsheviks countered that the law only came into force once the assembly
had officially convened. Further arrests of Cadet delegates followed on
1 December. A number of SR deputies were imprisoned on 16 December
and Kerensky was forced to go into hiding.

The Bolsheviks also passed a decree on 21 November on the right to
recall delegates. While seemingly democratic, these powers were only
given to local soviets – who were allowed to recall deputies even before

the assembly opened. The Smolensk Soviet recalled three SRs, including Ekaterina Breshko-Breshkovskaya, while the Pskov Soviet recalled one SR. The delegates ignored the notices, however, claiming that they answered to their electorate and not the soviets. Shortly after that, on 3 December, over 100,000 people rallied in support of the Constituent Assembly in both Petrograd and Moscow. A week later, forty were killed when Red Guards opened fire on a demonstration in support of the assembly in Kaluga.

On 22 December, the All-Russian Central Executive Committee finally announced that the Constituent Assembly would open on Friday 5 January 1918. The Third All-Russian Congress of Soviets was also scheduled to open on Monday 8 January – ostensibly 'to support the left half of the Constituent Assembly against the right bourgeoisie and conciliatory half'.[2] But because almost the entire 'left half' were also delegates to the Third Congress of Soviets, it was clear that the Bolsheviks were planning to set up a rival assembly. That same day, Zinaida Gippius – who had written campaign leaflets for the SRs – observed in her diary: 'The Constituent Assembly (no matter in what form) and the Bolsheviks cannot co-exist for a single minute.'[3]

Most of the arriving delegates were provincials in the capital for the first time and without money. The Soviet government assigned half a million roubles for their upkeep and booked all 320 rooms in the Astoria Hotel for their accommodation. However, only the Bolsheviks and thirty-six Left SRs took up residence at the Astoria, where they occupied three floors.[4] Most SRs lived in a former hospital on Bolshaya Bolotnaya Street, five to ten in a room with no furniture except military cots. Another group from Siberia settled in a hostel on Ligovsky Prospekt, which only had camp beds and small bedside tables.[5]

On 1 January 1918, shots were fired at Lenin's car after he gave a speech at the Mikhailovsky Manège. Ironically, this was the exact same place where Tsar Alexander II had been, just before he was blown up by terrorists as he rode home to the Winter Palace on 1 March 1881. The Bolsheviks blamed the SRs and, the following day, three of their delegates – including Pitirim Sorokin, who later founded the sociological faculty at Harvard University – were taken hostage in case of fresh assassination attempts against the Soviet leader.

On 3 January, the Bolsheviks banned all demonstrations in the vicinity of the Tauride Palace. All approaches to the building were guarded by Latvian riflemen and Chinese mercenaries, specially employed instead of

Russian soldiers and sailors, who might balk at shooting their compatriots. The SRs debated taking Lenin and Trotsky hostage and calling loyal troops from the Semyonovsky, Preobrazhensky and Izmailovsky regiments onto the streets. But the majority rejected these plans and it was decided instead to hold a peaceful march to the Tauride Palace on opening day.

On 5 January, nine different processions set off from all over the city towards the Field of Mars, where they converged and marched as one enormous group towards the Tauride Palace. As many as 100,000 demonstrators were estimated to be on the streets of Petrograd that Friday morning.[6] But they never reached their destination. Red Guards opened fire on the crowd in a number of different locations, killing over twenty marchers, including an SR delegate from Siberia and the granddaughter of a Decembrist. Similar attacks took place in other Russian cities, such as Moscow, where at least fifty supporters of the Constituent Assembly were killed.

The victims of 'Bloody Friday' were buried at the Preobrazhenskoe Cemetery on 9 January. This was the thirteenth anniversary of Bloody Sunday and they were buried alongside the victims of the 1905 massacre. Maxim Gorky published a newspaper article on the day of their funeral, entitled 'The Ninth of January – The Fifth of January', which drew parallels between the two events: 'On 5 January, the Petrograd workers were mowed down, unarmed. They were mowed down without warning that they might be fired on, they were mowed down from ambush, through cracks in fences, in a cowardly fashion, as if by real murderers.'[7]

At the end of his article, Gorky asked the Soviet government: 'Do they understand that by putting the noose around their own necks, they will inevitably strangle the entire Russian democracy and ruin all the conquests of the revolution? Do they understand this? Or do they think, on the contrary – either we have power or let everyone and everything perish?'[8] The answer would not be long in coming.

'Friends, I Have Lost a Day!'

'The breaking up of the Constituent Assembly by the Soviet power is the complete and public liquidation of formal democracy in the name of the revolutionary dictatorship. It will be a good lesson.'

Vladimir Lenin to Leon Trotsky

The Constituent Assembly was scheduled to start work at noon. At ten in the morning, 200 SR delegates met in a canteen on the corner of Liteiny Prospekt and Führstadt Street and walked to the Tauride Palace through increasingly large and hostile crowds of Bolshevik soldiers and sailors. They found the main gates closed but were let in through a side entrance. Sailors had taken the place of the usual staff inside the building and the corridors and public galleries were filled with armed Red Guards. Most deputies preferred to remain in their overcoats in the chamber. Trotsky later mocked: 'They brought candles with them in case the Bolsheviki cut off the electric light and a vast number of sandwiches in case their food be taken from them. Thus democracy entered upon the struggle with dictatorship heavily armed with sandwiches and candles.'[9]

Lenin arrived at the Tauride Palace at one o'clock and spent the next three hours in conference with the rest of the Bolshevik faction. The SRs wanted to start without them, but the sailors would not let them into the chamber. When the Bolsheviks finally appeared, they were admitted and immediately occupied the centre and right of the hall. To their right sat three of the four Popular Socialists and several members of the 'national-bourgeoisie' groups. To their immediate left sat the Left SRs, followed by the Bolsheviks. A total of 410 of the 767 elected delegates were present, so the assembly had a quorum.

The father of the house, sixty-two-year-old Yegor Lazarev, was supposed to open the session. But the SRs thought it wiser to give this honour to the second oldest deputy, Sergei Shvetsov, who was a much bigger man. A Bolshevik delegate, Fyodor Ilin (Raskolnikov), described what happened after Shvetsov rang the bell to open the sitting: 'We start a frenzied obstruction. We shout, whistle and kick our feet against the thin wooden lecterns. When none of this helps, we jump from our seats and... throw ourselves on the platform. The Right SRs rush to the defence of the father of the house. Some fisticuffs take place... One of our lot grabs Shvetsov by the sleeve of his jacket and tries to pull him off the dais.'[10] Victor Chernov also described the scene:

From various sides, guns were trained on Shevtsov. He took the bell, but the tinkling was drowned in the noise. He put it back on the table and somebody immediately grabbed it and handed it over, like a trophy, to the representative of the Sovnarkom, Sverdlov. Taking advantage of a moment of comparative silence, Shevtsov managed to pronounce the sacramental phrase: 'The session of the Constituent Assembly is open.' These words evoked a new din of protest. Shevtsov slowly left the dais and joined us. He was replaced by Sverdlov, who opened the session for the second time, but now in the name of the Soviets.[11]

The first item of business was electing the chairman, which took three hours. The SRs nominated Victor Chernov, while the Bolsheviks proposed a popular revolutionary and Left SR delegate, Maria Spiridonova, hoping that she might attract votes from the other peasant deputies. But the voting ran along party lines and Chernov won the election (244 to 153). His inauguration address lasted two hours and was interrupted sixty times, either by applause or insults. Attempting to reach out to the radical deputies, the SR leader gave quite a revolutionary speech. He spoke of the need for democracy to unite 'under the red banner of socialism', condemned 'international imperialism' and stated that the election results reflected the popular 'will for socialism'.

The following day, Lenin wrote his own account of the session, beginning with the words of the Roman emperor Titus – *Amici, diem perdidi!* ('Friends, I have lost a day!'). He complained: 'It was terrible! To be transported from the world of living people into the company of corpses, to breathe the odour of the dead, to hear those mummies with their empty "social" Louis Blanc phrases, to hear Chernov and Tsereteli, was simply intolerable.'[12] This coincides with Victor Chernov's own recollection: 'Lenin, in the government box, demonstrated his contempt for the assembly by lounging in his chair and putting on the air of a man who was bored to death.'[13]

Yakov Sverdlov, representing the Soviet government, proposed 'the complete recognition by the Constituent Assembly of all the decrees and resolutions of the Council of People's Commissars', including its declaration that Russia was a republic of soviets of workers', soldiers' and sailors' deputies. The assembly rejected the motion by 237 to 146 votes, whereupon the Bolsheviks asked for the sitting to be suspended so that they could consult with their left-wing allies. This copied the tactics regularly employed by the third largest party in the House of Commons, the Irish Parliamentary Party, aimed at depriving the chamber of a quorum. The Bolsheviks were absent for four or five hours, but the centre-right majority continued without them.

When the Bolsheviks reappeared shortly after midnight, they read out a resolution charging the delegates with counter-revolution and dissolving the Constituent Assembly 'due to its refusal to accept the declaration of the All-Russian Central Executive Committee'. The Bolsheviks then trooped out of the hall, followed shortly afterwards by the Left SRs (putting on his overcoat, Lenin discovered that his Browning pistol had been stolen). The armed guards remained in the chamber and amused themselves by training their rifles on whoever was speaking and playing with their grenades and hand bombs. When one of the deputies tried to win the soldiers over to the side of the Constituent Assembly, he was told: 'Don't worry. Lenin will stop a bullet too if he deceives us!'

The remaining delegates sat long into the night. They passed an SR resolution calling for an international conference to end the First World War and condemned the Bolsheviks for starting peace negotiations without consulting Russia's allies. Instead of a soviet republic, they declared Russia to be a 'federative democratic republic' and outlawed 'the private ownership of land on the territory of the Russian Republic forever more.'

At half past four in the morning, when the assembly planned to elect a new head of state – who would probably have been Victor Chernov – an anarchist sailor suddenly mounted the rostrum and uttered one of the most famous phrases in the history of Russian democracy. The sailor was Anatoly Zheleznyakov, who had been arrested during the July Days, but escaped from prison. He told the representatives: 'I have received instructions to tell you that everyone present must leave the chamber, because the guard is tired.' When the deputies replied that they did not need a guard, Zheleznyakov pointed to the exit and said: 'I am the head of the palace guard and I have instructions from Commissar Dybenko... Your chatter is not needed by the working people. I repeat, the guard is tired!'

The deputies agreed to disperse and meet again at five in the evening. But when they turned up at the Tauride Palace, they found the doors firmly bolted and a notice on the door signed by the commandant: 'The Tauride Palace is closed by order of the commissar.' The entrance was blocked by Red Guards armed with machine guns and two light artillery weapons.[14] Two other events happened nearby at almost the exact same time. The All-Russian Central Executive Committee met and passed a decree officially dissolving the Constituent Assembly. Meanwhile, the two arrested Cadet deputies, Fyodor Kokoshkin and Andrei Shingaryov, were murdered by their guards in the Mariinsky Prison Hospital.

The following day, on 7 January, fifty factories and businesses went on strike in support of the Constituent Assembly. The workers of the Semyannikov (Nevsky) Shipbuilding Works and the Obukhov Armaments Factory invited the deputies to move there and reconvene under their protection. But the delegates thought that this would undermine the prestige of the supreme legislative organ and only lead to more bloodshed.

The factions met on 8 January and declared a temporary break in the work of the Constituent Assembly, pledging to resume 'in an appropriate place and at an appropriate time'.[15]

The Constituent Assembly never met again and Russia slid instead into civil war. After the Czechoslovak legion liberated Samara from the Reds in June 1918, five SR deputies met there and formed the first post-revolutionary alternative government to the Bolsheviks – the Committee of Members of the Constituent Assembly (*Komuch*). At the height of its powers, Komuch was joined by ninety-seven former delegates and raised a small army, which fought alongside the Czechoslovaks against the Reds. In September 1918, Komuch combined with the Provisional Siberian Government in Omsk to form a Provisional All-Russian Government. This coalition government had five members – two SRs, one Cadet, a Siberian regionalist and General Vasily Boldyrev, commander of its military forces – and became known as the Directorate, after the five-member *Directoire* which held office in France after the dissolution of the National Convention in 1795.

Just as the Directoire was overthrown by Napoleon in the Coup of 18 Brumaire (9 November), the Russian Directorate was overthrown on 18 November 1918 by its minister of war, Admiral Alexander Kolchak. He assumed power as a military dictator and arrested or shot any deputies who did not manage to go into hiding. Ironically, the Constituent Assembly had been dissolved in Petrograd by the Bolsheviks and now its remnants were overthrown in Siberia by the Whites, who had no more respect for democracy than the Reds. As Admiral Kolchak himself later said: 'I considered that although the Bolsheviks had few positive features, their dispersal of the Constituent Assembly was a service for which they should be given credit.'[16]

Victor Chernov escaped abroad in 1920 and died of poverty in the Bronx in 1952. Few of the deputies elected to the Constituent Assembly lived into old age. At least 350 are known to have died violent deaths – over 50% of the Bolsheviks and 85% of their opponents. A fifth of those who later fled the country, such as Leon Trotsky, were also murdered. At least eleven committed suicide. Meanwhile, the dissolution of the Constituent Assembly paved the way for the suppression of all other forms of democracy in Russia. The new constitution adopted by the Bolsheviks in July 1918 disenfranchised large sections of the population – mostly 'former people' and members of the 'exploiting classes', but also rich peasants (*kulaks*) and even such arbitrary cases as people living in the same house as a priest. Representatives of all other socialist parties were expelled from the soviets in June, ushering in a one-party system for the next seventy years.

What would Russia have looked like had the Constituent Assembly been able to complete its work? There would likely have been no Red Terror or Civil War, no Gulag or Holodomor, no Stalin or collectivisation, no Molotov-Ribbentrop Pact or Cold War. As Victor Chernov wrote: 'That terrible night, I understood back then, decided the fate of Russia for long, long years. But it now becomes even clearer to me that it decided the fate not only of Russia, but also of Europe and the whole world.'[17]

Why Did Democracy Fail?

'As far as Russia is concerned, we will carry to the grave the greatest disappointment in the world.'

Ivan Bunin, 6 May 1919

Why did the Constituent Assembly fall so quickly after being so eagerly awaited in Russia? There are several reasons for this. Firstly, the transition period was too long. In most countries, provisional governments usually only held power for an average of three months. In January 1919, two months after the November Revolution, Germany was already holding elections for its Constituent National Assembly in Weimar. The Zemsky Sobor which elected Michael Romanov opened in January 1613 – just two and a half months after the liberation of Moscow in 1612. But the Provisional Government of 1917 took two months to even start writing the electoral law.

The country had no real democratic traditions and had to create everything *ex nihilo*. While the Special Council genuinely wanted to write the world's most democratic electoral law – and probably succeeded – it possibly went too far at a time when circumstances dictated something quicker and simpler. As Pitirim Sorokin wrote about the voting law: 'It is most democratic, allowing for full proportional representation – only it seems to me that it is about as suitable for poor Russia as an evening dress would be for a horse.'[18]

Constituent assemblies belonged to the Western democratic tradition. In Russia, the masses better understood the soviets as organs of direct democracy similar to the *veche* or the village assemblies. The decisions taken in the soviets were blunt and based on common sense, without any need for the flowery language or convoluted debate of the parliamentary chamber. It took seventy years of life under these same soviets for Russians to finally warm to the idea of democratic parties, parliamentarianism and civil society.

Russian politics lacked the experience of peaceful decision-making. Power had previously only changed hands through violence and the events of 1917 continued this tradition. As Admiral Kolchak said in 1918 to General Alfred Knox, head of the British military mission in Siberia: 'The organisation of political power at a time like the present was possible only under one condition: this power must rely on the armed force which it has at its disposal.'[19] The Constituent Assembly was not prepared to use this force – and so power passed to the Bolsheviks.

Back in Petrograd, the Third All-Russian Congress of Soviets opened on 10 January 1918 in the Tauride Palace – in the very same hall where, less than a week earlier, the democratically elected Constituent Assembly had sat for just one day. Anatoly Zheleznyakov received a standing ovation when he vowed on behalf of the revolutionary sailors: 'We are prepared to do anything to defend the power of the soviets! We are ready to shoot not a handful, but hundreds and thousands; if it takes a million, then a million.'[20]

Civil War

Central Asia

'There was a buzz about the place. Meetings and rallies every day, elections to some committee every second day... People interpreted and understood freedom in their own way. When some started to treat others insolently or to commit misdeeds, their reply to any reproach was: "Hey, this is free-dum!"'

Kazakh poet Saken Seifullin

Turkestan

The Bolshevik seizure of power in Petrograd hastened the break-up of the rest of the country. One month after the October revolution, on 26 November 1917, the Fourth Kurultai of Muslims met in extraordinary session in Kokand to discuss the situation. Although it was termed a 'congress of Muslims', the Kurultai reflected the composition of the whole of Turkestan – both secular and religious authorities. The 200 delegates included representatives of the town dumas, Tatars and even members of *Poale Zion* ('Workers of Zion').

The Kurultai voted to declare autonomy in Turkestan, creating the first ever democratic state in Central Asia – and only the second secular state in the Muslim world (after Albania in 1912). The new nation was officially titled *Turkiston muxtoriyati* (Turkestan Autonomy) with Kokand as its capital. Until the opening of the Constituent Assembly, executive power on its territory was entrusted to a twelve-member Provisional Council, chosen from among the thirty-two delegates elected to represent Turkestan in Petrograd.

The driving force behind the decision to declare autonomy was a liberal party called *Shura-i Islamia* (Council of Islam), which was founded in Tashkent in March 1917. This was a movement of moderates who did not seek independence from Russia – only national sovereignty in a single economic and political space. *Shura-i Islamia* wanted to use the democratic forces existing in Russia to build a modern society based on civil liberties and economic freedoms, while upholding local cultural, historical and ethnic traditions.[1]

The Provisional Council was headed by prime minister Mukhamedzhan Tynyshpaev. He resigned in December 1917 and was replaced by the foreign minister, Mustafa Shokay, a Kazakh statesman who had previously been elected to the Duma. The legislative and representative organ was called the National Assembly (*Milli Mejlis*) and had fifty-four seats. Eighteen places were reserved for members of other ethnic groups, giving a third of all seats to the non-native inhabitants (who only made up 7% of the population).

In January 1918, after the dissolution of the Constituent Assembly in Petrograd, the Provisional Council announced its intention to hold its own constituent assembly on 20 March. The assembly would consist of 234 delegates, elected on the basis of a universal, direct, equal and secret vote, with a third of the places again guaranteed to non-Muslim candidates. This was a direct threat to the Bolsheviks, who could not allow an alternative democratic state to emerge. They sent troops and heavy artillery to Tashkent and launched an attack on the Kokand government on 6 February – opening one of the first fronts in the Civil War.

Turkestan Autonomy was only defended by a small force of several thousand policemen and Kipchaks on horseback. Armed with truncheons, axes, pitchforks, knives and stones, they were no match for the Bolshevik machine-guns. The Turkestan state fell on 9 February, after only seventy-two days of independence. Kokand was sacked by the Red Army and an estimated 10,000 people were killed. In April 1918, the Turkestan Autonomous Soviet Socialist Republic was established in Tashkent, led by a fourteen-member government without a single representative of the native population.

Kazakhstan

Just two weeks after the proclamation of Turkestan autonomy, the Second All-Kazakh Congress met in Orenburg on 5-13 December 1917 and took a similar decision to establish national-territorial autonomy inside

Russia. The congress ruled that, as 'there is no reliable and authoritative government in the Russian state,' they had unanimously decided 'to take power into their own hands'.

As in Turkestan, the congress elected a provisional government, which was known as the Alash Orda ('Kazakh Horde'). This was a national council of twenty-five members, headed by Alikhan Bukeikhanov, with ten seats reserved for representatives of other nationalities. The capital was the city of Semey (formerly Semipalatinsk), which was renamed Alash-qala. The Alash Orda introduced local self-government, banned the private ownership of land and created a national police force to maintain law and order.

The Kazakh provisional government planned to hold elections for a national constituent assembly, which would adopt a new constitution. However, the Alash Orda only controlled part of its territory and was opposed by both sides in the Civil War. The Whites wanted a single and united Russia, while the Bolsheviks – although pretending to uphold national autonomy – similarly suppressed any separatist tendencies. Throughout 1919, the Red Army gradually conquered the territory of the Alash Autonomy, which was officially dissolved by the Bolsheviks in March 1920. Five months later, the Kyrgyz (Kazakh) Autonomous Soviet Socialist Republic was established as a constituent part of the RSFSR.[2]

The two short-lived autonomies of Central Asia were more like modern Western republics than national democracies, with their secular governments and guarantees of representation for ethnic minorities. The establishment of parliaments and ministries introduced innovations from Europe, far removed from the traditional forms of government in the region. In the West, the Allies helped to secure the independence of Poland, Lithuania, Latvia, Estonia and Finland as buffer states protecting Europe from communism. But the democratic governments of autonomous Turkestan and Kazakhstan received no foreign support against the Bolsheviks – despite being islands of democracy in Central Asia.

The Crimean Democratic Republic

The story of the Crimean Democratic Republic, which existed from December 1917 to February 1918, was very similar, even though the Crimean Tatars moved faster, further and earlier than their Muslim counterparts in Central Asia. But they still suffered the same fate at the hands of the Bolsheviks.

On 17 November 1917, the Crimean Tatars held elections to their Qurultay. Although the name was a deliberate reference to the Mongol kurultai of 1206, which elected Temüjin Borjigin as Genghis Khan, everything else about this body was modern, especially with regards to women's rights. The vote was given to all men and women over the age of nineteen – the first time in the Muslim or Turkic world that all women were able to vote or stand for election. While this development had yet to reach Britain or the United States, it was typical of the Crimea, which had already become the first place inside Russia where women had voted. This was in early 1917, when the Muslim Revolutionary Committee held three weeks of elections to the All-Crimean Muslim Congress, which convened on 25 March 1917 with a number of women among the 1,500 delegates.[3]

The elections to the Qurultay were based on a simple majority system (not party lists). The ballot was held in the same month as the elections to the Constituent Assembly in Petrograd, but the turnout was higher for the Qurultay elections (over 70%). A total of seventy-nine delegates were elected, including five women. The Qurultay started work in the former Khan's Palace in Bakhchisarai on 26 November 1917, two days later than scheduled as a cyclone prevented all the deputies from arriving on time. The session was opened by Noman Çelebicihan, who said that he dreamt of the Qurultay 'transforming the Crimea into a real cultural Switzerland'. The eldest delegate, Adji Ali Efendi, was elected chairman. The presidium also included a woman, Şefiqa Gaspıralı, who was elected by a vote of 46-16.[4]

On 13 December, the Qurultay proclaimed the world's first ever Turkic republic, officially titled the Crimean Democratic Republic. It had a written constitution called the 'Crimean Tatar Fundamental Laws', which gave each nationality the right to complete self-determination (Article 1), annulled all titles and classes (Article 17) and proclaimed the equality of the sexes (Article 18). The constitution guaranteed the full separation of the legislative, executive and judicial powers (Article 7) and left the final decision on the fate of the peninsula to an All-Crimean Constituent Assembly (Article 16).

Article 2 of the Fundamental Laws established a permanent parliament (*Mejlis-i Mebusan*), electable by the whole population on the basis of a free, equal, direct and secret ballot. However, as the aftermath of the Bolshevik revolution made it impossible to hold immediate elections, it was decided that the Qurultay would continue sitting as the national parliament. One of the leaders of the National Party (*Milli Firqa*), the

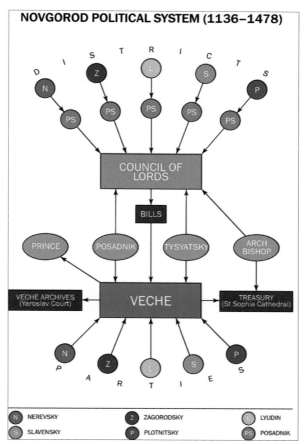

NOVGOROD POLITICAL SYSTEM (1136–1478)

DISTRICTS

N · Z · L · S · P

PS · PS · PS · PS · PS

COUNCIL OF LORDS

BILLS

PRINCE · POSADNIK · TYSYATSKY · ARCH BISHOP

VECHE ARCHIVES (Yaroslav Court)

VECHE

TREASURY (St Sophia Cathedral)

N · Z · L · S · P

PARTIES

N NEREVSKY	Z ZAGORODSKY	L LYUDIN
S SLAVENSKY	P PLOTNITSKY	PS POSADNIK

Right: The Republic of Novgorod had five political 'parties' which competed at elections to appoint all public servants. Top officials only remained in power for as long as they held public confidence or their party controlled the *veche.*

Below: Martha Boretskaya is taken to Moscow, along with the veche bell, after Ivan III's conquest of Novgorod in 1478. Alexei Kivshenko, *The Annexation of Novgorod the Great – The Expulsion of Distinguished and Eminent Novgorodians to Moscow,* 1880, Central Naval Museum, St Petersburg, Russia.

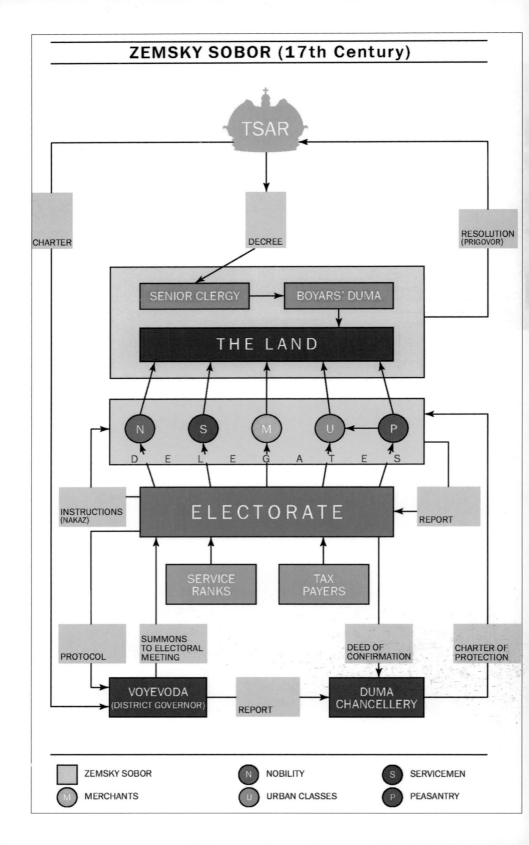

Ilya Repin, *17 October 1905*, 1907–11, State Russian Museum, St Petersburg, Russia. University students, professors and workers sing revolutionary songs and carry a freed political prisoner on their shoulders. The crowd includes linguist Mstislav Prakhov (left), actress Lydia Yavorskaya (holding a red bouquet) and art critic Vladimir Stasov (bearded man in centre).

In his first speech from the throne on 17 January 1895, Nicholas II had dismissed calls for democracy as 'senseless daydreams'. But on 27 April 1906 he was forced to welcome elected representatives into St George's Hall of the Winter Palace for the opening ceremony of the Imperial Duma.

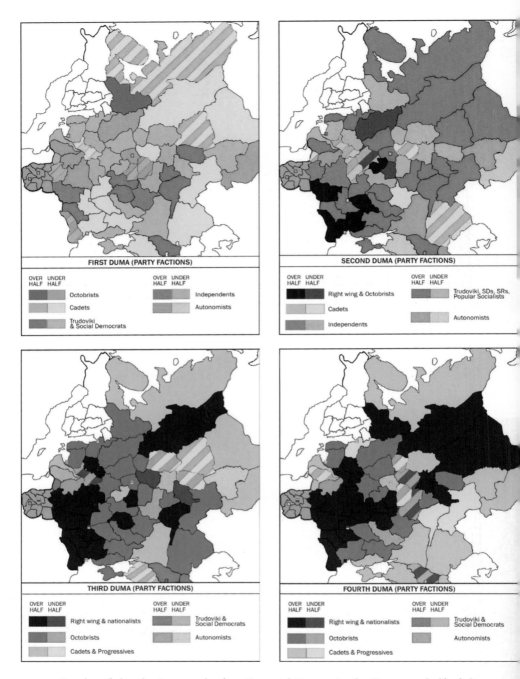

FIRST DUMA (PARTY FACTIONS)

OVER UNDER
HALF HALF

OVER UNDER
HALF HALF

Octobrists

Cadets

Trudoviki
& Social Democrats

Independents

Autonomists

SECOND DUMA (PARTY FACTIONS)

OVER UNDER
HALF HALF

OVER UNDER
HALF HALF

Right wing & Octobrists

Cadets

Independents

Trudoviki, SDs, SRs,
Popular Socialists

Autonomists

THIRD DUMA (PARTY FACTIONS)

OVER UNDER
HALF HALF

OVER UNDER
HALF HALF

Right wing & nationalists

Octobrists

Cadets & Progressives

Trudoviki &
Social Democrats

Autonomists

FOURTH DUMA (PARTY FACTIONS)

OVER UNDER
HALF HALF

OVER UNDER
HALF HALF

Right wing & nationalists

Octobrists

Cadets & Progressives

Trudoviki &
Social Democrats

Autonomists

Results of the elections to the four Imperial Dumas in the European half of the Russian Empire. The First and Second Dumas were dominated by liberal and radical parties. Nicholas II then changed the voting laws in the 'coup of 3 June 1907', and the Third and Fourth Dumas were more conservative and loyal to the throne – though still joined in his overthrow in February 1917. Maps originally compiled by and reproduced with the kind permission of Alexei Titkov.

Pyotr Stolypin's first speech as prime minister to the Second Duma on 6 March 1907. He talked of 'perestroika' and his willingness to work with parliament to reform Russia. A Cadet deputy recalled: 'Many of us were only prevented by party discipline from applauding.'

Election posters in Petrograd during the Constituent Assembly election campaign in November 1917. The Soviet-style poster for List 2 was actually for the centre-right Cadets. The slightly indiscernible poster for the All-Russian League for Women's Equality (List 7) was designed by famous Russian artist Boris Kustodiev.

'Democracy will defeat anarchy'. After the February revolution, the Cadets abandoned their previous radicalism and targeted voters tired of violence and bloodshed. They repositioned themselves as a centre-right party defending the interests of Russia and the 'great Russian people'.

'Elect the Socialist Revolutionaries'. The SRs ran the best campaign and easily won the Constituent Assembly elections in 1917. They employed colour psychology in their posters and leaflets – red for their past revolutionary struggle and yellow for corn and abundance.

'Vote only for the Social Democrats'. Poster for the Mensheviks in Moscow, where they came a disappointing fifth in the Constituent Assembly elections. Too many parties competed for the moderate socialist vote and first place in Moscow went to the Bolsheviks.

Only known photograph of the single sitting of the Constituent Assembly on 5 January 1918. Lenin can be seen lounging in the government box in the top left 'putting on the air of a man who was bored to death'.

A military genius with a mesmerising gaze, Nestor Makhno was said to have paranormal powers which made him invincible in battle. He conquered a third of Ukraine and set up an anarchist 'non-state' called the Free Territory from 1918 to 1921.

Above: Anarchist leader Nestor Makhno and the commanders of his Revolutionary Insurrectionist Army, which grew into an enormous host of 100,000 troops, posing for a photograph in the Ukrainian port city of Berdyansk in 1919.

Left: Lubsan-Samdan Tsydenov, 'king of the three worlds', established the Kudun state in Eastern Siberia in 1919. Combining elements of Buddhist theocracy, constitutional democracy and Western republicanism, it gave the vote to all men and women aged over fifteen.

Right: Stalin voting in a 1950 propaganda poster designed by Victor Ivanov. Stalin once hired a handwriting expert to identify those who had voted against him in Party elections. Ten years later 'they would receive a bullet in the back of the neck.'

Below: Striking workers in Novocherkassk in 1962. This was the first uprising against Communist rule since Kronstadt in 1921 and it was just as brutally suppressed.

In the early hours of 20 August 1991, Mikhail Gorbachev recorded a ten-minute video denying he was ill and condemning the military coup. He then hid copies of the film around the house where he was being held captive in the Crimea.

ПОЧТА СССР 1991 · ВЛАДИМИР УСОВ · 1954–20.08.1991

ПОЧТА СССР 1991 · ДМИТРИЙ КОМАРЬ · 1968–20.08.1991

ПОЧТА СССР 1991 · ИЛЬЯ КРИЧЕВСКИЙ · 1963–20.08.1991

Stamps commemorating the three men killed defending the Russian parliament during the military coup of August 1991. Vladimir Usov, Dmitry Komar and Ilya Krichevsky were posthumously awarded the titles of 'Heroes of the Soviet Union' for 'defending democracy'.

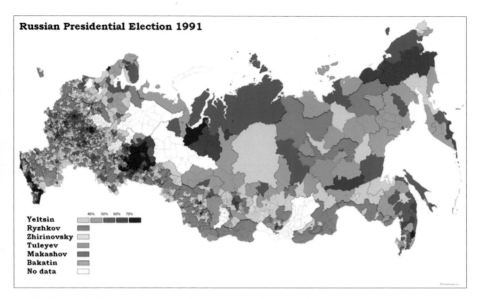

© Electoral Geography, https://www.electoralgeography.com

Nationalist politician Vladimir Zhirinovsky ran for president six times and won the Duma elections in 1993. The secret of his success was being down-to-earth (his poster claims 'I am just the same as you') and his apocryphal promise of 'a husband for every woman and a bottle for every man'.

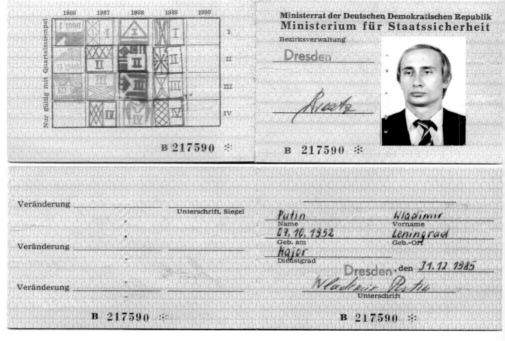

Vladimir Putin's *Stasi* identity card issued in Dresden in 1985. The fall of the Berlin Wall in 1989 left him with a permanent distrust of democracy and 'people's power'.

Posters showing heavy-metal musical support for Vladimir Bryntsalov and pop backing for Gennady Zyuganov in the 1996 presidential elections; an anti-Zyuganov poster ('Buy food for the last time!'); advertisements for the 'Bloc of Juna' and the Beer Lovers' Party in the 1995 Duma campaign.

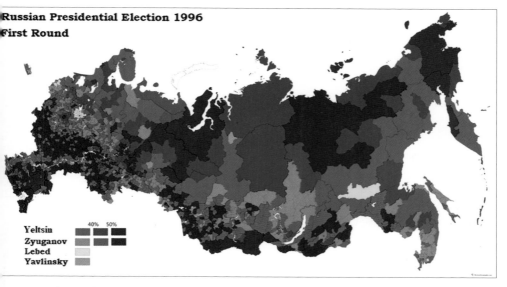

© Electoral Geography, https://www.electoralgeography.com

Above left: Alexander Lebed ran for president in 1996 and governor of Krasnoyarsk Region in 1998. The latter campaign was supported by his friend, French film star Alain Delon, who flew thousands of miles to help him get elected.

Above right: Grigory Yavlinsky was Ukrainian youth boxing champion in 1967 and 1968, winning 43 of 44 fights. A liberal economist, he headed the Yabloko party from 1993 to 2008 and ran for president in 1996, 2000 and 2018.

Boris Yeltsin is serenaded by US President Bill Clinton at Novo-Ogaryovo outside Moscow in 1994. (Courtesy of the National Archives and Records Administration)

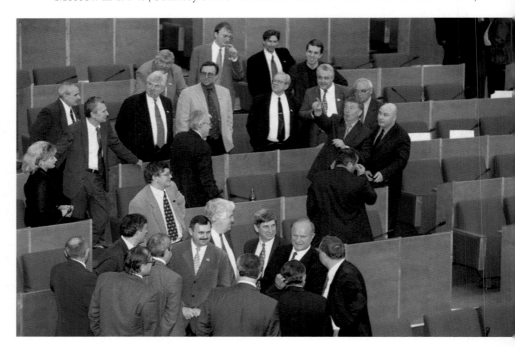

The Duma attempts to impeach President Yeltsin in May 1999. The charges were led by Communist leader Gennady Zyuganov (bottom centre), but were defeated when Vladimir Zhirinovsky's LDPR (top group) sided with the Kremlin. (Courtesy of Duma.gov.ru under Creative Commons)

Eduard Limonov founded the National Bolshevik Party with Alexander Dugin and took part in the events of October 1993 (on the side of parliament). A constant thorn in the authorities' side, he unsuccessfully stood for the Duma in 1997 and 2002 and for president in 2012. (Courtesy of Svklimkin under Creative Commons)

US President Barack Obama with Vladimir Putin. Obama wrote that Putin reminded him of the old Chicago political barons – 'tough, street-smart, unsentimental characters ... who viewed patronage, bribery, shakedowns, fraud and occasional violence as legitimate tools of the trade.'

President Barack Obama meeting with Russian opposition leaders in July 2009. Left to right: Leonid Gozman, Boris Nemtsov, Gennady Zyuganov, Elena Mizulina, Sergei Mitrokhin.

Mikhail Gorbachev died at the age of 91 at the Central Clinical Hospital in Moscow on 30 August 2022. He was not given a state funeral and Putin was 'too busy' to attend. Gorbachev's daughter Irina banned Russia's state media from the burial ceremony at the Novodevichy Cemetery. (Courtesy of Sergey Korneev under Creative Commons 4.0)

Crimean writer Asan Sabri Aivazov, was elected chairman. The Qurultay
held its first sitting as the Crimean parliament on 13 December, when it
discussed the need to elect, as soon as possible, the planned All-Crimean
Constituent Assembly.

On 18 December, the Qurultay set up a provisional government called
the Directorate. Like its French revolutionary predecessor, it had five
members headed by Noman Çelebicihan as the president and minister
of justice. In March 1917, he had become the first ever elected mufti in
Russian history (one of his first acts was to ban the wearing of the burqa).
Three months later, he founded the National Party with Cafer Seydahmet,
who was the minister of defence and foreign affairs in the Directorate and
replaced Çelebicihan as president after his resignation on 4 January 1918.

When it became clear that the rights and equalities guaranteed
under the Crimean constitution were incompatible with a Bolshevik
Russia, the Tatars began to increasingly consider full independence
from both Russia and Ukraine.[5] The republic also expressed a desire
to take part in the future post-war peace conference in Europe and
other international forums. On 19 December, a Crimean army was
created under the civil command of Cafer Seydahmet and the military
command of Lieutenant Colonel Vladimir Makukhin. The armed forces
consisted of the Crimean cavalry regiment, a Tatar infantry battalion,
two units of Ukrainian soldiers and some Russian officers – a total of
around 6,000 troops.

The following day, armed clashes broke out between the Crimeans
and the Bolsheviks, who had captured Sevastopol on 16 December and
established military-revolutionary headquarters in the city. During peace
negotiations in Simferopol on 26 January, Noman Çelebicihan was arrested
and flown to prison in Sevastopol. On 23 February, he was murdered and
his body was thrown into the Black Sea. By the end of February 1918,
the Bolsheviks had established full control over the whole peninsula. They
dissolved the Crimean Tatar government and parliament – ending what
was, on paper, one of the world's most democratic republics.[6]

The Idel-Ural State

In July 1917, the First All-Russian Muslim Congress in Kazan proclaimed
the 'national-cultural autonomy of the Turkic-Tatars of Inner Russia
and Siberia'. A constitution was written and adopted by a provisional
government in October, giving the vote to all citizens, male and female,
who had reached the age of twenty.

Elections were held in November 1917 for the National Parliament (*Milli Mejlis*), which was elected for three years with each delegate representing 50,000 inhabitants. At the same time, over a million roubles were raised from among the local population as the 'national treasury' (*Milli hazine*).

The parliament opened in Ufa on 20 November and sat until 11 January 1918. The delegates elected a National Government (*Milli Idare*), which consisted of three ministries (education, religion and finances) and two committees (defence and foreign affairs). On 29 November, the National Parliament proclaimed a republic called the Idel-Ural state, which covered the whole of Kazan and Ufa provinces, as well as neighbouring regions.[7]

The whole Turkic-Tatar population of European Russia and Siberia was divided into national districts. Each canton would have its own organs of self-government for religious and cultural affairs, leaving the central authorities responsible for law, finance, taxation, customs, transport, communications, defence and foreign policy. Several districts were exclaves, making the Idel-Ural state more like a multinational federation than a national republic. The total area was inhabited by seven million people – 3.7 million Tatars and Bashkirs, 2.7 million Russians and about half a million Chuvash, Mari and Udmurts – with each nationality receiving a proportional share of parliamentary seats.

Sadrí Maqsudí, a liberal statesman who had headed the Muslim faction in the Second and Third Dumas, was appointed president of the Idel-Ural state. The ministry of religion (*Diniya Nazaraty*) was led by Galimjan Barudi, a Jadidist (see note 3) who had been elected mufti of Inner Russia and Siberia in May 1917. He issued a fatwa calling on Muslim women to actively participate in all elections, from the local councils right up to the Constituent Assembly. His fatwa stated that Sharia law 'does not restrict the political rights of women in any way' and condemned opposition to the female suffrage as 'a great crime'.

A Military Council (*Harbi Shuro*) had been formed in Kazan back in May 1917 – even earlier than the National Parliament – and included all national Tatar and Bashkir regiments. The founder and leader was a twenty-two-year-old socialist called Ilias Alkin. His forces took an oath of loyalty to the parliament and numbered 60,000 troops by January 1918. So the Tatars already had a parliament, a government, financial reserves and even an army – something no other ethnic minority in Russia could boast.

The Idel-Ural state was due to officially start functioning on 16 February 1918. But instead of bringing the date forward after the dispersal of the Constituent Assembly in Petrograd, the Tatars kept to their original timetable – by which time the Bolsheviks controlled the surrounding territory. The only attempt at resistance was in Kazan, where Ilias Alkin and the Military Council took up positions in the Tatar district beyond the River Bulak. They created a Tatar autonomous zone which became known as the Zabulachnaya Republic ('the republic beyond the Bulak'), but they were surrounded by Red Guards on 15 March and surrendered to avoid bloodshed.

The National Parliament ceased functioning on 13 April and the National Government was abolished on 1 May. Sadrí Maqsudí escaped to Finland at the end of 1918 and attended the Versailles Peace Conference, where he delivered a note on behalf of the Muslims of European Russia. The remnants of the Idel-Ural state appealed for help to Admiral Kolchak in September 1918, but he banned all democratic ethnic organisations after his forces captured Ufa in March 1919. Ilias Alkin later served as the chief of staff of the neighbouring Bashkir republic, which was one of the only autonomous units to successfully put an army into the field.

Bashkurdistan

On 15 November 1917, the Bashkir National Council (*Shuro*) proclaimed the national-territorial autonomy of Bashkurdistan inside a federative Russia. A constituent assembly was held in Orenburg between 8 and 20 December, creating a government and a pre-parliament (*Kese-Kurultai*). The government was headed by Junus Bikbov and adopted a constitution with ninety-three articles in January 1918. The territory was divided into self-governing cantons with a central parliament elected every three years by all men and women over the age of twenty-one. On 5 January 1918, the Bashkirs started recruiting their own army under the command of Zeki Velidi Togan.

The Bolsheviks captured Orenburg on 31 January 1918 and arrested the government on the night of 3/4 February. Two of the deputies were shot on 7 March, but a group of Bashkir officers managed to free the others from prison on the night of 3/4 April. The Bashkir regiments joined forces with the Czechoslovak Legion on 27 May and helped to drive the Reds out of Orenburg and the south Urals in the summer of 1918. However, three days after proclaiming himself 'supreme ruler' of

Russia on 18 November, Admiral Kolchak issued a decree liquidating the Bashkir government and disbanding its army. The Bashkirs switched sides in February 1919 and joined the Reds against the Whites. The following month, the Bashkir government agreed to join the RSFSR as the Bashkir Autonomous Soviet Socialist Republic.

Theocracy

While the tsardom was never restored in Russia, something similar – a form of constitutional monarchy with spiritual attributes – emerged in 1919, when the only Buddhist theocracy in Russian history was founded and headed by a lama in Buryatia.

In April 1917, the Buryat National Committee took over the functions of local government in the Transbaikal region of eastern Siberia. Protests broke out in 1918 after the committee agreed to conscript young men into the White Army, as the nomadic Buryats had previously been exempt from mobilisation under the tsars. In Khorinsk, the local Buddhists appealed to a famous ascetic, Lubsan-Samdan Tsydenov, who lived in a hillside retreat near the River Konda. He had once been the abbot of the Kizhinga (Kudun) datsan and was famous for having refused to kneel before Tsar Nicholas II ('a spiritual king does not bow to a secular king'). Tsydenov responded to their request in the democratic spirit of the times by creating an independent state.[8]

In April 1919, a Great Loam (constituent assembly) of 102 delegates was held on the holy mountain of Chelsana. The result was the establishment of a Buddhist theocracy called the 'Kudun State of Balagats' (*Kudunai Erketei Balgasan*). Tsydenov was proclaimed its supreme religious and civil leader with the title 'Dharma Raja Khan, king of the three worlds and lord of doctrine'.[9] Over 13,000 local inhabitants responded to his appeal: 'As fighting is contrary to the Buddha's law, let he who does not wish to fight come to me and be subject to my rule.'

A draft constitution was written on 4 May 1919. Consisting of thirty-six articles, it classified the theocracy as a 'sovereign state of balagats', divided into twelve administrative units – balagats. Officials at the balagat level were elected by residents for a two-year term. The balagats were further subdivided into several smaller units called toskhons, whose administrators (dargas) were elected for one year. The salaries of all officials were set by the electorate. The seat of government was at Soorkhoi ('lama's gully') near the village of Ust-Orot, where the head of state continued to live in his retreat, communicating only by letter. The capital was officially named 'Soyempkus' after the Soyombo, a sacred Buddhist symbol included in the flag of independent Mongolia in 1911.

The Kudun state was a unique fusion of traditional Buddhist theocracy, constitutional democracy and Western republicanism. Although regarded as a living deity – equal, if not superior, to the spiritual leaders of Tibet and Mongolia – Tsydenov chose not to become a reincarnating ruler (he nominated his own successor). There was an elected parliament called the Great Suglan (Congress of Deputies), which appointed the president, vice-president and ministers and passed the budget. Deputies were elected by universal, direct, equal and secret ballot for a two-year term on the basis of one representative for every hundred inhabitants. The vote was given to all subjects, male and female, over the age of fifteen.

The theocracy had its own judicial system – balagat courts consisting of one chairman (the balagat's head of administration) and two judges elected for two years – and all the customary state institutions. The only thing that the pacifist state lacked was an army and, as with the Constituent Assembly in Petrograd, this is what caused its downfall.

When news of the unsanctioned state reached the Buryat National Committee, they asked the White Army to arrest its leaders. The theocratic government responded by warning that anyone threatening its borders would be stopped by 'the supernatural force of Dharma Raja, who could drain his enemies of all strength and turn them into miserable creatures.'[10] But the plan to defend the capital by 'encircling Soyempkus with magic fortifications' failed to halt the White forces, who arrived on 11 May 1919 and arrested the head of state and nine ministers.[11]

Tsydenov was freed after voluntarily renouncing his title but was rearrested on three more occasions for continuing to preach non-violence. He was still in prison in Verkhneudinsk when the Red Army conquered the Kudun Valley in October 1920, and he remained a captive of the Soviets, who accused him of spreading counter-revolutionary propaganda. Meanwhile, his followers tried to revive the Kudun state by creating small self-governing communities based on the balagat principle. They refused to pay government taxes and established their own police force.

In July 1921, Tsydenov sent a secret edict from his prison cell, appointing his heir, the eight-year-old Bidia Dandaron, as the new head of state. According to the official records, the Dharma Raja died of pleurisy in May 1922 in a military hospital in Novo-Nikolaevsk (now Novosibirsk). However, a witness claimed to have seen him, dressed in an elegant European pin-striped suit, at Verkhneudinsk railway station in 1924. When asked where he was going, the spiritual leader simply replied, 'to Italy.'[12]

Anarchy

'Anarchism is primarily a creation of the Russian national spirit.'
Nikolai Berdyaev, 1907

Between 1918 and 1921, in the chaos of the Civil War, a Ukrainian anarchist managed to conquer a large enough territory to launch the world's first ever experiment in stateless anarchism. Nestor Makhno had been sentenced to life in prison in 1910 but was freed by the February revolution and returned to his hometown of Hulyai Polye in July 1918. His pledge to implement his anarchist ideas, including 'the dispersal of all government institutions', found a willing response among the local population, who associated any form of authority with taxes, food requisitions and forced conscription into the various warring armies.

Although only five foot two inches in height (160 cm), Makhno had a magnetic personality. He had a piercing, hypnotic gaze and a deep scar running across his face. It was rumoured that he possessed extrasensory and paranormal powers, which made him invincible, 'because he had never been wounded during all the years of warfare in spite of his practice of always personally leading every charge'.[13] He wore dark glasses and had only one lung, after contracting tuberculosis in prison, where he spent his time reading anarchist literature and writing sentimental poems.

Despite having no formal education, Makhno was a military genius. His original band of several thousand anarchists grew into a host of 100,000 troops, who were known collectively as the Revolutionary Insurrectionary Army of Ukraine. They employed unorthodox tactics, such as making lightning dashes on horse-driven carts mounted with machine guns, which could cover a hundred miles in a day. Marc Wolff, a Jewish émigré in London, recalled the sight of one of Makhno's detachments in Yalta: 'The appearance of the unit was rather picturesque, because quite a part of it wore ladies' fur coats over which bandoliers of ammunition were worn like decorations.'[14]

Starting from their 'revolutionary headquarters' in Hulyai Polye in November 1918, the Makhnovites conquered one region after another.

In October 1919, they occupied the city of Ekaterinoslav, where Makhno had once sat on death row (he burnt the prison down as an act of revenge). The anarchists eventually controlled a third of the modern state of Ukraine, inhabited by seven million people, which they renamed the Free Territory. Operating out of their capital, renamed 'Makhnograd', they established a stateless society based on the anarcho-communist theories of Peter Kropotkin.[15] There was no government – only self-government based on 'free worker-peasant soviets'. But unlike the soviets in the rest of the country, all political parties were banned.

Delegates from the anarchist soviets and Makhno's army attended the Regional Congress of Peasants, Workers and Insurrectionists, which was the closest thing the Free Territory had to a parliament. The first regional congress opened in January 1919 in the village of Bolshaya Mikhailovka and discussed the twin military threats posed by the Ukrainian national army of Symon Petliura and the White Army of General Anton Denikin. The second congress in Hulyai Polye in February 1919 created a supreme executive organ called the Military-Revolutionary Council, composed of the representatives of the army and thirty-two districts with responsibility for all political, military and public affairs.

The third congress in Hulyai Polye in April 1919 adopted an anarchist programme, including the socialisation of land and factories, a system of free exchange between urban and rural communities and complete freedom of the press, speech, assembly and conscience. Makhno hoped to one day turn the whole country into a Ukrainian Anarchist Labour Federation and dreamt of a worldwide federation of anarchist communes. He later recalled his system of anarchist non-government: 'The popular assembly made the decisions. In military life, it was the War Committee composed of delegates of all the guerrilla detachments... everyone took part in the collective work, to prevent the birth of a managing class which would monopolise power. And we were successful.'[16]

All private land was seized and redistributed by the village assemblies. But the plan to create a system of agricultural communes failed, as the peasants hated the communal living conditions and preferred private farming. The workers were more receptive to Makhno's ideas, which gave them control over the means of production. All factories, workshops and mines were run as cooperatives and the employees established their own quotas and hours of work. In Oleksandrivsk, the railway workers drew up the train timetables and set the fares themselves.

Makhno announced that all shops, banks and businesses were now the property of the poor, who could help themselves to 'whatever they needed' – although any abuse for personal gain was punished by death. The economy was based on bank robberies, raids on pawnshops and attacks on the surrounding towns and villages. The result was not the promised 'free soviets without communists and requisitioning', but an orgy of violence and looting. Gold reserves were acquired by intercepting a train delivering bullion from the Whites to the Allies and killing a rival warlord who had robbed the Odessa State Bank.

The Revolutionary Insurrectionary Army was run along anarchist lines. Officers and commands were abolished, tactics were debated at general assemblies and discipline was left to the soldiers' committees. In February 1919, when fresh recruits were urgently required, it was decided to hold a 'voluntary mobilisation' based on moral persuasion. The only anarchist principle not implemented was the free election of commanders, who were instead appointed by Makhno himself. The Free Territory also had a diplomatic corps and foreign relations. A diplomatic mission was elected in September 1920 and sent to Kharkiv as 'envoys' to the Soviet government, while a trade agreement was signed with the French military on the sale of coal seized in the port of Mariupol in March 1919.

Makhno planned to abolish all forms of currency and introduce a system of free barter between the towns and villages. But this idea never took off and money continued to circulate. The insurgents designed their own banknotes, which were called coupons and depicted Makhno in his trademark Cossack hat (*kabana*). Because of a shortage of paper, they were printed on old notebooks or wrapping paper from a sweet factory. When there was no more paper, the anarchists simply stamped the dozens of other currencies circulating in those years with humorous or crude inscriptions, such as 'anyone not accepting this note gets their tits ripped off' or 'you cannot even buy lice with this dough.' Some banknotes were stamped with the words 'Makhno's money is guaranteed by the head of the bearer.' Others depicted a skull and crossbones and the warning 'counterfeit is punishable by firing squad' (such notes were popularly known as 'skulls').[17]

The anarchist experiment ended when the Red Army invaded and ousted Makhno from the Free Territory in August 1921. Heavily wounded and accompanied by seventy-seven followers, he crossed the River Dniester into Bessarabia and surrendered to the Romanians. Makhno later settled in Paris, where he died in 1934 and was laid to rest near the Communards in the Père Lachaise Cemetery.

The Red Rebellions

'...and they shall spoil those that spoiled them'

Ezekiel 39:10

The Civil War ended in Russia in December 1920, when Baron Wrangel was defeated in the Crimea and the White Army evacuated to Constantinople. But this did not bring peace to Russia or any benefits to those who had sided with the Reds. All the ideals for which so many had fought, such as the promised 'withering away of the state', were quietly abandoned by the Communists – who actually increased the power of the state.[18]

The only Marxist ideas to be implemented were economic policies under the name of 'War Communism'. Industry was nationalised, private trade was banned and the peasants had to surrender all agricultural surpluses to the state. Discontent over these policies sparked a second wave of democratic counter-revolution and mass uprisings in 1920 and 1921 – including among those who had led the Bolshevik revolution.

The Red Army of Truth

In June 1920, the commander of the Ninth Cavalry Division of the Red Army, Alexander Sapozhkov, was dismissed from his post for drunkenness and replaced by a 'military expert' from the former tsarist army – a policy initiated by Trotsky to help the Reds win the Civil War. Sapozhkov held a meeting with his fellow commanders, who were also committed revolutionaries now disgruntled with the Bolsheviks. Together, they formed the First Red Army of Truth on 14 July and raised the banner of revolt in the village of Pogromoye in Orenburg Province.

Sapozhkov issued Order No. 1, declaring that the aim of their rebellion was 'to unite all the poorest workers and peasants' under the slogan 'All power to the soviets according to the real programme of the Bolshevik Party on the basis of a constitution!' The following day, the Army of Truth adopted the 'Declaration of the Rights of Man and a Citizen of the RSFSR', which called for fresh elections to the soviets. They proposed a new electoral law only giving the vote to those whose pre-war possessions had been worth less than 10,000 roubles.

Although numbering only 500 men, the Army of Truth defeated a much larger government force and captured the nearby town of Buzuluk in just one hour. They disarmed the garrison, dissolved the local soviet and elected a new administration. The rebels were widely supported by the local peasants and soon joined by 5,000 deserters from the Red Army.

The Bolsheviks immediately assembled 12,000 troops and recaptured Buzuluk. Sapozhkov retreated towards his home village in Samara Province and fought running battles with the pursuing Red Army throughout the whole of August. The rebels were eventually forced to retreat into the steppe in Astrakhan Province, where they held their last stand near the village of Koim. The Army of Truth was surrounded and Sapozhkov was killed on 6 September. His corpse was beheaded and his head was taken back to his former division headquarters as a warning to any other potential rebels.

Tambov

The Sapozhkov revolt sparked a wave of other rebellions in neighbouring provinces in the summer of 1920. The Tambov uprising was accompanied by the establishment of a 'provisional democratic republic' and ended in a poison-gas attack – the first time in history that a government employed chemical weapons against its own people.

In the Constituent Assembly elections, the results in Tambov Province had reflected the overall picture in the whole country – SRs 71%, Bolsheviks 21%, Cadets 4%, Mensheviks 2%. Although the province supported the Reds against the Whites in the Civil War, many peasants took to the forests to avoid being conscripted into the Red Army, while the Bolsheviks were expelled from the local soviets after signing the Treaty of Brest-Litovsk with Imperial Germany in March 1918. In spring 1920, the local SRs created a network of 300 'unions of working peasantry' across Tambov Province as alternatives to the soviets. Each local union sent delegates to the district union, which then sent its representatives to the central provincial committee.

The uprising began in the village of Khitrovo on 15 August 1920, after a grain requisitioning unit stole everything it could find ('even pillows and kitchen utensils') and 'beat up elderly men of seventy', while the confiscated corn was left to rot in the open air.[19] Armed with hunting rifles, pitchforks and clubs, the local union of working peasantry disarmed and drove off the government unit. After news spread, they were joined four days later by other villages and by Alexander Antonov, a former SR terrorist who had led an anti-Bolshevik partisan force in the forest since December 1918.

The rebels advanced on Tambov on 30 August but were halted just outside the provincial capital. Their numbers had now reached 6,000 and, except for the towns, they soon controlled the entire province.

A unified Partisan Army was formed in November 1920 under the overall command of Pyotr Tokmakov, who was also elected chairman of the Tambov Provincial Committee (he was killed in February 1921 and replaced by Ivan Ishin).

In December 1920, the committee issued a manifesto, which stated that 'the primary aim of the Union of Working Peasantry is the overthrow of the Communists-Bolsheviks, who have led the country into poverty, destruction and disgrace.' The committee issued a programme of seventeen points, which included freedom of speech, press, conscience, union and assembly, the summoning of a constituent assembly and self-determination for all ethnic minorities inhabiting the former Russian Empire. The first point called for 'the political equality of all citizens, independent of class, except for the House of Romanov' – although the reference excluding the former imperial family was removed a month later.[20]

By February 1921, the size of the rebel army had swollen to 50,000 combatants and the uprising spilled over into Saratov, Voronezh and Penza provinces. In May 1921, at a meeting in the village of Karai-Saltykovo, the Union of Working Peasantry proclaimed the Provisional Democratic Republic of the Tambov Partisan Region, which would rule until the holding of a democratically elected constituent assembly.

The conclusion of the Soviet-Polish War in March 1921 allowed the government to redeploy its main forces against Tambov. In May 1921, Mikhail Tukhachevsky was appointed commander of a punitive army of 44,500 troops with 706 machine guns, four armoured trains and eight warplanes. Armed with direct orders from Lenin to suppress the Tambov uprising 'by setting fire to everything',[21] Tukhachevsky's tactics included mass terror and executions, artillery bombardments of peasant villages, the taking of thousands of hostages and the incarceration of women and children in concentration camps.[22]

The Tambov rebels were defeated in a series of battles between 25 May and 7 June. They decided to change tactics by dividing into smaller groups and taking to the forests, where they engaged in guerrilla warfare. Tukhachevsky sent the local commander 250 barrels of chlorine along with the following order on 12 June: 'Remnants of the defeated gangs… are gathering in the woods… I hereby order you to clear these woods using poison gas in such a way that it will spread and destroy anything hiding in there.' Surviving reports by Bolshevik commanders suggest that chemical weapons were consistently deployed against the partisans throughout the summer and autumn of 1921.[23]

Around 70,000 inhabitants of Tambov Province are estimated to have died in battle or from Soviet repressions between 1920 and 1922, while the Red Army suffered over 6,000 casualties in seven months in 1921.[24] The chairman of the Tambov Provincial Committee, Ivan Ishin, was executed in Moscow in July 1921. Alexander Antonov evaded capture for a whole year, before he and his brother Dmitry were cornered and shot in June 1922.

Western Siberia

The Western Siberian rebellion of 1921 was the largest in terms of its territory. It began on 31 January 1921, when an assembly of women in the village of Peganovo in Tyumen Province passed a resolution condemning the seizure of bread surpluses. After they successfully disarmed a government requisition unit of nine men, news spread to the nearby villages and soon the whole province had joined in the revolt.

The peasants blocked the Trans-Siberian Railway for three weeks in February and captured a number of cities: Petropavlovsk and Tobolsk in February, Surgut and Beryozov in March, Obdorsk and Karkaralinsk in April. The rebels established a Provisional Siberian Government but were gradually defeated by regular Soviet troops and switched to guerrilla tactics after their last stronghold of Obdorsk fell in June 1921. The exact number of casualties is unknown, but easily ran into the tens of thousands.

The rebel slogans were a mixture of economic and political demands. Their main political points were freedom of speech, assembly and unions. In one part of Tyumen Province, there were calls to restore Grand Duke Michael as emperor, but this was an exception and the most common phrases on the banners were 'Down with communism! Long live the soviets!' and 'All power to the peasants'.[25] In the liberated territories, free elections were held to vote in new district and village soviets.

Lenin considered such uprisings more dangerous than the Whites, as they were popular movements in support of democracy. In response, the Bolsheviks abolished grain requisitions in March 1921 and permitted private trade under their New Economic Policy (NEP). But while economic concessions were possible, any democratic or political compromises were out of the question.

Kronstadt

Even before the Civil War ended, workers who had supported the Reds began to realise that the new regime was even worse than their old capitalist masters. Many began to openly protest against the Bolshevik monopoly on power, which had turned from a 'dictatorship of the proletariat' into the dictatorship of the Communist Party.

A wave of strikes in Petrograd reflected the immediate disenchantment with the new government. On 8 May 1918, anti-Bolshevik protests broke out at the Putilov and Obukhov factories. The following day, government troops opened fire on unarmed workers at the Izhora Factory in Kolpino. This was the first ever case of the Soviet government shooting striking workers – only six months after the revolution. In June 1918, the workers of the Obukhov Factory and the sailors of the Baltic Fleet's mine division attempted an armed uprising, which was brutally suppressed by the authorities.

A fresh wave of strikes swept Petrograd in March 1919, when 20,000 workers in seventeen plants downed tools. More protests were held in summer 1919 and throughout 1920. In February 1921, the workers of several factories and the Putilov Shipyard went on strike. On 24 February, there were armed clashes between workers and troops on Vasilyevsky Island, accompanied by a series of anti-Bolshevik demonstrations demanding democratic freedoms and fresh elections to the soviets.

Four days later, the crew of the battleship *Petropavlovsk* stationed at the fortress of Kronstadt on Kotlin island in the Gulf of Finland passed a resolution expressing solidarity with the striking workers of Petrograd.[26] Their motion contained fifteen points, including calls for freedom of speech, press and assembly and re-elections of the soviets by secret ballot. They also demanded the release of all imprisoned workers, peasants and members of other socialist parties and an end to commissars in the armed forces, grain requisitions and privileged food rations for Party members.

On 1 March, 16,000 sailors and workers congregated on Anchor Square – popularly known as the 'Kronstadt *veche*' – to protest against the 'autocracy of the Communists' under the slogans 'All power to the soviets and not the parties' and 'For soviets without Communists!' The fifteen-point programme of the *Petropavlovsk* sailors was adopted by an overwhelming majority of votes (only two voted against). The next day, a Provisional Revolutionary Committee was formed to keep order in Kronstadt and to organise the defence of the fortress. The committee was headed by Stepan Petrichenko, a Ukrainian sailor who had previously led a 'soviet republic' on the Estonian island of Naissaar between December 1917 and February 1918.[27]

The Provisional Revolutionary Committee assumed power on Kotlin island in a bloodless revolution on 2 March. The sailors arrested the leaders of the Kronstadt Soviet and prepared to hold new elections by secret ballot, now allowing all left-wing parties to stand and campaign. When news of the uprising reached Ukraine, Nestor Makhno sent his fraternal greetings in a special radio message. After Trotsky warned Kronstadt on 4 March to surrender or face death, an assembly of 202 sailors voted to reject his ultimatum and defend their freedoms.

The following day, the government assembled an army of 17,600 men under the command of Mikhail Tukhachevsky, who was ordered to immediately launch an attack on the island. The Tenth Party Congress was due to start in Moscow on 8 March and the Bolshevik leaders wanted to announce the crushing of the rebellion on the opening day to demonstrate their intolerance of any dissent. Tukhachevsky began an artillery bombardment on the evening of 7 March and ordered his troops to advance across the frozen sea, but they were forced to retreat with heavy losses (some of his army deserted and joined the rebels).

A second attack was launched on the night of 16/17 March. This time, Tukhachevsky gave the command to use chemical weapons, although unfavourable weather conditions meant that they were not deployed. Several hundred delegates from the Tenth Party Congress were also ordered to help suppress the revolt (fifteen of them were killed). Twenty-five warplanes bombed the fortress on 17 March and, by midday on 18 March, Kronstadt was back in Bolshevik hands. During the assault, both sides suffered around 10,000 casualties, while 8,000 rebels – including Stepan Petrichenko – escaped over the ice to Finland.

12

Soviet Union

Winter

> 'Like Saturn, the revolution devours its own children.'
>
> Jacques Mallet du Pan, 1793

The RSFSR Constitution of 1918 proclaimed that all power belonged to the soviets. But all power in Soviet Russia really belonged to the Communist Party, where there was even less freedom after Lenin banned factions in 1921. As Lenin's health deteriorated and Stalin slowly accumulated power from 1921 to 1924, Trotsky suddenly realised that this prohibition could be used against him. Even though he had written after the dispersal of the Constituent Assembly in 1918 that 'as Marxists, we have never been idol-worshippers of formal democracy,'[1] he now performed a *volte-face* and published a letter in October 1923 calling for the restoration of democracy inside the Communist Party.

A declaration repeating Trotsky's demands for 'inner-party democracy' was signed by forty-six prominent Party members and sent to the Central Committee a week later. In December 1923, this letter was mocked by Stalin, who pointed out the dubious backgrounds of its signatories, all of whom had innocent blood on their hands. Writing in *Pravda*, he expressed amazement at the sudden conversion to democracy of Alexander Beloborodov, who had organised the execution of the tsar and his family in July 1918 and 'whose "democratism" is still remembered by the workers of Rostov' or 'Pyatakov, whose "democratism" made the whole Donbass not only cry out, but positively howl.'[2]

The growing opposition inside the Party – especially among the lower ranks – to the lack of democracy and the rise of a new bureaucratic elite was the subject of an OGPU report in December 1923.[3] The briefing warned that in most Party organisations, including Moscow, the majority of members were now voting against the Central Committee. By this time, due to Lenin's illness, the country was being ruled by a *troika* or 'triumvirate' of Stalin, Lev Kamenev and Grigory Zinoviev, and they met to discuss the matter. Their conversation is described by Stalin's former secretary, Boris Bazhanov, who defected to Persia in 1928:

> Stalin kept quiet and pulled on his pipe. In truth, his opinion was of no interest either to Zinoviev or Kamenev: they were sure his advice was useless in questions of political strategy. But Kamenev was a man of great courtesy and tact. That was why he asked, 'And you, Comrade Stalin, what do you think of this question?' 'What,' asked Stalin, 'of what question?' (In fact, they had raised several questions.) Forcing himself down to Stalin's level, Kamenev said, 'Of the question of capturing the majority of the Party.' 'Do you know what I think about this?' Stalin replied, 'I believe that who and how people in the Party vote is unimportant. What is extremely important is who counts the votes, and how they are recorded.' Kamenev, who knew Stalin well, coughed significantly.[4]

After Lenin died in January 1924 and the triumvirate collapsed in 1925, Stalin had Kamenev and Zinoviev removed from their positions of authority in 1926. They now attempted to ally themselves with Trotsky, but Stalin – 'wielding his power like a club' – expelled all three from the party in 1927. Kamenev and Zinoviev were later shot after show trials in 1936, while Trotsky was deported to Turkey in 1929. He moved about Europe in the 1930s, continuing all the time to write and campaign against Stalin.

In 1937, Trotsky published a programme for a liberated, post-Stalin USSR, which included freedom of speech, freedom of the press and even free elections. As long as other political parties did not try to restore capitalism, they would be allowed to freely exist and compete with the Communist Party for power. Trotsky now called for a new political revolution to overthrow the Stalinist dictatorship and install a socialist democracy: 'Bureaucratic autocracy must give place to soviet democracy.'[5] But Trotsky had no power to make this happen, having been consigned to the same 'dustbin of history' to which he himself had condemned the Mensheviks following the October revolution. In 1940, he was murdered in Mexico by an NKVD agent sent by Stalin.

Back in the Soviet Union, the only traces of democracy left in the Communist Party were the elections to the central organs at party congresses. Although the delegates voted for a single list of candidates, they could still cross out any of the names and replace them with another. The approved names were always successfully elected, but the number of votes against each candidate was still important.

After the Thirteenth Party Congress in May 1924 – the first after Lenin's death – Stalin's assistant, Ivan Tovstukha, hired a handwriting expert to study which of the delegates had crossed out Stalin's name on the ballot papers. Because the alternative choice had to be written by hand, this made it possible to find the culprit by comparing the ballot papers with the handwriting on the delegates' registration forms: 'Comparing these samples with the questionnaires, Tovstukha and the chekist graphologist identified those who voted against Stalin and were therefore his hidden enemies. The time would come, in ten or so years, when they would receive a bullet in the back of the neck.'[6]

In February 1934, at the Seventeenth Party Congress, Stalin received 'never-ending ovations' from the hall.[7] But when the delegates voted in a secret ballot to elect the Central Committee, the tellers found that the largest number of votes 'against' had been given to Stalin (almost 300). While these numbers were not enough to prevent his election, their revelation would have had unthinkable consequences, so the tally was altered to show only three votes against Stalin – ostensibly, the lowest number of all. In reality, the poll was won by the popular Leningrad party boss, Sergei Kirov, who only had three votes cast against his name. Kirov's results were changed to show that four delegates had voted against him – one more than Stalin – and he himself was assassinated later that year in his office at the Smolny in Leningrad.

The Seventeenth Congress of 1934 became known as the 'congress of victors', because Stalin used it to announce that the revolution was victorious and all enemies – both external and internal – had been defeated. As socialism had been established, changes could now be made to the constitution. There was no longer any need to disenfranchise anyone and equal suffrage with direct and secret elections could be safely introduced. Stalin appointed a commission to write a new constitution and suggested to the members that they might base the Soviet document on the Swiss model.

The draft constitution, which was published in June 1936, gave the franchise to all citizens aged eighteen and over (except for lunatics and prisoners). The document stated that the USSR is 'a socialist state of workers and peasants' and 'all power belongs to the working people of town and country as represented by the soviets.' All organs of state power would be directly elected by secret ballot – right up to the national parliament called the Supreme Soviet of the USSR. The Supreme Soviet would elect a presidium, which would then elect a chairman as the head of state.

One aspect of the constitution which immediately attracted foreign criticism was the clause providing for the existence of only one party – the Communist Party. Stalin addressed this subject at the Eighth Congress of Soviets in November 1936:

> Several parties and, consequently, freedom for parties, can exist only in a society in which there are antagonistic classes... In the USSR there are only two classes, workers and peasants, whose interests – far from being mutually hostile – are, on the contrary, friendly. Hence, there is no ground in the USSR for the existence of several parties and, consequently, for freedom for these parties. In the USSR there is ground only for one party, the Communist Party.[8]

The new constitution was adopted in December 1936 and a general election was scheduled for a year later – on 12 December 1937. Thousands of candidates, both Communists and non-Communists, were nominated for the first ever Supreme Soviet. As just under one and a half million people (less than 1% of the population) were Party members in 1937, some of the places were given to non-Communists. Everyone standing for election ran as the single candidate of the 'bloc of Communists and non-Party members' – or, as one voter described them on a ballot paper in 1947, the 'bloc of hunger and death'.

A specimen ballot paper printed in *Pravda* on 6 March 1937 showed more than one candidate, while as late as 21 November the newspaper was still claiming, in a guide to voting, that there could be 'two, three or more' candidates competing for one seat. In the end, the additional candidates were limited to a select list of thirty-two Party bosses, including members of the Politburo, who could theoretically be nominated in any constituency. But this system was abandoned after they started losing in primaries. The NKVD reported a case on a collective farm in Smolensk Region, where one woman criticised Stalin's nomination to the Supreme Soviet and voted against him. Nine others abstained and the farmwoman was arrested. In Belorussia, the political instructor of the Twenty-Fourth Infantry Regiment misunderstood the electoral law. There were four candidates on the ballot paper, but he told the voters that they could only choose two, which resulted in Stalin and the commissar of defence, Marshal Voroshilov, losing the election.[9]

Some voters genuinely believed that alternative parties could stand, including the Russian Orthodox Church, as Article 124 of the new constitution guaranteed religious freedom. The NKVD reported a month before the elections: 'In the village of Petrovinka, four churchgoers refused to vote for comrade Stalin... the group has been arrested... The priest Sheichuk and four sectarians went around the villages and openly campaigned against voting in the elections to the Supreme Soviet. The guilty have been arrested.'[10] Soviet citizens who attempted to stand as alternative candidates were also arrested.

The night before the elections, on 11 December 1937, Stalin gave a speech at a campaign rally held at the Bolshoi Theatre for voters in his constituency. The dictator announced to the assembled crowd: 'Never in the history of the world have there been such really free and really democratic elections – never! History knows no other example like it... our universal elections will be carried out as the freest elections and the most democratic of any country in the world.' Stalin heaped scorn on elections in 'capitalist... so-called democratic countries', where 'the deputies flirt with the electors, fawn on them, swear fidelity and make heaps of promises of every kind', only, once elected, to 'undergo a radical change... until the next elections.'[11]

Voting in favour of the 'bloc of Communists and non-Party members' involved simply dropping your paper in the ballot box, as it already had the single candidate's name on it. But if you wanted to vote against the candidate, you had to cross out the name by going into a special booth – after presenting your passport or other identity document. In 1937, which was the peak of the purges, most people were too afraid to do so, especially as the polling stations were closely monitored by the NKVD. According to the official results, the turnout was 96.8% of the electorate and 98.6% voted for the 1,143 single candidates.

On the eve of polling day, the central electoral commission issued a secret directive, warning the local commissions not to publish any figures or any other information except the name of the 'winning' candidate. The Soviet Union only ever released the total results for the whole country or a separate republic or region. No results were published for any individual polling station or even constituency. The figures were probably never recorded because the results were a foregone conclusion – while any real data might leak out and cause international embarrassment.

During Soviet elections, the secret police carefully recorded and studied any anti-government slogans or abuse directed at candidates and the Party in general. For example, in December 1937, one ballot paper in Vologda was found to contain the words 'Fascism and Communism are the one and the same.' The authors of such messages were normally tracked down and given long prison sentences. During the elections to the Supreme Soviet of the USSR in February 1946, the head of a fire department was imprisoned for six years for writing 'Stalin's death will save Russia' on his paper.[12] The following year, when electing the Supreme Soviet of the RSFSR, a book-keeper wrote the single word 'comedy' on his ballot paper; this was classified as anti-Soviet agitation and he was sentenced to eight years in prison.

One of the earliest foreign criticisms of Soviet elections came in November 1939, when Reuters reported on the voting for the People's Assembly of Western Ukraine. The elections were held on 22 October 1939 on the former territory of south-east Poland, which had been occupied by Soviet troops under the secret terms of the Molotov-Ribbentrop Pact. The turnout was only 50% in the towns and 25% in the villages – even though Red Army soldiers were allowed to vote and locals were marched at gunpoint to polling stations (one woman from Lviv was 'taken from home dressed only in slippers and a bathrobe'). But the official figures still reported a turnout of 92.83% with 90.93% voting for the single candidates.[13]

Wartime Republics

Nazi Germany broke the terms of the Molotov-Ribbentrop Pact and invaded the Soviet Union on 22 June 1941. In the course of the war, 40% of the population – almost eighty million people – found themselves in occupied territory. While most of these areas suffered unspeakable horrors under the Nazis, who regarded the local populations as 'sub-humans' useful only for slave labour or medical experiments, some pockets were left entirely on their own – and used this opportunity to set up small democracies.

The German military commanders usually appointed representatives from among the local population to administer the conquered territories on their behalf. Each village was headed by an elder, who was formally elected by the population, but in reality appointed by the German commandant or, sometimes, the district burgomaster. This official was 'chosen' at a rural gathering of male citizens not unlike a *veche*, although none of the voters dared to vote against the Nazi nominee.

The elder was expected to keep a close watch on the local population and sometimes surpassed Soviet officialdom in corruption and the extent to which he interfered in people's lives. In several villages in Oryol Region, the elder decided whom girls could or could not marry.[14] In the village of Zhukovka, the district burgomaster was forced to act on a complaint and wrote to the elder: 'You were ordered by the head of police to take one goose from every household for the German army. But you took four geese from Bolshunov. You must therefore comply with the order of the head of police and return to him three geese.'[15]

Two main alternatives to Nazi rule sprung up among Soviet citizens behind enemy lines. The most numerous were 'partisan republics'. At the end of 1943, twenty such zones existed in Belorussia, covering a territory of 20,000 square miles. The largest was the Klichaw zone, where 18,000 partisans defended a civilian population of over 70,000 people. These areas had their own administrative organs (Party committees) and system of justice (prosecutors and judges), which largely replicated the Stalinist order.

The partisan zones operated on a war footing and were solely concerned with fighting the Nazis. But there were other republics in the west of the USSR which remembered life before the revolution and developed democratic alternatives to Soviet rule in their three years without Stalin.

Zuyev's Republic

The Belorussian village of Zaskorki lay deep in impenetrable forests and was inhabited by 3,000 Old Believers. In September 1941, the villagers held a *veche* to appoint a new leader and elected fifty-year-old Mikhail Zuyev, who had been arrested by the NKVD and imprisoned for most of the 1930s. When Soviet partisans came to the village in November 1941, Zuyev recognised one of them as an NKVD agent. The villagers killed them in the night and successfully fought off attacks by other partisans until their ammunition ran out in December 1941. The following month, Zuyev went to the nearby town of Polotsk and secured fresh supplies from the Germans. The surrounding villages joined them and formed a 'republic of Old Believers' with its capital in Zaskorki.

'Zuyev's Republic' restored private property and reopened the churches. Serious crimes were judged by an assembly of elders and respected citizens, who could only pass the death sentence by collective decision. The republic was protected by a small army of self-defence units, which followed a policy of armed neutrality, driving away both Soviet partisans and an Estonian SS police battalion in May 1942. Colonel von Nikisch, the German commandant in Polotsk, turned a blind eye to the republic in return for payment of a fixed tax in kind.

When the Germans were forced out of Polotsk in the summer of 1944, Zuyev and 2,000 other citizens of the republic retreated to Poland and then East Prussia. The rest remained and fought as guerrillas against the Red Army until they were finally defeated in 1948. Zuyev's own fate is unknown. He joined General Andrei Vlasov's Russian Liberation Army, served as a lieutenant in his Second Infantry Division and either settled in France, before emigrating in 1949 to first Brazil and then Australia, or surrendered to the British in 1944 and was repatriated to the USSR, where he died in a corrective labour camp.[16]

Republic of Rossono

A more short-lived republic was established in marshy forestland around Lake Rossono near the town of Rossony in Belorussia. It all began with an experiment by the German occupiers in spring 1942 to return eight pre-revolutionary estates to their former owners. But the local peasants, who had just got rid of the hated Soviet collective farms, were not prepared to now live under their old tsarist landlords. The resistance movement was led by two former SRs: Karl Libik (a land surveyor) and Stepan Gryaznov (chief of the town police). They were joined by an anarchist teacher, Martynovsky, who had also been imprisoned under the Communists.

After an unsuccessful attempt to capture the small town of Idritsa in April 1942, Libik and Gryaznov led their associates into the nearby woods and swamps, where they founded the Republic of Rossono in autumn 1942. The small state began to attract deserters from SS police units, dislocated Red Army soldiers and anti-Soviet partisans. By early 1943, they controlled a territory inhabited by 15,000 people with an army of several thousand men. They raided nearby towns controlled by the Germans but had an agreement not to touch the Soviet partisans.

Each village was governed by a soviet with one representative for every ten adult citizens. Libik was elected 'chairman of all the soviets' (president) with Gryaznov as prime minister. Their ideology was 'a mixture of socialism, Russian nationalism and utopianism', sometimes described as 'Russian socialism without Nazis and Stalinists'. The official title of the state was the 'Free Soviet Republic of Rossono without Germans, Stalin and Communists' or the 'Free Partisan Republic of Rossono'. The government implemented the old SR programme, awarding six acres of land to each member of a peasant family, who paid a tax in kind of 20% of the harvest. The forests, lakes and rivers were communally owned. Everyone over the age of fourteen performed public duties twice a week.

After their forces captured a freight train transporting food, clothes, soap and tobacco to the front, the Germans directed Operation Winterzauber against the Rossono Republic from 15 February to 30 March 1943. Libik and Gryaznov were both killed in battle and Martynovsky took over as the head of the republic, which was reduced to just half a dozen villages. He made the mistake of breaking the peace agreement with the Soviet partisans and moved onto their territory. In August 1943, the republic was bombed in retaliation by Soviet aviation. Martynovsky was wounded in a battle with Soviet partisans on 5 November 1943 and his subsequent fate is unknown.

Lokot Republic

The Lokot Republic was an autonomous zone in Russia which collaborated with the Nazis from 1941 to 1943. The republic was based around the small town of Lokot in Brasovo district, now in Bryansk Region, which had previously belonged to the imperial family (Grand Duke Michael had an estate in Lokot and his morganatic wife was given the title of 'countess of Brasovo'). Serfdom had never existed there and the local peasants only suffered after the revolution from the civil war and collectivisation.

The rapid advance of the Germans in autumn 1941 caused the Communist authorities to panic and flee, leaving Lokot without any form of government. The village elders held a meeting and elected a local engineer, Konstantin Voskoboinik, as 'governor of Lokot and the surrounding lands' with schoolteacher Bronislav Kaminsky as his deputy, backed by a small militia to maintain order.

When the Germans arrived on 6 October, they allowed Voskoboinik and Kaminsky to remain in charge of the civil administration as an experiment in collaborationist government. The Lokot Republic had its own court system and police force, which took part in military operations against Soviet partisans. Collective farms were abolished and private enterprise was reintroduced. On 26 November, Voskoboinik founded the 'Viking' National Socialist Party of Russia, although it was never legalised by the Germans.

The Lokot Republic eventually covered an area the size of Belgium with a population of 600,000 people. After Voskoboinik was killed in a partisan attack in January 1942, Kaminsky took over as leader. The Lokot Republic existed until July 1943, when it was forced to evacuate to Belorussia, where it continued as the Lepel Republic. Although Kaminsky actively helped the Nazis crush the Warsaw Uprising, he was executed for excessive looting by direct order of Heinrich Himmler in August 1944.

Ukraine

One week after the Nazi invasion in summer 1941, the 'restoration of Ukrainian statehood' was proclaimed in Lviv by the Organisation of Ukrainian Nationalists (OUN) led by Stepan Bandera. The OUN set up a provisional government, which pledged to cooperate with the German invaders, but the Nazis were not interested in any independent Ukraine and deported Bandera to Germany for the rest of the war.

The remaining nationalists formed the Ukrainian Insurgent Army (UPA), which fought both Communists and Nazis and engaged in ethnic cleansing of the local Polish inhabitants. Because the Germans avoided the dense forests and marshlands of western Ukraine, the UPA was able to establish itself in small 'republics'. In May 1943, the Generalkommissar of Volhynia-Podolia, Heinrich Schoene, confessed that 'only the territory along the highways and railway lines lies in German hands.'

The largest Ukrainian wartime state was the Kolky Republic, which covered 1,000 square miles inhabited by 3,000 people in Volhynia. The republic lasted for six months and was created after the UPA occupied the town of Kolky on 13 May 1943 and then extended control over forty nearby villages. A civil administration was elected at a mass meeting outside the church and a sign was placed at the entrance to the town: 'Kolky is the provisional capital of Ukraine pending the liberation of Kiev.'

The Kolky Republic was a fully functioning state with its own police force, court system, postal service, ambulances and even a counter-intelligence unit, which foiled an attempt at a Communist coup. The local currency was a bond called a *bofon*, which the UPA used to pay for food, clothes and other essential items and were redeemable 'at a later date'. The word was an abbreviation of *boevoi fond* ('fighting fund') and the notes were designed by Robert Lisovsky, to whom the Lufthansa corporate logo is sometimes also attributed. The unofficial exchange rate was one *bofon* to one Reichsmark, one Soviet rouble or two *młynarki* (the currency in German-occupied Poland).[17]

The UPA units operating from the Kolky Republic fought fifty skirmishes against German forces in September and October 1943, killing 1,500 enemy soldiers. Ukrainian Reichskommissar Erich Koch decided to crush the republic and assembled a German SS unit, two Hungarian regiments, Kazakh and Uzbek troops, tanks and four planes. The operation against Kolky began with an air raid on 2 November and ended two days later after a battle in which 3,000 Axis troops, 1,237 UPA fighters and 500 villagers were killed.

Besides Kolky, several smaller republics existed in western Ukraine between 1941 and 1944. There was a 'state' of forty villages in Galicia with its capital in the village of Dusaniv. At the start of the war, Taras Bulba-Borovets established the Olevsk Republic in Zhytomyr region, along with a Cossack army called the Polesia Host, which collaborated with the Germans in shooting the entire Jewish population on 15 November 1941.

Most of these republics regarded themselves as the nucleus of an independent Ukrainian state. At their peak, they controlled 60,000 square miles inhabited by fifteen million people. On 27 August 1943, acting as the 'highest and single sovereign power' on the liberated territories, the UPA Supreme Command called for the holding of elections to rural and district soviets in September 1943. These councils were elected by direct, universal and equal suffrage in a secret ballot of all local residents who had reached the age of twenty-one. The soviets appointed the local administrations and could themselves issue executive orders.

Other UPA decrees abolished the collective farms and reintroduced the private ownership of land, which was democratically distributed by the local soviets and elected commissions. Military courts and revolutionary tribunals operated until the establishment of a proper judicial system. Free primary and secondary education was restored and schools started teaching in Ukrainian in September 1943. However, the advance of the Red Army put an end to all these plans and the attempts to create an independent Ukrainian state during the Second World War.

After the War

'I tried to make the voters happy by petitioning for repairs to their stairways and roofs, to their plumbing and switches, their doors and

locks, knowing that, on the eve of voting, any old lady could say: "You
do all that, my dear, or I won't vote!"'

Mikhail Gorbachev's student memories, 1951

Just one month after the Japanese surrender, in October 1945, the Soviet
government announced plans to elect a new Supreme Soviet of the USSR
on 10 February 1946. This was a very unusual campaign, because not all
of its territory was under the full control of the Red Army. In November
1945, the Ukrainian resistance called for a 'boycott of the Stalinist pseudo-
democracy'. Both the Communist Party and the UPA distributed leaflets
and held rallies throughout the winter of 1945/46. On polling day, Soviet
troops went round Ukrainian houses and churches – it was a Sunday – to
lead everyone out to vote. Despite their best efforts, the estimated turnout
was as low as 45% in some places – and only 5% voted of their own
free will. Nevertheless, the official results for the whole USSR reported a
record turnout of 99.74% with 99.18% of all votes cast in favour of the
single candidates.

The following year, elections to the Supreme Soviet of the Ukrainian
SSR were disrupted not by nationalists, but by Leonid Brezhnev. He was
standing in a constituency in Zaporozhye and was determined that
nothing should go wrong. Officials were instructed to keep a tenth of all
ballot papers in reserve and substitute them for any with his name crossed
out – potentially falsifying the results by 20%. Presiding officers were
encouraged to either remove or break the pencils in the polling booths
and generally do all they could to prevent anyone from voting against
Brezhnev. This was unusual even by Soviet standards and the minister of
state security, Victor Abakumov, submitted a report to Stalin in February
1947 on 'constitutional distortions in the recent elections'. The problem
was not the act of falsification itself, but the danger of any deviations from
the previously agreed figures, which always included a specific turnout
and a minimum number of votes 'against'.

None of this appears to have done any harm to Brezhnev's career. On
the contrary, it seems to have impressed Stalin, who rapidly promoted
Brezhnev after holding a personal meeting with him in 1952. Stalin was
already planning his next round of purges and possibly saw Brezhnev
as a useful assistant who could be relied upon to carry out his duties
assiduously. But the world will never know what Stalin planned to
do next, as the dictator fortuitously died on 5 March 1953 after three
decades in power.

Thaw

'He was like an old Bolshevik – instead of saying "good morning", he
tended to punch you in the stomach.'

János Kádár to Margaret Thatcher on Nikita Khrushchev

After Stalin's death, there was a brief period of collective rule, before
Nikita Khrushchev emerged as the new leader. He consolidated his
position against the old guard with his 'secret speech' at the Twentieth
Party Congress in February 1956, which revealed Stalin's crimes and
criticised his 'cult of personality'. This ushered in a period of relative
liberalism known as the Thaw. Khrushchev's following speech at the
Twenty-First Congress in January 1959 was peppered with such words as
'democratisation' and 'perestroika' and even referenced *The Economist*
and *The New York Times*. In addition, he announced that the Soviet
Union was now ready to move onto its next historical phase – the
'full-scale construction of communism'.

On 14 December 1959, the Soviet leadership met to discuss the
'Programme for the Construction of Communism' and to imagine what
life under this system would really be like. Khrushchev supposed that
communism would be similar to the 'all-you-can-eat' buffets in capitalist
countries combined with democracy. He told his Party colleagues:

It is necessary to think about the democratisation of our system.
Take, for example, the leadership of the country, the presidium of the
Central Committee. We are limited neither in time, nor in power. We
have been elected, but are we the most ingenious – and everyone else
completely unworthy? Bourgeoisie constitutions are constructed more
democratically than ours; the American president is limited to two
terms, while changes in our top leadership only occur through natural
death.[18]

The planned move from living under socialism to building communism
required a new Party programme, which was adopted at the Twenty-
Second Party Congress in October 1961. The speeches at this congress
went much further than in 1956. For the first time, in the radio and
newspaper reports, the public learnt of the 'monstrous crimes' – arrests,
tortures and murders – committed against innocent citizens and the need
to restore 'historical justice'. Khrushchev spoke emotionally on the second
day about telling the truth to people and promised to open a monument

in Moscow 'to the memory of the comrades who fell victims to arbitrary power'.[19] The decision was unanimously taken to remove Stalin's body from the Mausoleum after Dora Lazurkina, a Party member since 1902, told the conference that Lenin had appeared to her in a dream and said: 'I do not like being next to Stalin, who inflicted so much harm on the Party.'[20]

Khrushchev informed the congress that the Soviet Union would finish building communism by 1980. One delegate asked if the date could not be brought forward, but was told that this was impossible, as everything was based on 'strictly scientific calculations'. It was also announced that as the 'dictatorship of the proletariat' had fulfilled its historical role, it would now be replaced by a new concept – 'a state of the whole people' (*obschenarodnoye gosudarstvo*). The Communist Party would likewise be not just for the working class, but 'an organ expressing the interests and will of the people as a whole'.[21]

Khrushchev's first steps in this direction were reforms to transfer power from the state and Party organs to the soviets and public organisations, such as the trade unions and Komsomol.[22] In April 1962, he established a commission of ninety-seven members to draft a new constitution, which he hoped to put directly to the people in a consultative referendum. Among ideas discussed by the commission were the devolution of power to the union republics, limitations on terms of office, legislation to allow the replacement of Party leaders, convening the Supreme Soviet more than twice a year and transforming it into a truly representative assembly. Academician Yury Frantsev proposed creating a two-chamber parliament, while Khrushchev even floated the idea of multi-candidate elections.

Back in 1956, there had been an attempt to add a touch of competition to low-level elections by standing more candidates than the number of available places. But this small experiment in democracy had been terminated after local Party leaders failed to get elected. When sixty-nine candidates competed for sixty-five places in Yadrin district in Chuvashia, the losing four included the first secretary of the district committee, who only got eighty-one of 286 possible votes. In Uglich district in Yaroslavl Region, there were seventy-seven candidates for seventy-five places – and the losing two also included the first secretary of the district committee. After the chairman of a district executive committee lost an election in Kuibyshev (now Samara) Region, the Party leadership decided to abandon the initiative.[23]

The lack of alternative candidates meant that the only way voters could make their views known at elections was by writing messages on the ballot papers, which were always carefully read and closely studied by the authorities. When elections to the Supreme Soviet of the USSR were held in March 1962, Khrushchev was standing in Kalinin district in Moscow. Many constituents made use of this opportunity to let him know their feelings – and some of the inscriptions bore what the Moscow Party Committee called 'unhealthy, backward sentiments':

For the first time in my life I am voting against Soviet power – life is very difficult... Expecting manna from Khrushchev is like expecting milk from a billy goat... Why is there no lowering of prices for manufactured goods and foodstuffs? You cannot just think about satellites and rockets all the time... You are a fine fellow, but it would be good to let us have a bit more dough... Let the Russian people live and not just exist...[24]

Not long after the elections, on 1 June 1962, the government hiked meat prices by 30% and milk prices by 25%, setting off a wave of protest in many large cities. 'Fight for your rights and a lowering of prices' was the message on leaflets pasted along Lilac Boulevard in Moscow. 'Today a rise in prices, what will it be tomorrow?' was scrawled on a building on Gorky Street. The mechanics of the October Revolution Factory in Minsk went on strike, while the KGB reported that a small crowd had shouted 'anti-Soviet slogans' at a meeting in the centre of Riga.[25] The largest protests were in Novocherkassk in southern Russia, where several thousand workers walked out *en masse*. The next day, 2 June, they marched into the town centre, carrying red flags and portraits of Lenin.

The striking workers held a demonstration outside the Communist Party headquarters. The building was then occupied by protesters, who made speeches from the balcony. Soldiers tried to disperse the crowd in the square outside by firing a volley above their heads – inadvertently killing several boys who had climbed into the surrounding trees to watch. One of the boys to luckily escape was twelve-year-old Alexander Lebed, who lived on nearby Sverdlov Street. When the shooting started, he jumped out of the tree and ran home, but the two boys sitting directly above and below him were hit by bullets.

When the dead children started falling out of the trees, the crowd roared and the soldiers began firing into them, killing at least seventy more people. The number of casualties would have been even higher had General Matvei

Shaposhnikov not disobeyed a direct order to advance on the demonstrators with his tanks. Novocherkassk was the first popular uprising since Kronstadt in 1921, but all details of the massacre were covered up. It remained a secret for decades in the Soviet Union and no word of it seeped abroad.

Khrushchev was the first Soviet leader to travel to the West. He visited the United Kingdom in April 1956 and addressed both Houses of Parliament in the Royal Gallery – although his memoirs only record his amazement at the sight of the Lord Speaker wearing a wig and sitting on the Woolsack in the House of Lords and seeing Winston Churchill fall asleep in the House of Commons. He seems to have been more taken by Nordic democracy when he visited Scandinavia between 16 June and 4 July 1964. The Soviet leader was immediately struck by the down-to-earth nature of their monarchs and even mistook King Frederick IX of Denmark for a palace gardener. He praised the democratic conduct of King Gustaf VI Adolf of Sweden – 'the king was dressed in an ordinary grey suit and did not stand out in any way from those around him' – and was astonished when the Norwegian prime minister, Einar Gerhardsen, turned up for a reception at the Soviet embassy on a bicycle.[26]

Such observations possibly generated radical thoughts inside Khrushchev's mind. On the last leg of his tour, the Soviet ambassador to Norway, Nikolai Lunkov, overheard part of a conversation he was having with his son-in-law Alexei Adzhubei (the editor of *Izvestiya*) and Pavel Satyukov (the editor of *Pravda*). Khrushchev was asking them: 'How about we create two parties – a workers' party and a peasants' party?' The ambassador later repeated what he had heard to the Soviet foreign minister, Andrei Gromyko, who replied: 'Interesting... but I would not mention this to anyone.'

Khrushchev returned to Moscow, where he spoke at a plenum of the Central Committee on 11 July about 'the necessity of creating all the conditions for the development of democracy'. Four days later, he told his Party colleagues that he would soon be presenting them with the draft of his new constitution. Before leaving Moscow on 30 September to spend two weeks at the Black Sea resort of Pitsunda, he asked for all the documents of the constitution commission, so that he could write the final version before the next Central Committee plenum in November. Although he did not divulge any details, it was rumoured that he planned to introduce multi-candidate elections and the post of president of the USSR.

'Unfortunately,' as his son Sergei later wrote, 'we will never know how far my father planned to go.' On 12 October, Khrushchev was unexpectedly called back to Moscow by Leonid Brezhnev for an extraordinary meeting of the presidium of the Central Committee. Brezhnev had been plotting Khrushchev's overthrow since March 1964. He had considered having him arrested upon his return from Scandinavia, poisoned or killed in a car accident or plane crash. In the end, it was done peacefully on 14 October, by a simple vote. Khrushchev was dismissed as first secretary of the Communist Party and replaced by Brezhnev – becoming, in the process, one of the few rulers in Russian history to be peacefully removed from power.[27]

For Khrushchev, this was his greatest legacy and his proudest achievement. He had been elected by the presidium and he was removed by the presidium – in a legal act, without arrests or bloodshed – showing just how much the Soviet Union had changed since he took over from Stalin a decade ago. As he said to his closest ally, Anastas Mikoyan: 'Could anyone have dreamt of telling Stalin that he didn't suit us anymore and suggesting he retire? Not even a wet spot would have remained where we had been standing. Now everything is different. The fear is gone and we can talk as equals. That's my contribution.'[28]

Stagnation

'The unfair election is the same in the Soviet Union as in the United States, except that in the Soviet Union it's one candidate and in the United States it's two.'

Eduard Limonov

Although Brezhnev replaced Khrushchev as the general secretary of the Communist Party, the Soviet leadership again initially operated as an oligarchy. Alexei Kosygin was appointed premier and attempted limited economic reforms in 1965, but they were abandoned after the crushing of the Prague Spring in 1968. By this time, some citizens were growing brave enough to hold more political demonstrations. In December 1965, dozens gathered on Pushkin Square in Moscow in support of two arrested writers, Andrei Sinyavsky and Yuly Daniel. In August 1968, eight protestors unfurled banners on Red Square against the Soviet invasion of Czechoslovakia – although they were instantly beaten, arrested and given various prison sentences.

The following year, a nineteen-year-old student, Valeria Novodvorskaya, formed an underground group with the aim of overthrowing the Communist Party. On 5 December 1969, she went to the Kremlin Palace of Congresses and threw anti-Soviet leaflets from the balcony at a concert celebrating Constitution Day. She was arrested and taken to Lefortovo Prison, where she tried to organise an uprising among the inmates. Novodvorskaya was sentenced to two years in a psychiatric hospital in Kazan, where she was physically tortured using internationally banned drugs. She later co-founded the first ever legal opposition party in the USSR – Democratic Union – in May 1988.

The 1970s were known in the Soviet Union as the age of 'stagnation' (*zastoi*). While the economy was kept afloat by high oil prices, the general malaise and stupor infecting society were reflected in the writings on ballot papers during elections to the Supreme Soviet of the USSR in 1974: 'When will this charade of elections end? ... you can only vote for Brezhnev... I protest against our idiotic electoral system... This is not an election, this is fraud... The truth is in the Mausoleum along with Lenin...'[29] But there were no longer any repercussions for this mild form of dissent, or for openly voting against the official list of candidates. Soviet dissident Lyudmila Alexeyeva recalled: 'I would go to vote and cross out the name of the candidate. I was possibly the only one who did so at my polling station. Yet I never suffered any negative consequences.'

In 1979, twenty-five dissidents formed a bloc called 'Elections-79' and petitioned to stand candidates in the elections to the Supreme Soviet of the USSR. One of them was the famous historian Roy Medvedev, who illegally published bestselling books on Stalin in the West. However, they were refused permission by the central electoral commission. These 1979 elections had the highest ever turnout in Soviet history (99.99%). A further record was set at the next elections to the Supreme Soviet of the USSR, in March 1984, when the 'bloc of Communists and non-Party members' achieved its best ever results – 99.94% for the Soviet of the Union and 99.95% for the Soviet of Nationalities.[30] These were the last non-alternative elections ever held to the supreme legislative body of the Soviet Union.

By the early 1980s, the average age of the Politburo was seventy. Soviet leaders died in such quick succession that their funerals became popularly known as 'the hearse races'. Leonid Brezhnev had been terminally ill for so long that when he finally died, in November 1982, the news came as a great shock. After his reform-minded successor, Yury Andropov, died in February 1984, Raisa Gorbachev was shaken by the unconcealed glee of other Politburo members: 'It's an awful thing to recall, but at his funeral I saw some openly happy faces.'[31] British prime minister Margaret

Thatcher attended Andropov's funeral with a doctor, who published his prognosis on the lifespan of the new general secretary, Konstantin Chernenko – and was only out by a couple of weeks.[32]

Mikhail Gorbachev later recalled: 'Looking at Chernenko, who was not only unable to work, but had difficulties in speaking and breathing, I often wondered what had kept him from retiring... the main problem was that we had no normal democratic process by which power could change hands. The system existed according to its own laws, and a hopelessly sick, even senile person could sit at the top of the pyramid.'[33] This situation also caused problems for the Americans. When President Reagan was woken up in the middle of the night to be told that another general secretary had died, he grumbled to his wife: 'How am I supposed to get anyplace with the Russians if they keep dying on me?'[34]

Konstantin Chernenko was confined to the Central Clinical Hospital with breathing problems at the end of 1984. When rumours swept the country that he had died, the Soviet leadership proved that he was still alive by showing him taking part in the elections to the Supreme Soviet of the RSFSR on 24 February 1985. A hospital room was turned into a makeshift polling station and he was filmed dropping his ballot paper into the box, voting for himself. Four days later, Soviet television showed Chernenko receiving his parliamentary credentials and congratulations on being elected. Two weeks later, on 10 March 1985, he was dead.

13

Perestroika – Gorbachev

'Across Russia dashes a troika – Mishka, Raika, Perestroika.'
Popular saying, second half of the 1980s

'Democratising Change' – East-West Chemistry
'I was searching for someone like him.'
Margaret Thatcher

'Thatcher discovered Gorbachev for the West. She immediately believed in his sincerity, supported Perestroika and generally created a special aura around Mikhail Sergeyevich.'
Leonid Mlechin

When Mikhail Gorbachev came to power in the Soviet Union in 1985, he was already known in the West. He had visited Britain in December 1984, when he had been introduced to the world by Margaret Thatcher as 'a man I can do business with.' The prime minister's foreign policy adviser, Sir Percy Cradock, later wrote that 'Mrs Thatcher came close to claiming that she had discovered, even invented, Gorbachev.'[1] But, in many ways, this was true.

In September 1983, wishing to seek dialogue with Russia, Margaret Thatcher held a special seminar at Chequers 'to pick the brains of experts on the Soviet Union'. One of the eight invited specialist academics was Archibald Haworth Brown, emeritus professor of politics at Oxford University. Using the example of the Prague Spring, he suggested that 'a movement for democratising change can come from within a ruling Communist Party as well as through societal pressure.' As he spoke, Thatcher underlined the words 'democratising change' in her copy of his paper. Brown went on to identify a man called Mikhail Gorbachev as 'the best-educated member of the Politburo and probably the most open-minded' – although he believed that 'a transition to political pluralism is not in prospect for the foreseeable future.'

Thatcher sought a way to invite Mikhail Gorbachev to Britain. After he was appointed head of the Foreign Affairs Committee of the Supreme Soviet in April 1984 (a post traditionally held by the second-in-command of the Party leadership), she had his British counterpart – Sir Anthony Kershaw, chairman of the House of Commons select committee on foreign affairs – send Gorbachev an invitation to visit London. He came with his wife Raisa for a week in December 1984 and, while the programme included meetings with ministers, opposition leaders and business people, the highlight was lunch and a five-hour discussion with the prime minister at Chequers on Sunday 16 December.

Gorbachev and Thatcher found that they were very similar to one another. Both were staunch advocates of their two polar opposite ideologies – due to which they almost did not make it through their first hour together. Thatcher remembered: 'We went into lunch... It was not long before the conversation turned from trivialities – for which neither Mr Gorbachev nor I had any taste – to a vigorous two-way debate. In a sense, the argument has continued ever since and is taken up whenever we meet; and as it goes to the heart of what politics is really about, I never tire of it.'[2] Gorbachev himself recalled: 'At some point, our conversation became so tense that some of those present thought that it would have no continuation. And then I said to Margaret that I had no instructions from the Politburo to persuade her to join the Communist Party of the Soviet Union. She broke into laughter.'

After lunch, while Denis Thatcher gave Raisa a tour of the house, Margaret and Mikhail retired to the sitting room to continue their intense debate. Sitting down in front of the open log fire, Mrs Thatcher took off her shoes and reached for her notes. As Gorbachev reached into his pocket for his own notes, he suddenly said: 'Could we do without these papers?' She replied: 'Gladly!' and put them aside. Thatcher recalled: 'As the day wore on, I came to understand that it was the style far more than the Marxist rhetoric which expressed the substance of the personality beneath. I found myself liking him.'[3]

Many thought that the British leader went beyond merely 'liking' Gorbachev. Tony Bishop, her interpreter, felt that he was 'witnessing something akin to a flirtation between two people with much to gain from and offer to each other'.[4] Gorbachev's interpreter, Viktor Sukhodrev, thought the exact same thing when they met again in 1985 – although another interpreter, Pavel Palazhchenko, claimed that it was Anatoly Chernyaev, Gorbachev's foreign policy adviser, who was himself in love with Thatcher. Chernyaev himself confesses in his diary on 28 May 1991: 'I "adore" her and my office is decorated with her portraits.'[5]

Although the talks were due to end at 4.30 pm, to allow Gorbachev to get back to London for a reception at the Soviet embassy, he said that he wanted to continue. It was 5.50 pm when he left and he was two hours late for the event. The following day, Thatcher gave a television interview to the BBC in which she said: 'I like Mr Gorbachev. We can do business together.' Likewise, Gorbachev later wrote that 'Margaret Thatcher did much to support our Perestroika. Needless to say, she had her own views on the reforms, perceiving them as winning the Soviet Union over to Western positions, as a Soviet version of "Thatcherism". Nonetheless, she genuinely wanted to help us and to mobilise the efforts of the Western countries in support of our policies.'[6]

Their following meeting took place at Chernenko's funeral in March 1985, when Gorbachev was now the head of the Soviet Union. Although only fifteen minutes was earmarked for each meeting with the attending foreign leaders, Gorbachev spent almost an hour with Thatcher, who told him that his visit to Britain had been 'one of the most successful ever'. A Foreign Office official observed that 'the PM seems to go uncharacteristically weak at the knees when she talks to the personable Mr Gorbachev.'

During their first meeting in 1984, Gorbachev had invited Thatcher to come to the USSR and 'see how the Soviet people lived – "joyfully".' Although Mrs Thatcher had underlined the last word and written '!' beside it, she kept her promise and visited Moscow, Zagorsk and Tbilisi in March 1987. The highlight of her trip was when she was grilled on Soviet television by three top political journalists – an event often described as the starting point of Glasnost. Her biographer Charles Moore wrote: 'It was an hour-long interview where she said exactly what she thought about the Soviet Union. People were absolutely amazed by her. Soviet viewers had never ever seen anything like it.'[7] Russian television producer Sergei Skvortsov recalled: 'The Iron Lady wiped the floor with them.'[8]

After Thatcher's trip to the USSR in 1987, Sir Percy Cradock found it 'harder to talk about Gorbachev with her entirely objectively' and believed that she became 'dangerously attached to Gorbachev in his domestic role'. However, as the prime minister explained, this was not the case:

I was convinced that we must seek out the most likely person in the rising generation of Soviet leaders and then cultivate and sustain him, while recognising the clear limits of our power to do so. That is why those who subsequently considered that I was led astray from my original approach to the Soviet Union because I was dazzled by Mr Gorbachev were wrong. I spotted him because I was searching for someone like him.[9]

No British prime minister held as many meetings with a Soviet leader as Thatcher did – not even Winston Churchill with his wartime ally Stalin. She met Gorbachev for two hours in December 1987 at a stop-over at RAF Brize Norton – where Soviet aircraft had never been before – and told the press after he left that 'as on previous occasions, I have had a thoroughly valuable and, of course, stimulating talk with Mr Gorbachev and the atmosphere was very good and very warm, as we have come to expect.' She visited the Soviet Union again in June 1990 and in May 1991, when she was invited to address the Supreme Soviet of the USSR.

Gorbachev first learnt of the Armenian earthquake of 7 December 1988 from a telegram sent to him in the USA by Thatcher. Likewise, the Soviet ambassador to the UK, Leonid Zamyatin, only heard about the military coup when Thatcher telephoned him on 19 August 1991: 'She called me at eight in the morning and said very angrily: "Mister Ambassador, do you know what is happening in Russia?" – "I am sorry, madam, I don't." – "Well, then turn on your TV set and see for yourself. I need permission for the flight of an English aircraft to Russia. You are flying with me. I will take a doctor along. Gorbachev must be sick. Maybe dying. I must be in Russia!"'[10] Noticeably, while all Western leaders denounced the coup, Thatcher was the only one genuinely concerned about Gorbachev's health.

Gorbachev held his last meeting with Thatcher as prime minister in Paris on 20 November 1990, two days before she was forced into resignation. 'We bid farewell at the entrance to my residence. "God bless you!" she said in a soft voice.'[11]

'We Can't Go on Living Like This'

'No matter how valid the ideas that inspire a party, no matter how wise its programme, no matter how strong the initial support from the people, sooner or later there will be an inevitable degeneration of a revolutionary party into a conservative party.'

Mikhail Gorbachev

Hours after Chernenko died, Mikhail Gorbachev called a meeting of the Politburo, which appointed him to head the funeral arrangements – the traditional sign that he would be the next Soviet leader. Returning home at four o'clock in the morning, he found his wife, Raisa, waiting up for him. They went for a long walk in the garden and Gorbachev told her, as dawn was breaking: 'We can't go on living like this.'[12] The following day, he was elected general secretary of the Communist Party at a plenum of the Central Committee.

As a committed communist, Gorbachev was not an obvious reformer. He had never stepped out of line as he slowly climbed the Party ranks from head of Stavropol in the 1960s to secretary for agriculture in the 1970s and a full member of the Politburo in 1980. He had been the protégé of Yury Andropov, who had suggested him for the post of deputy chairman of the KGB in 1969. There were even fears, among some observers, of a return to Stalinism under the new fifty-four-year-old leader.

Nevertheless, there were a few hints in Gorbachev's past that he might be different from all previous general secretaries. In the early 1950s, he had been considered a 'dissident' among his young friends because of his 'radicalism'.[13] As a law student at Moscow University, his friend and roommate had been Zdeněk Mlynář, a future leader of the Prague Spring (although this was taken as further evidence of his closeness to the security services, as all foreign students were spied upon).[14] He once openly criticised a professor in a class on Stalin's writings. Both of his grandfathers had been imprisoned during the purges.

Gorbachev's first major policy decision, in May 1985, was a war on drunkenness. He made himself unpopular by cutting alcohol production, increasing prices and limiting the sale of drink. While this campaign had been the initiative of his then Politburo ally, Yegor Ligachev, it was rumoured to be the work of Gorbachev's wife, whose younger brother was an alcoholic.[15] In 1991, Raisa wrote of Yevgeny Titarenko, who had been a talented and successful writer of children's stories until one of his books was censored: 'My brother drinks and spends many months in hospital... For me it is a constant source of pain which I have carried in my heart for more than thirty years now.'[16]

Raisa Gorbachev caused further resentment by appearing alongside her husband at public and formal occasions. This was the tradition in Western countries, but not in the Soviet Union, where leaders' wives were only ever seen at their husbands' funerals. People remarked that Raisa meant 'master' or 'leader' in Arabic – she was actually named after the Russian word for 'paradise' (*rai*) – and when Gorbachev started sidelining the Politburo, they said that she was now his principal adviser. Gorbachev's close friend Vladimir Lieberman probably best described the couple's relationship: 'Raisa Maximovna is Gorbachev's *alter ego*.'

Tales spread of Raisa's domineering habits and Western shopping trips, allegedly with an American Express gold card. Boris Yeltsin's bodyguard, Alexander Korzhakov, related a story he had been told by a colleague: 'Raisa marched around the Grand Kremlin Palace, pointing with her finger – repair this, replace that... In her husband's office, at her command, the elderly General Plekhanov, head of the president's security, was ordered to shift heavy bronze standard lamps around in the presence of his subordinates.' The press also talked of a 'cold war' between Raisa and Nancy Reagan, who complained after their first meeting that 'the conversation was dry, impersonal and tedious. She was lecturing me about communism and I couldn't wait for her to stop.'[17]

Ronald Reagan had been fully briefed on Gorbachev by Margaret Thatcher and the two men got along well at their first summit in Geneva in November 1985. Although they argued over Reagan's 'Star Wars' missile defence programme – Gorbachev wondered 'was it science fiction?'[18] – the turning point came when Gorbachev assured Reagan that he would help defend the USA from any attack by aliens from outer space ('No doubt about it!'). The summit ended with the signing of a joint communiqué that 'nuclear war cannot be won and must never be fought' and a series of measures to improve bilateral relations, including an annual exchange of New Year addresses in each other's country.

Closer relations with the West were just one of Gorbachev's new policy initiatives, which became collectively known as Perestroika ('restructuring') and Glasnost ('openness'). Although Perestroika was not officially adopted as the state ideology until January 1987, Gorbachev first used the word in May 1985, when he unexpectedly went on a walkabout to meet people in Leningrad. He started travelling around the country and, to the alarm of his security and the surprise of onlookers, he would get out of his car to talk and listen to people.

At first, Gorbachev only envisaged minor changes to make the socialist economy work better. In 1985, he talked more about 'acceleration' (*uskoreniye*) – modernising the Soviet system by introducing incentives and reducing inefficiencies. But then a catastrophe occurred which, he believed, shed light on the sickness of the system. On 26 April 1986, one of the reactors exploded at the Chernobyl nuclear power plant, killing several workers and releasing radioactive gas into the atmosphere. But news of the disaster was not reported until three days later – in a fourteen-second announcement on the evening news – and the traditional May Day parade still went ahead in the nearby city of Kiev.

Gorbachev later said that Chernobyl divided his life into two halves. He was now convinced that he had to put an end to the tradition of cover-ups and secrecy. The country needed a free flow of information, an end to censorship, the introduction of genuine public debate and the democratisation of society. He decided that reforms were required in every aspect of Soviet life and that political change was the key to everything. As he explained at the plenum of the Central Committee in January 1987: 'Perestroika itself is only possible through democracy and thanks to democracy.'

Censorship was eased and thousands of previously banned works of literature were published. Many of them dealt with Stalin's crimes and the purges, such as Anatoly Rybakov's novel *Children of the Arbat,* Lydia Chukovskaya's novella *Sofia Petrovna* and Anna Akhmatova's poem *Requiem.* Tengiz Abuladze's anti-Stalinist film *Repentance* was finally cleared for release. Alexander Solzhenitsyn's seminal work of research into the prison-camp system, *Gulag Archipelago,* was serialised in *Novy mir.* Works by émigré writers, philosophers and historians could also be read for the first time in the Soviet Union.

The avalanche of books, films, art and information had unforeseen consequences. So many archive documents were released, contradicting the official textbooks, that the school history exams had to be cancelled in 1988. Condemnation of Stalin's crimes led to attacks on Lenin, the October revolution and the whole Soviet system. Rock bands like Nautilus Pompilius and Kino and popular films like *Little Vera* (1988) and *Intergirl* (1989) shed light on many modern problems. Stanislav Govorukhin's documentary *This Is No Way To Live* (1990) was highly critical of the Bolshevik legacy. Alexander Nevzorov's nightly current-affairs programme *600 Seconds* covered everything from corruption, murders, racketeering and prostitution to radioactive vegetables on sale in Soviet shops.

The general loosening of restrictions unleashed a wave of ethnic violence, starting with bloody riots in Alma-Ata in 1986. In 1987, Crimean Tatars forcibly resettled by Stalin demonstrated for three days outside the Kremlin, demanding to be allowed to return home. The Nagorno-Karabakh conflict exploded in 1988, leading to a full-scale war between Armenia and Azerbaijan. The violent crackdown on a demonstration in Tbilisi in April 1989 sparked calls throughout Georgia for independence. There was civil unrest in Moldova in November 1989 and anti-government riots in Dushanbe in February 1990. Hundreds died in Kyrgyz-Uzbek clashes in the Fergana valley in June 1990, while fifteen people were killed after Lithuania declared 're-independence' and Soviet troops attacked the TV tower in Vilnius in January 1991.

1987 – The Small Leap Forward

'It is too early to speak of a school of democracy, for we are still in its nursery.'

Yevgeny Yevtushenko, 1989

After Gorbachev encountered what he believed to be resistance inside the Party to his limited economic reforms – there were many reasons for their failure, mainly the falling price of oil – he became convinced that he could not rely on the apparatus to bring about change and had to seek 'fresh forces'.[19] This could only be done by mobilising the human resources lying outside the Party and handing real power to the people – although, for now, he did not describe it as political pluralism, but 'the transfer of real power to the soviets'.[20]

The first mention of multi-candidate elections came at the Central Committee plenum of January 1987, when Gorbachev said that the key to 'strengthening socialism through democracy' was reform of the electoral process. It was decided to hold a small experiment in free elections later that year, on 21 June, when voters went to the polls to elect new district, urban and rural soviets. In 5% of these local elections, instead of the usual single candidate, the ballot paper would contain more than one name. For the first time in Soviet history, some voters were being offered a choice.

A total of 94,000 seats were contested by over 120,000 candidates. Although this was only a limited trial, it threw up some interesting results. In the majority of multi-candidate constituencies, the incumbent was defeated (57%). While all candidates still represented the 'bloc of Communists and non-Party members', the majority of those elected in alternative votes were non-Party members (58%). The losing candidates included the heads of 14% of district committees, 15% of rural soviets, 23% of urban soviets and 35% of municipal committees.

The messages left on ballot papers reflected the overall displeasure with the old system: 'As long as there is only one party, one cannot expect anything good... Appoint non-Party members to leadership posts, as the Communists have shown themselves to be crooks, one and all... We have a one-party system, but it should be multi-party.' However, there were many encouraging remarks: 'Now I already believe in the reality of elections and will vote with pleasure... This is looking something like real democracy... The measures for perfecting the electoral system and guaranteeing a secret ballot are very correct and timely... I am voting for Perestroika and the beneficial changes taking place in our country.'

Looking back on the experiment, Gorbachev said: 'Competition enlivened the elections, increased the interest of voters and raised the accountability of deputies. We now need to go further, assimilating and strengthening new approaches to the electoral system.'[21]

Boris Yeltsin – 'Demolition Man'

'Boris, I believe that historians will say you were the father of Russian democracy.'

Bill Clinton to Boris Yeltsin

Like Gorbachev, Boris Yeltsin came from a provincial family which had suffered under Stalin. His grandfather had been exiled as a *kulak* in 1930, while his father had been arrested in 1934 and sentenced to three years hard labour on the Moscow-Volga Canal. Boris was born in a village in Sverdlovsk Region in 1931 and, as a child, had several narrow escapes from death. He nearly drowned during his baptism when the tipsy priest left him in the font. Growing up, he broke his nose in a fight, caught typhus from drinking swamp water, then lost two and a half fingers of his left hand while playing with a wartime grenade.

Yeltsin had a complex personality and frequently suffered from depression. His prime minister, Yegor Gaidar, compared him to the mythical Russian giant Ilya Muromets – either energetically smashing his enemies or lying prone on a stove. Before he suffered his first heart attack in 1995, he made several suicide attempts when political events did not go his way. In December 1992, after the Russian parliament rejected his choice of premier, he locked himself in a sauna and his bodyguard had to break down the door. After the death of his mother and an impeachment attempt in March 1993, he took out a gun and threatened to shoot himself in the head in his Kremlin office.

In many ways, Yeltsin was the perfect example of the 'Russian dream'. He rose from working as a builder in 1955 to chairing the Sverdlovsk

Regional Party committee in 1976 – although he became more famous in that role for deconstruction. In 1977, he carried out government orders to pull down the Ipatiev House, scene of the murder of the former imperial family in 1918, after the KGB noticed an 'unhealthy interest' in the building ahead of the sixtieth anniversary of their deaths.[22] In 1985, he was appointed the head of the Moscow city committee, where Gorbachev needed someone to dismantle the old guard. But Yeltsin secretly harboured higher ambitions. Like his namesake, Boris Godunov, he was regarded by others as just an *oprichnik*[23] – while, all the time, he was dreaming of ascending the throne himself.

Yeltsin was not originally a democrat and was privately described by one of his Moscow colleagues as 'an orthodox Stalinist bastard'. But he genuinely embraced Perestroika and won popularity by openly travelling on public transport, while his wife was seen standing in food queues. He made unannounced visits to factories, where he delighted the workers by openly berating their managers. Throughout 1987, Yeltsin had frequent disagreements with Ligachev over bureaucracy and the slow pace of reforms. He believed that reactionaries in the Party leadership were sabotaging Perestroika and sent Gorbachev a written request to resign from the Politburo in September 1987.

When Gorbachev failed to respond to his letter, Yeltsin repeated his request openly – in an unexpected tirade at the Central Committee plenum in October. This was the first time that anyone had ever asked to quit the Politburo. Even more outrageously, Yeltsin said that the Moscow city committee should be allowed to decide for itself whether he stayed on there as first secretary. Gorbachev accused him of 'political immaturity' and 'complete irresponsibility' and the plenum descended into 'screeching and swearing'. Meanwhile, a fabricated version of Yeltsin's 'secret speech' was printed and sold outside underground stations, further increasing his popularity as a rebel and a victim of the Party bosses.

On 9 November 1987, two days after the seventieth anniversary of the Bolshevik revolution, Yeltsin stabbed himself in the chest with a pair of scissors at work. He was rushed to hospital. Summoned three days later to a meeting of the Moscow city committee, he was sacked as first secretary by Gorbachev. Yeltsin was told that his career was over and that he would never be allowed back into politics. Ironically, it would be Gorbachev's own democratic reforms which would allow him to return and, four years later, throw Gorbachev himself out of politics. But, for now, he started plotting his revenge.

1988 – 'A Watershed Year'

'But now comes a man who has stirred up the sleeping kingdom. He did not come from outside, but arose within this very system... he dared, it would seem, the impossible – a revolution of minds while preserving the socialist order of society.'

Chingiz Aitmatov

In 1988, Gorbachev pushed through a set of far-reaching political reforms which proved to be a watershed in the history of the Soviet Union. Building on his first small experiment in 1987, he now enshrined free elections in law. These transformations had the added advantage of providing Gorbachev with an alternative powerbase, allowing him to bypass the growing opposition to his policies inside the Party. Because while the previous year had belonged to radicals like Boris Yeltsin, it was now the turn of the conservatives, led by Yegor Ligachev, to make their voices heard and opinions known.

In March 1988, *Sovetskaya Rossiya* newspaper printed a lengthy article attacking Gorbachev's reforms and the recent criticism of Stalin. Written by a chemistry lecturer from Leningrad called Nina Andreyeva, it was titled 'I Cannot Forsake My Principles' and included a fake quotation attributed to Winston Churchill that 'Stalin came to Russia with the plough and left her equipped with nuclear weapons.'[24] As the piece contained information known only to a small clique of politicians, Gorbachev and his pro-reform allies – Alexander Yakovlev and Eduard Shevardnadze – suspected Ligachev either of direct involvement or of being the author himself. The Politburo discussed the matter and, in response, *Pravda* published an article the following month by Alexander Yakovlev entitled 'The Principles of Perestroika: Revolutionary Thinking and Actions', which confirmed the official course towards the democratisation of public life.

There were more clashes that summer, when 5,000 delegates met to discuss electoral reform at the Nineteenth All-Union Party Conference. For the first time since the 1920s, the voting was not unanimous. Delegates were allowed to express independent opinions and even criticise one another – which Yeltsin and Ligachev did with relish. Yeltsin recommended removing Ligachev from the Politburo, while Ligachev publicly chastised him: 'You, Boris, have not drawn the correct political conclusion.' But Gorbachev was delighted by the result: 'The Party had not known such an open and lively debate since its first post-revolutionary congresses.' The proceedings were broadcast live and people were 'literally glued to their radios and televisions'.[25]

The Nineteenth Party Conference passed a resolution calling for direct elections to all soviets with multiple candidates and secret voting. This was an historical decision, as the Communist Party was voluntarily abandoning its own dictatorship by reverting to a multi-party system and allowing the existence of a legal political opposition. Gorbachev later wrote that the conference 'was a personal landmark for me. It was a watershed, a clear line between "before" and "after".'[26] He believed that he was returning the country to the days immediately after the revolution and wrote that 'it was the transfer of power from the Communist Party into the hands of those to whom it should belong according to the constitution – to the soviets, through free elections.'[27] But it was more a radical step into the unknown – an attempt to combine the Soviet system with parliamentary democracy.

Later that year, when visiting Krasnoyarsk in September 1988, Gorbachev felt for the first time that he was losing popular support. Going out to meet people on the streets, he was shaken to encounter a complete lack of optimism. He was assaulted with a barrage of complaints about empty shelves in shops, red tape, poor services and ecological problems. Nevertheless, as the year drew to a close, he firmly believed that 'a new, democratic era was dawning in the country.'[28] Meanwhile, the Soviet Union began to prepare to hold its first free nationwide elections.

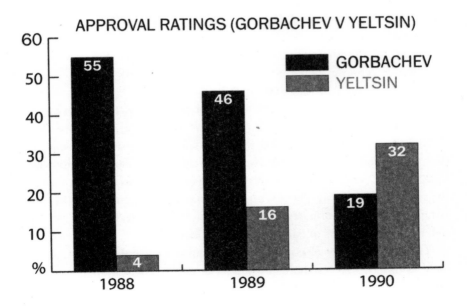

1989 – Thirteen Days that Shook the Soviet Union

'Perestroika is often described as a revolution. If it is one then it is practically unprecedented in Russia, a country of revolutions, because the main task Mikhail Sergeyevich has set himself is to carry it through democratically, without bloodshed or the use of force.'

Raisa Gorbachev

The term of office of the Supreme Soviet of the USSR elected in March 1984 expired in spring 1989. As it could not be re-elected under the old rules, the decision was taken to create a new form of parliament. Trying to steer a middle course between the complete abdication of power by the Communist Party and the need for greater democracy, Gorbachev came up with something resembling the old Zemsky Sobor – an assembly representing the whole of Soviet society. Some delegates would be appointed by organisations, while others would be directly elected by 'the land'. Known as the Congress of People's Deputies of the USSR, the new parliament would meet twice a year and elect a permanently operating Supreme Soviet for everyday legislative matters. The draft electoral laws were published in October and the Soviet constitution was amended accordingly in December 1988.

The Congress of People's Deputies had 2,250 members. Two-thirds of the membership (1,500 deputies) was directly elected – 750 in constituencies and 750 in national-ethnic territories. Multiple candidates stood in 1,101 of these 1,500 seats, while the other 399 ran old-style single-candidate elections. The remaining third of the congress (750 deputies) was 'semi-elected' by public and professional bodies, which held caucuses to choose their representatives. This included a hundred seats specially reserved for the Communist Party.

The Central Committee held a plenum in January 1989 to vote on its list of parliamentary representatives, who were nicknamed the 'Red Hundred'. The voting reflected the deep split and hostilities inside the Party between reformers and conservatives. Yegor Ligachev came last (100th place) with seventy-six votes cast against him. Alexander Yakovlev was second-last (99th place) with fifty-seven votes against his name and later remarked: 'Another two candidates and both Ligachev and I would have found ourselves outside the body of deputies.'

The first round of elections to the Congress of People's Deputies was held in March 1989, signalling the start of real political change. In many ways, the country picked up from where it had left off in November 1917.

Campaigning was mainly by word of mouth or telephone. Candidates addressed electors wherever they could be found in large numbers, mostly outside shops and underground stations. Photocopiers were still illegal and typewriters were expensive, so leaflets were usually written out by hand. The most advanced forms of electoral technology were the use of megaphones and the holding of televised debates.

Attempts to bribe voters generally had the opposite effect. The director of a sewing factory standing for the Communist Party sold heavily discounted clothes at her campaign stands, but her rivals in the democratic camp identified her as 'a regional committee member' on all her posters, which was enough to make her lose the election. In Leningrad, the Party was about to rubberstamp the single candidacy of the first secretary of the city committee when a man rushed onto the stage and begged: 'I have never voted in my life, please let me vote!' – only to drop dead from a heart attack.

There were few reports of serious violations or falsifications. The only major scandal occurred in the Proletarian constituency of Moscow, where the democrats boycotted the elections after several popular candidates were refused registration to improve the chances of a high-up official. Independent observers in the constituency subsequently claimed that ballot stuffing and other irregularities were employed to artificially raise the turnout above the required 50% threshold.

Almost 173 million people – 89.9% of the electorate – voted in the first round of the elections on 26 March. The highest turnout was 96.6% in Tambov Region, while the lowest was still a very respectable 75.9% in Leningrad. When Margaret Thatcher met Gorbachev a week later at Heathrow Airport, she told him that she had been 'very impressed by the recent Soviet parliamentary elections, especially by the turnout of the voters' – which was much higher than in her own recent election victory in June 1987 (75.3%).[29]

Although the Communists technically won the elections with 1,957 deputies (87%), compared to 292 independents (13%), the results were really a defeat for the Party. Gorbachev ensured that the 'Red Hundred' included many reformers, who subsequently used the Congress to attack the Soviet system. A fifth of all Party secretaries, including thirty heads of regional committees, were defeated. In Leningrad – 'the cradle of the revolution' – all seven Communist candidates were defeated, including the first secretary of the regional committee, who was a candidate member of the Politburo.

The elections signalled the political rebirth of Boris Yeltsin, who won 89.4% of the vote in Constituency No. 1 in Moscow. They also launched the careers of many other prominent politicians of the 1990s, including Anatoly Sobchak, Gavriil Popov, Galina Starovoitova, Gennady Burbulis, Ella Pamfilova and Yevgeny Primakov. Besides Yeltsin, the deputies included seven other future heads of state – Vytautas Landsbergis (Lithuania), Stanislav Shushkevich (Belarus), Petru Lucinschi (Moldova), Nursultan Nazarbayev (Kazakhstan), Askar Akayev (Kyrgyzstan), Islam Karimov (Uzbekistan) and Saparmurat Niyazov (Turkmenistan).

Two future presidents took part in the election campaign. Dmitry Medvedev was a post-graduate student of Anatoly Sobchak and helped to distribute his leaflets and stick up posters. Alexander Lukashenko narrowly lost in the second round (45.7% to 51%) to the deputy prime minister of Belorussia, Vyacheslav Kebich, after a bitter campaign in which Lukashenko – then still only a state-farm chairman – attacked corruption, privileges and 'the fat, sleek particrats with their limousines, special rations and rest homes', while Kebich responded by spreading false rumours about him. The two rivals met again five years later, in the 1994 Belarusian presidential elections, when Lukashenko crushed Kebich 80.6% to 14.2%.

A twenty-seven-year-old physicist called Boris Nemtsov was one of eight potential candidates in a constituency in the city of Gorky (which reverted to its original name of Nizhny Novgorod in 1990). He used the hustings to 'say terrible things about the Communists and spoke of private property, a multi-party system and the need to remove Article 6 from the constitution'. This was one of the first times that a politician had called for the repeal of Article 6, the clause which guaranteed the 'leading role' of the Communist Party. Although Nemtsov did not make it onto the final ballot paper, he was elected a year later to the Russian parliament, winning 57% of the vote in his constituency.

There was a total of fifty-nine journalists, fifty-five writers, thirty-two actors and directors, sixteen artists, fourteen composers and seven religious leaders at the Congress, including novelists Chingiz Aitmatov and Valentin Rasputin, actor Oleg Yefremov and the future patriarch Alexius II.[30] A relatively large number of women were elected – 352 deputies (15.7%). The poet Yevgeny Yevtushenko was selected and wrote that, 'for me personally, these elections were a unique lesson in life – happy in some ways and bitter in others. Democracy is no place for delicate princesses.'[31]

The membership included several famous dissidents, led by Andrei Sakharov, who was elected by the Academy of Sciences. The father of the Soviet hydrogen bomb, Sakharov had been calling for multi-party elections since 1968. He was awarded the Nobel Peace Prize in 1975 but was prevented from accepting it and exiled to Gorky in 1980 for protesting against the Soviet invasion of Afghanistan (Gorbachev allowed him to return to Moscow in 1986). Dmitry Likhachev, an expert on medieval literature who had once been sentenced to hard labour on the White Sea Canal, represented the Soviet Cultural Foundation. Roy Medvedev was elected after taking 52.3% of the vote in Voroshilov constituency in Moscow.

All this promised high drama when the Congress of People's Deputies convened for its first session from 25 May to 9 June 1989. The parliamentarians did not disappoint and it was thirteen days that shook the Soviet Union. The Congress opened on the 200th anniversary of another famous assembly, the États-Généraux, which Louis XVI summoned in May 1789 to try to solve France's financial and social problems. Although the king did not know it at the time, he would only remain on his throne for another two and a half years. The same fate awaited Gorbachev, whose parliament would also demand sweeping changes and would start the countdown of the old regime within a similar timeframe.

The short history of Soviet parliamentarianism began at ten o'clock on the morning of Thursday 25 May. The deputies assembled in the Kremlin Palace of Congresses, scene of so many Party gatherings, but this was unlike any previous congress. The Politburo did not sit on the stage but in the hall, alongside the other deputies (albeit in the front rows). When Gorbachev entered, no one stood up or applauded. Instead of the general secretary, the congress was opened by the chairman of the central electoral commission.

Latvian deputy Vilens Tolpežņikovs caused a sensation right at the start by running onto the stage and grabbing the microphone. He first called for a minute's silence for the victims of recent events in Tbilisi, where troops had attacked a peaceful demonstration on 9 April, killing twenty-one people. The entire hall rose and stood in silence, including Gorbachev. Tolpežņikovs then demanded an inquiry into the events and a commission was convened under lawyer Anatoly Sobchak, whose report to the Second Congress in December 1989 condemned the military and recommended the prosecution of the guilty parties.

The most important business on the first day was electing the chairman of the Supreme Soviet, who would be the new head of state. A second surprise occurred when Alexander Obolensky – an unknown engineer from the Kola Peninsula who had won his seat by defeating the commander of the Leningrad Military District – proposed, in the interests of democracy, to stand against Gorbachev. However, he failed to secure enough votes to get onto the ballot paper (689 for and 1,415 against). The same thing happened when Gennady Burbulis proposed Boris Yeltsin. So there was only one candidate and Gorbachev was duly elected on 95.6% of the vote. But this was the only way in which the congress resembled the old Soviet politics.

Over the next two weeks, parliamentarianism and freedom of speech were reborn in the USSR. Most Soviet citizens had initially been sceptical of Gorbachev's reforms, but now saw that they were for real. People heard on their television screens things which had, up until then, only been whispered in kitchens. As Anatoly Sobchak wrote: 'In the holy of holies of Kremlin power were heard words which yesterday carried a sentence in prison camp or a psychiatric hospital.' Protected by parliamentary immunity and knowing that the whole country was watching, the emboldened speakers – their tongues untied for the first time in seventy years – addressed not just the congress, but the entire nation in their speeches.

Yury Vlasov, who won a gold medal for weightlifting at the 1960 Olympics, called the KGB a criminal organisation and an 'underground empire' which had 'tortured and tormented... the pride and flower of our nations'. He demanded the resignation of the government, telling Gorbachev that 'people are sick to the back teeth of promises of a better life and absolutely insist on change.' Anatoly Sobchak proposed an investigation into the Novocherkassk massacre of 1962, while writer Yury Karyakin called for the names of all forty million victims of the KGB to be carved on the walls of their Lubyanka headquarters in the centre of Moscow.

Andrei Sakharov was allowed to make eight speeches. He described the invasion of Afghanistan as 'a criminal adventure' and condemned atrocities which had caused a million Afghan deaths. Two investigators into the 'cotton affair' in Uzbekistan, Telman Gdlian and Nikolai Ivanov, attempted to expose the prosecutor general on live television for covering up corruption. Yevdokia Gaer, a representative of the Nanai nation, spoke of the terrible living conditions of the indigenous peoples of the

Far North. Boris Yeltsin asked: 'Why do tens of millions live below the poverty line, while others wallow in luxury?' Sergei Belozertsev from Karelia demanded radical reform of the army and parliamentary control of the military and intelligence services. Alexei Yemelyanov, a professor of economics, called for the repeal of Article 6, proclaiming: 'The Supreme Soviet is above the Central Committee, the Congress of Deputies is above the Party Congress!'

The whole nation avidly watched the daily broadcasts on television. One Moscow journalist remembered:

> A crowd of people gathered on Smolensk Square at the windows of a radio store displaying several working televisions. Such crowds gathered wherever the Congress could be seen or heard. Televisions and radios were switched on everywhere – in cars (drivers opened the doors on a hot day and the sound spread throughout the streets, creating the strange feeling that the Congress was being transmitted directly from the sky), in offices, apartment buildings, on ships and in trains. Those who did not have the chance to watch or listen to the live broadcasts during working hours felt deeply deprived. One alarmed deputy said: 'Nobody is working, everyone is watching the Congress.'[32]

People stayed up until the broadcasts ended at two in the morning – 'no one went to bed' – and labour output declined by an estimated 20%.

The congress declared a day of mourning on 5 June after 575 people lost their lives in the Ufa train disaster. This was also unprecedented, as tragic events had previously been hushed up. When the deputies returned to work, they passed a motion condemning the massacre on Tiananmen Square on 4 June. The Baltic deputies established a commission chaired by Alexander Yakovlev to examine the secret protocols of the Molotov-Ribbentrop Pact. Roy Medvedev was appointed to investigate high-up corruption and was amazed at his new powers: 'Now I, a dissident, could look at any classification of secret documents; I could summon [interior minister] Pugo, [KGB chairman] Kryuchkov or anyone else for "a chat".'

On 7 June, 268 liberal deputies (12% of the Congress) established the first legal opposition group since the 1920s. They were known as the Inter-Regional Group (IRG) and included Andrei Sakharov, Boris Yeltsin, Gavriil Popov, Anatoly Sobchak, Galina Starovoitova and the youngest general in KGB history, Oleg Kalugin. Gorbachev privately called them *les enragés* after the radical faction at the National Convention during the French Revolution. Other oppositions groups soon followed. The conservative 'Union' (*Soyuz*) group was founded in February 1990 and included such hardliners as Yegor Ligachev and Sazhi Umalatova from Chechnya, who loudly demanded Gorbachev's resignation at the Fourth Congress in December 1990. Everything was exciting, new and confusing – some deputies joined both groups and one member of the IRG was even elected to the leadership of Union – but opposition parties, parliamentary debate and real democracy seemed to be finally gaining a foothold in the USSR.

Dmitry Likhachev observed these revolutionary developments with mixed feelings. While happy that 'the Congress liberated us from fear and taught us to speak the truth,' he could not avoid seeing parallels with the sudden feeling of liberty in February 1917, which had led to anarchy and violence and ended with the Bolshevik coup and civil war. Was Russian history going to repeat itself?[33]

1990 – The Parade of Sovereignties

'Take as much sovereignty as you can swallow.'

Boris Yeltsin, August 1990

The spread of democracy and the accompanying political battles entered a new phase in 1990 with elections to republican and local parliaments and loud calls for further constitutional reforms. All this happened on a background of growing nationalism, separatism and ethnic violence.

Although the Communists were still the only authorised political party, the opposition came together in January to create an informal umbrella organisation called 'Democratic Russia'. On 4 February 1990, over a quarter of a million people rallied outside the Kremlin in support of Democratic Russia and to demand the repeal of Article 6. Only three days later, an expanded plenum of the Central Committee agreed to amend the constitution, which was done at the Third Congress of People's Deputies on 14 March. Never before and never again did the government react so quickly to the voice of the people.

Article 6 was not removed but rewritten to include mention of other parties and organisations. The text now read:

The Communist Party of the Soviet Union and other political parties, as well as trade-union, youth, other public organisations and mass movements, through their representatives elected to the Soviets of

People's Deputies, and in other forms, participate in developing the policies of the Soviet state and in managing state and public affairs.

Although the amendment was a compromise, it was still revolutionary. This was the day when the Communist Party lost its monopoly on power and the USSR officially became a multi-party state.[34]

The constitutional amendments included the establishment of the post of president of the USSR. This was a deliberate move by Gorbachev to allow him to remain in power even if the Communist Party lost a general election – and protect him from suffering the same fate as Khrushchev in 1964 and being ousted by the Central Committee. Fearing that he might lose a public vote, Gorbachev decided that the presidential election would be held at the forthcoming Congress of People's Deputies. However, this move deprived him of the legitimacy of being democratically elected by the whole population – a serious disadvantage when the union republics started holding their own direct presidential elections. Gorbachev was elected president of the USSR by the Congress of People's Deputies on 15 March 1990. The two other nominees, Nikolai Ryzhkov and Vadim Bakatin, withdrew their candidacies and Gorbachev won without any opposition by 1,329 votes in favour and 495 against (the votes against came from both extreme reformers and hardliners).

The amendments also introduced the post of vice-president. Gennady Yanayev – Gorbachev's third choice after Eduard Shevardnadze and Nursultan Nazarbayev – was narrowly approved by the Fourth Congress of People's Deputies in December 1990. Yanayev had previously worked for twelve years as the head of the Committee of Youth Organisations, a lucrative post with much foreign travel (he once vanished on a pub crawl in Glasgow). Yanayev's main merit was his complete lack of ambition; he was described by a senior Soviet official as 'Gorbachev's Quayle – a conservative nonentity, no threat to Gorbachev' – although even this 'grey, unremarkable figure with bags under his eyes' would later attempt to overthrow Gorbachev.[35]

The changes to Article 6 allowing for the participation of other parties, blocs and organisations came just in time for the elections that year to the parliaments of all fifteen union republics, from Uzbekistan on 18 February to Georgia on 28 October. The most important political battle was the Russian elections on 4 March, as the RSFSR was the largest republic with over 51% of the population and 76% of the land area. As long as Gorbachev and the union centre could keep Russia under control, they could stabilise the whole country. But if the opposition came to power in the RSFSR, there would be problems everywhere.

The RSFSR adopted the same political system as the USSR. A Congress of People's Deputies would be elected for a term of five years and would itself elect a Supreme Soviet of 252 deputies. One major difference was that the RSFSR did not have its own republican communist party, so there were no guaranteed 'Red Hundred' in its parliament. The country was divided into constituencies in which multiple candidates competed for a single place in a first-past-the-post contest. Because the old totalitarian system had been abandoned while the practice of political spin had not yet been introduced, the 1990 elections are often regarded as the most democratic in Russian history.

A total of 8,254 candidates competed for 1,068 seats. The average number of candidates running for one place was 8.6 in Moscow and 9.2 in Leningrad. Boris Yeltsin faced eleven opponents in Sverdlovsk, but still won 64.4% of the vote. He was now firmly in the opposition camp as the leader of Democratic Russia. The liberals were only popular in large cities and did not have any visible leader with mass appeal after the death of Sakharov in December 1989. Yeltsin stepped into this role as a popular figurehead who could speak to the masses in their own language, while he benefitted from having the support of the democratic party machine at elections and inside parliament. In the end, this marriage of convenience proved fateful for the USSR – just as it did in the late 1990s for many liberals, who made the mistake of allying themselves with Vladimir Putin.

The turnout in the first round of voting was 77%. Violations were only reported in two of the 1,068 constituencies, where the results were annulled – one in the first round and one in the second round. The Communists won 920 seats (86%), which matched their result of 87% in 1989 – meaning that the Communist Party can claim to have never lost a Soviet election. However, almost a quarter of their deputies belonged to the 'Democratic Platform' – a faction created in January 1990 to push for becoming 'a genuinely democratic parliamentary party' – while even more were opposed to the Party leadership in general. As a result, while only 148 places (14%) went to non-communists, Democratic Russia ended up with around 205 seats. The Communists were initially the largest group with 367 deputies, but their numbers gradually declined as members left the Party.

The first free city council elections were held on the same day. For the first time since 1917, Russia now had legislative organs in which non-communists had a majority. In Moscow, 285 of the 465 deputies (61%) were members of Democratic Russia. In Leningrad, the democrats did even better and won two-thirds of the 381 seats. Gavriil Popov was elected chairman of the Moscow City Council, while Anatoly Sobchak headed the Leningrad City Council. Two months later, the opposition was allowed to join the traditional May Day parade on Red Square and marched with banners attacking communism, the Soviet system and even Gorbachev. When they started shouting 'Down with Leninism', 'Down with the KGB' and 'Down with the Communist Party', Gorbachev and the other members of the government left the podium.

The Congress of People's Deputies of the RSFSR opened on 16 May 1990 in the Grand Kremlin Palace, although they later moved to a permanent home on Krasnopresnenskaya Embankment in the House of Soviets, which soon became better known as the 'White House'. The first session lasted thirty-eight days, which was much longer than its Soviet counterpart a year earlier. As it did not have so many famous names, there was less public interest in this assembly – but it proved to be even more important in terms of subsequent history.

The first item of business was electing the chairman of the Supreme Soviet, who would become the leader of the RSFSR. The winning candidate needed an absolute majority of votes (531 of 1,060 deputies). The Communist candidate was Ivan Polozkov – a grey hardliner described by *The Washington Post* as 'scowling, grumpy and blessed with a permanent five o'clock shadow' – while Democratic Russia nominated Yeltsin. In the first round of voting, Yeltsin only just defeated Polozkov by 497 to 473 votes. In the second round two days later, Yeltsin did slightly better, but still only got 503 votes (Polozkov dropped to 458). He needed to find another twenty-eight votes and there were no more democrats left.

At this point, the Communists replaced Polozkov with the slightly more charismatic Alexander Vlasov, while Gorbachev spoke at the Congress in a last-ditch attempt to prevent Yeltsin's election. However, his personal attack ('I cannot work with this man') had the opposite effect – particularly among hardliners who hated Gorbachev even more than they did Yeltsin. Yeltsin's supporters held an advance showing of Stanislav Govorukhin's documentary *This Is No Way To Live* to bolster the anti-communist vote, while Yeltsin held last-minute negotiations with a group of military delegates, who were promised government posts if they supported his candidacy.

The following day, Yeltsin secured the necessary majority of votes – although only by four – when he defeated Vlasov with a result of 535 to 467. As Nikolai Ryzhkov wrote in his memoirs: 'These four votes, approximately half a percentage of deputies of the Congress, ultimately defined his subsequent political fate and, at the same time, the fate of Russia!' This was not only a victory for Yeltsin, but a defeat for Gorbachev. Yeltsin now had his own powerbase, cabinet of ministers and an office in the Kremlin – all the things that Gorbachev had at the union level. The only thing Yeltsin lacked was a chauffeur-driven limousine, which the Kremlin garage refused to issue him, so he demonstratively drove himself to work in an old banger belonging to a friend.

Yeltsin entrenched his position two weeks later, when the Congress adopted a 'declaration of Russian sovereignty' on 12 June 1990. This act was initiated by Yeltsin and established the supremacy of RSFSR laws over USSR laws on Russian territory. Unlike the narrow vote to elect Yeltsin as chairman of the Supreme Soviet, the declaration of Russian sovereignty passed by a large majority – 907 for and only 13 against. All factions supported the act for different reasons. Democrats believed that economic and political reforms were impossible in the union parliament, which had a built-in conservative majority. Nationalists regarded the other republics as a drain on Russian resources. Hardliners bitterly opposed the reforms introduced by the union leadership, while other communists saw sovereignty as a way to grab part of the common state property and Party membership fees.

The Russian communists finally set up their own republican party and held the founding congress of the 'Communist Party of the RSFSR' on 19 June 1990. They positioned themselves to the left of the Communist Party of the USSR and rejected Gorbachev's preferred candidate for the post of first secretary, electing Ivan Polozkov as their leader. The Communist Party of the RSFSR was banned by Yeltsin in August 1991, but reborn as the Communist Party of the Russian Federation under the leadership of Gennady Zyuganov in February 1993.

The rise of the Communist Party of the RSFSR coincided with the demise of the Communist Party of the Soviet Union, which held its last gathering in July 1990. Gorbachev faced attacks from all sides at the Twenty-Eighth Congress, which continued the break with Bolshevism by condemning totalitarianism and swearing allegiance to democracy and freedom. Led by Ligachev, the conservatives raged against Gorbachev for giving up their monopoly on power, while Yeltsin championed the democratic wing and proposed: 'We must change the name of the party. It should be a party of democratic socialism.' When his motion was defeated, Yeltsin announced that he was resigning from the Party and demonstratively left the hall – to a barrage of curses and abuse from the other delegates.

The final item of business was the nominations for the post of party leader. Gorbachev recalled: 'I thought how much the situation in the party had changed. The election of the general secretary was contested, and no one now was afraid that someone would twist his arms behind his back and ship him off who knows where.'[36] In the end, only one other candidate stood against Gorbachev. This was Teimuraz Avaliani, a miner who had written a brazen letter to Brezhnev in 1978, calling on him to resign. Gorbachev easily defeated Avaliani by 3,411 to 501 votes, although 1,116 votes were still cast against his candidacy. Commenting on the widespread hatred for Gorbachev inside the Communist Party, one delegate sarcastically proposed applying for an entry in the *Guinness Book of Records*: 'We are the only party that does not want its leader to be the president.'[37]

After walking out of the Party congress, Yeltsin embarked on a three-week tour of Russia, which is when he gave his famous advice to the smaller regions and autonomous republics: 'Take as much sovereignty as you can swallow!' He first said these words in Tatarstan on 6 August and repeated them later in Bashkortostan. This was not so much a call for devolution as a political ruse against Gorbachev, who had attempted to weaken Yeltsin by diminishing the role of the RSFSR. On 26 April 1990, straight after the Russian elections, the USSR had passed a law giving autonomous regions the same rights as union republics. This would have made sixteen smaller republics independent of the RSFSR and given the likes of Tatarstan or Mordovia the same status as Russia in the union. Yeltsin countered this move by offering them as much sovereignty as they liked – as long as they stayed in the RSFSR. The plan worked. There was a 'parade of sovereignties' as a dozen autonomous republics passed their own 'declarations of sovereignty' in 1990. Although this later led to constitutional crises in Tatarstan and Chechnya, Yeltsin's compromise held the RSFSR together and averted a 'state coup' by Gorbachev.[38]

Around this time, Yeltsin overtook Gorbachev in the popularity ratings. Tatyana Zaslavskaya, director of the country's first ever polling agency, the All-Union Centre for the Study of Public Opinion, traced the explosion in Yeltsin's approval ratings to May 1990, when he started opposing the union centre. He overtook Gorbachev in June and his approval ratings continued to sharply climb in July. Similarly, while opinion polls showed 56% actively supportive and 14.5% broadly supportive of Perestroika in autumn 1989, the number of active supporters had now fallen to 21.1% a year later – while 46.5% believed that the reforms had done more harm than good. As the country entered the fateful year of 1991, those who wanted change increasingly looked to Yeltsin and the Russian democrats, rather than Gorbachev and the Communist Party.

A terrible year for Gorbachev ended with him nearly being assassinated on Red Square on 7 November, during the last ever parade to celebrate the October revolution. Alexander Shmonov, a thirty-eight-year-old mechanic from Leningrad, drew a sawn-off rifle from under his overcoat as he approached the Mausoleum among the other marchers. Just as he was taking aim at Gorbachev, he was spotted by a policeman, who grabbed the barrel of the gun and sent his two shots astray. Shmonov blamed Gorbachev for the deaths of demonstrators in Tbilisi in April 1989 and Baku in January 1990 and hoped that his assassination would lead to the democratic election of a new president.[39]

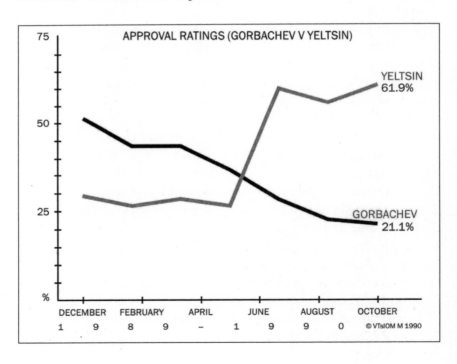

14

1991 – Transfiguration

The Union Strikes Back

'The regime which is destroyed by a revolution is almost always an improvement on its immediate predecessor, and experience teaches that the most critical moment for bad governments is the one which witnesses their first steps toward reform.'

Alexis de Tocqueville

Observing the 'parade of sovereignties' and growing nationalism in 1990, Gorbachev concluded that the only way to hold the Soviet Union together 'was the preparation without delay of a new union treaty'.[1] In a reflection of the democratic revolution taking place in the USSR, the government decided to consult directly with the people on the matter. For the first and only time in Soviet history, there was to be a national referendum. The question asked in March 1991 was: 'Do you consider it necessary to preserve the Union of Soviet Socialist Republics as a renewed federation of equal sovereign republics in which the human rights and freedoms of every nationality will be fully guaranteed?'

Unfortunately, in a sign of the already deep cracks in the union, only nine of the fifteen republics agreed to take part. Estonia, Latvia, Lithuania, Armenia, Moldova and Georgia all refused, saying that they had already decided to leave the USSR. Several of the republics which did hold the referendum altered the words, which had been carefully chosen to maximise a 'yes' vote. In Kazakhstan, there was no mention of a 'renewed federation' or 'republics', just the question: 'Do you consider it necessary to preserve the USSR as a union of equal sovereign states?' Ukraine added a second question: 'Do you agree that Ukraine should be in the composition of a Union of Soviet Sovereign States on the basis of the declaration of the state sovereignty of Ukraine?'[2] In Russia, a second question turned the referendum into another Gorbachev-Yeltsin showdown: 'Do you consider it necessary to introduce the post of president of the RSFSR, electable by popular vote?'

The campaign saw the first ever use of American political consultants in the Soviet Union. Back in 1989, when Gorbachev first thought about holding a referendum on a new union treaty, President George Bush expressed an interest in finding informal ways to support him. This led to Ralph Murphine, a political consultant who began as a door-to-door volunteer for John F. Kennedy in 1960, getting a phone call inviting him to the White House. Murphine was told of the plan to send an American expert in referendum campaigns to Moscow to observe the situation, offer comments and ideas, and generally provide advice, if asked or needed. The role would carry no formal title and there would be no salary.

In the run-up to the referendum on 17 March, a survey of public opinion suggested that the new treaty would probably be approved in most of the Soviet Union, but not in Moscow. Murphine spotted that the Party had been mobilising well-known but uninspiring political veterans in support of a 'yes' vote. The American consultant recalled: 'My suggestion was to conduct a survey to discover the names of persons in Moscow credible with voters. Four persons with good credibility were then selected to appear in television commercials endorsing the treaty change – the trainer of Spartak Moscow, a high-level priest from the Russian Orthodox Church, a well-known author from Moscow State University and the female anchor on the nightly television news network.'[3]

The mobilisation of Soviet 'celebrities' appears to have worked, because Moscow defied the opinion polls and narrowly voted in favour of the treaty (50.02%). Support for the union was generally low in large cities – 50.54% in Leningrad and 34.17% in Sverdlovsk. Nevertheless, every area in the nine participating republics returned a majority for 'yes' with the single exception of Boris Yeltsin's native Sverdlovsk Region (49.33%). The overall turnout was 79.5% (148,574,606 voters) and the final results were 76.4% in favour and 21.7% against (1.9% of ballot papers were invalid). The main focus of attention was Russia, where the battle between Gorbachev and Yeltsin ended in a draw. 71.34% backed the union in the first question, while 69.85% supported the introduction of the post of president of the RSFSR. The eight other republics all voted more enthusiastically than Russia for a continued union – Ukraine (70.2%),

Belarus (82.7%), Azerbaijan (93.3%), Uzbekistan (93.7%), Kazakhstan (94.1%), Kyrgyzstan (94.6%), Tajikistan (96.2%) and Turkmenistan (97.9%).

Gorbachev ordered the Supreme Soviet of the USSR to finish work post-haste on the new union treaty, while the Supreme Soviet of the RSFSR started drafting a law introducing the post of president. One of the authors, Sergei Shakhrai, suggested using Mikhail Speransky's historical project from 1809. In the end, Russia adopted a mixture of the US and French models. The president would be the head of state and executive power, but not the head of government and was not allowed to dissolve parliament. The president could only be a Russian citizen aged between thirty-five and sixty-five and would be elected for five years – reduced to four years in 1993 and then extended to six years in 2008 – for a maximum of two terms. This initially ruled out a second term for Yeltsin, who would be sixty-five in 1996, but the upper age limit was removed in May 1995.

The law on the post of president was passed by the Congress of People's Deputies of the RSFSR on 24 May 1991, ending centuries of hereditary monarchy and one-party rule. Less than three weeks later, Russians went to the polls to directly elect their own head of state for the first time in history.

Independence Day
'We are convinced that democracy, human rights and market principles are irreversibly entrenched in the Soviet Union.'
Margaret Thatcher, Supreme Soviet of the USSR, May 1991

Back in 1558, as noted earlier, Nostradamus had predicted the fall of a kingdom and a 'new Babylon' lasting for 'seventy-three years and seven months'. If this 'holocaust' referred to Bolshevik rule in Russia, which began in November 1917, then the end would fall on June 1991.[4] This was when the country not only went to the polls to choose its president, but also held the first free mayoral elections in its two largest cities of Moscow and Leningrad. A single day of voting was held on 12 June – the first anniversary of the declaration of Russian sovereignty and a date subsequently celebrated by democrats as 'Independence Day'.

As the single democratic candidate and the nominee of Democratic Russia, Boris Yeltsin was the clear favourite in the presidential election. However, he left his choice of running mate until the very last day for submitting his papers, after rejecting both Gavriil Popov and

Gennady Burbulis.⁵ It was his speechwriters who proposed Alexander Rutskoi, a Soviet air force colonel who had twice been shot down over Afghanistan. They hoped that Rutskoi, who headed a political faction called 'Communists for Democracy', might draw the votes of moderate left-wingers, while as a 'hero of the Soviet Union', he would also attract the female vote. Rutskoi tearfully accepted the nomination and promised Yeltsin: 'I will never let you down, you have made the right choice.'

The Communist candidate was Nikolai Ryzhkov, who had been the Soviet prime minister until suffering a heart attack in December 1990. His running mate was Boris Gromov, a popular army colonel who was the last Soviet soldier to leave Afghanistan in February 1989. Although officially backed by the Communist Party, Ryzhkov tried to distance himself from Gorbachev's policies and promised a much slower pace of reforms. Gorbachev himself backed a very different candidate – Vadim Bakatin, his former interior minister and a moderate liberal who, he hoped, would take moderate votes away from Yeltsin. Bakatin later became the last ever chairman of the KGB and caused fury when, 'as a gesture of friendship and goodwill', he gave the US ambassador, Robert Strauss, a map of the bugs hidden inside the new American embassy in Moscow. The far left was represented by the radical extremist General Albert Makashov, while Aman Tuleyev, who was later elected governor of Kemerovo Region, campaigned on behalf of the provinces and 'the common worker'.

Two new political parties also nominated candidates. The Liberal Democratic Party was founded in March 1990 by Vladimir Bogachyov, a composer and former dissident. He was ousted as chairman in October 1990 by Vladimir Zhirinovsky, who made the party synonymous with Russian nationalism, although he himself was the son of a Ukrainian Jew, Wolf Eidelstein, whose family had been murdered by the Nazis in the Second World War. Ostensibly an opposition movement, the Liberal Democratic Party stated that it preferred not confrontation but 'partnership' with the Communists. This has fuelled long-standing accusations that it was all a Kremlin project to set up a fake 'puppet party' at the very dawn of Russian democracy.

Alexander Yakovlev recalled eating *borsch* soup with Gorbachev in the Kremlin canteen when the KGB chairman, Vladimir Kryuchkov, approached them and said: 'Mikhail Sergeyevich, fulfilling your instructions, we have begun to form a party. We will give it a modern-sounding name. We have selected several candidates for the leadership.' This was confirmed by Kryuchkov's deputy, Philipp Bobkov: 'The Central

Committee suggested creating a pseudo-party, under the control of the KGB, to direct the interests and moods of certain social groups.' Yakovlev believed that Bobkov chose the party's name simply by stringing together two words fashionable at that time – 'liberal' and 'democratic'. He also provided evidence that the party was awarded three million roubles ($2 million) from the Central Committee via Zhirinovsky's running mate, Andrei Zavidiya, who was a member of the Communist Party.[6]

Zhirinovsky capitalised on the 'liberal democratic' name by seeking to build alliances with similarly named parties in Western Europe. Otto Graf Lambsdorff, chairman of the Free Democratic Party in Germany from 1988 to 1993, recalled: 'In 1990, a representative of the "Liberal Democratic Party" of Russia came knocking at the Liberal International Congress in Helsinki and the FDP party conference in Hannover, where our first and last talks with Zhirinovsky were held. It was clear from the start that these were not the Russian liberals with whom we wanted to build relationships. The door to the next Liberal International Congress in Lucerne remained firmly closed to Zhirinovsky – despite loud knocking.'[7] Zhirinovsky also contacted the Friedrich Naumann Foundation in Germany in 1990, but its chairman, Fritz Fliszar, wrote back to him in February 1991 that 'we are convinced that the organisation which you represent is only a liberal party in name. There is therefore no basis for cooperation between the Naumann Foundation and the institution which you represent.'[8]

Zhirinovsky campaigned on the slogan 'I will defend Russians' and other nationalist and populist policies. While his legendary promise of 'a husband for every woman and a bottle for every man' appears to have been apocryphal and invented by journalists, he did propose lowering the price of alcohol and allowing its unlimited sale around the clock. This helped to attract the alcoholic vote, although he faced stiff competition from Nikolai Ryzhkov, who had been the only member of the Politburo to vote against Gorbachev's dry law in May 1985. This was reflected in the polling at a clinic for alcoholics in North Ossetia, where Ryzhkov came first (157 votes), followed by Zhirinovsky (69), Yeltsin (22), Tuleyev (15), Makashov (10) and Bakatin (4).[9]

The Libertarian Party was founded in May 1990 by Yevgenia Debryanskaya and campaigned for human rights, animal rights and the legalisation of all drugs. The party held demonstrations at Moscow Zoo ('Freedom for animals, put the Communists in cages!') and rallied outside the Intourist Hotel for the legalisation of prostitution. At a

ℰ ₒ̄рвеиs

FRIEDRICH-NAUMANN-STIFTUNG

Der Vorsitzende der Geschäftsführung
Dr. Fritz Fliszar

Herrn
Vladimir Zhirinovskiy
Sokolicheskiy Val Street 38
Flat 115

107113 Moskau UdSSR

Königswinter, den 28.02.91
Zeichen FF-6453
Telefon 02223 / 701-110

Sehr geehrter Herr Zhirinovskiy,

die Friedrich-Naumann-Stiftung ist eine Institution des politischen
Liberalismus. Ziel unserer Arbeit auch im Ausland ist die Stärkung
des politischen Liberalismus, seiner Organisationen und die Umsetzung
seiner politischen Wertvorstellung in praktische Politik.

Auf Grund umfassender Informationen sind wir der Überzeugung, daß
es sich bei der von Ihnen vertretenden Organisation lediglich dem
Namen nach um eine liberale Partei handelt. Mithin ist eine Grundlage
für eine Zusammenarbeit zwischen der Naumann-Stiftung und der von
Ihnen vertretenden Institution nicht gegeben.

Hochachtungsvoll

Fliszar

Dr. Fritz Fliszar
Vorsitzender der Geschäftsführung

cc: Dt. Botschaft, Moskau
     über Referat 213, Auswärtiges Amt
     Liberal International, London
     FDP Bundesgeschäftsstelle, Bonn

Friedrich-Naumann-Stiftung · Margarethenhof   Commerzbank Bonn   Deutsche Bank Bonn   Dresdner Bank Sankt Augustin   —Volksbank Siebengebirge
Königswinterer Straße 409 · 5330 Königswinter 41   Kto.-Nr. 129 228 300   Kto.-Nr. 0 294 900   Kto.-Nr. 5060 400 00   Kto.-Nr. 1004 444 015
Tel. (0 22 23) 701-0 · Telex 8 869 997 fnst d   BLZ 380 400 07   BLZ 380 700 59   BLZ 370 800 40   BLZ 380 612 88
Telefax (0 22 23) 70 11 88   S.W.I.F.T.-Code: COBADEFF 380   S.W.I.F.T.-Code: DEUTDEDK 380   S.W.I.F.T.-Code: DRESDEFF 370   S.W.I.F.T.-Code: DGWGDEDW 32889

Above and opposite: Vladimir Zhirinovsky contacted the Friedrich Naumann
Foundation in Germany in 1990, but chairman Fritz Fliszar replied on 28 February
1991 that the LDPR is 'only a liberal party in name' and so 'there is no basis for
cooperation between the Naumann Foundation and the institution which you
represent.' Vladimir Zhirinovsky's reply to the Friedrich Naumann Foundation
on 2 April 1991 (opposite), expressed 'concern' over the 'misunderstanding' and
hoped that it would not 'influence the positive development of our relations'.
Zhirinovsky was dogged by rumours that the Liberal Democratic Party was a
Kremlin project controlled by the KGB.

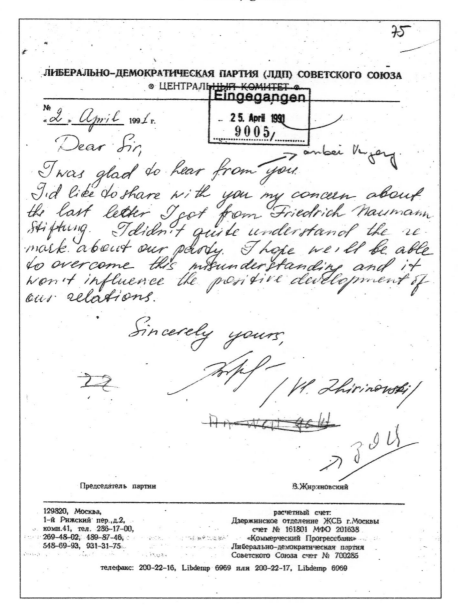

congress in woodland outside Moscow, the Libertarians nominated gay rights activist Roman Kalinin as their presidential candidate. Kalinin deliberately courted controversy with a series of outrageous interviews. When asked his opinion of Gorbachev, he said that he would not want to go to bed with him. When asked what would be his first policy decision on becoming president, he replied, 'To change sex.' His manifesto included plans to launch the first homosexual into space and increase the turnout at elections by automatically entering voters into a lottery. In the end, Kalinin was not registered because of the age restrictions – he was only twenty-five – and Russia lost its chance to become the world's first country with an openly homosexual head of state.

This was the shortest presidential campaign in Russian history, as the election date was not officially confirmed until nineteen days before polling day. Most of the campaign teams were headed by friends or party colleagues and it was an old-fashioned battle of ideologies, rather than personalities, without the use of spin doctors or image consultants. Negative campaigning was largely avoided, as smears tended to have the opposite effect – the government was so unpopular that anyone attacked by the authorities received even more votes. Nevertheless, as Zhirinovsky recalled in an interview in 2019: 'In 1991, it was fashionable to speak of democracy and that free, honest and competitive elections were finally being held. But it was actually a dishonest and corrupt campaign. The participants faced unequal conditions. The administrative resources operated at full throttle for those they wanted to win.'[10]

For the Communist Party, which still largely controlled the country, this was Nikolai Ryzhkov. During the campaign, Yeltsin's team reported physical attacks, technical problems, threats and bribery:

> Our demonstration was banned in Stavropol... our deputies were threatened with court proceedings when they tried to hold a meeting with voters... Sochi city council turned off the telephones of the democrats, who have been assaulted on the streets... Threats of sackings in Lipetsk if they do not vote for Ryzhkov... a kilogram of sausage meat was given to anyone voting for Ryzhkov at a factory in Tambov.[11]

On 16 May, a time-bomb exploded at the Moscow headquarters of Democratic Russia. A local parliamentarian blamed the KGB, who denied responsibility ('the KGB is neither here nor there') and pointed out that the main beneficiaries from all the publicity were Democratic Russia themselves. *Sovetskaya Rossiya* claimed that the explosion was an act of revenge by the Libertarian Party, after Roman Kalinin was beaten up by Yeltsin supporters, but a party representative went on television to deny the allegation as 'a lie and a provocation'.

Almost eighty million people voted on a turnout of 74.66% on 12 June. Boris Yeltsin won in the first round with approximately 45½ million votes

(57.30%). Ryzhkov came second (16.85%), followed by Zhirinovsky (7.81%), Tuleyev (6.81%), Makashov (3.74%) and Bakatin (3.42%). The option to vote 'against all' (none of the above) attracted 1.92%, while 2.16% of the ballot papers were spoiled or invalid. Yeltsin's main support base was in large cities (Novosibirsk 76%, Saratov 76%, Samara 74%, Moscow 72%, Leningrad 67%). His best result was in his native Sverdlovsk Region (84.80%) and his worst showing was in the Tuva Republic (15.25%) – where 10,000 votes were allegedly stolen from him in the capital of Kyzyl.

Ryzhkov was strong in rural areas, where the Communist Party had a well-established network and the party of power traditionally did well. He won four regions outright – Tuva, Altai, North Ossetia and the Agin-Buryat Autonomous District – although he was suspected of gaining an extra three to five million votes overall through ballot stuffing. Tuleyev won his native Kemerovo Region (44.71%), where similar falsifications possibly gave him an extra million votes.[12]

Zhirinovsky caused a sensation by coming from nowhere – some opinion polls had him on 0.5% – to take almost 8% of the vote. When the Central Committee met to discuss the results, Alexander Yakovlev reportedly said: 'This is not Yeltsin's victory, this is Zhirinovsky's victory.' Zhirinovsky was popular in the disputed South Kuril Islands near Japan and also performed well in the traditional Cossack regions – Krasnodar (12.87%), Stavropol (11.93%) and Rostov (11.63%). He explained the reasons for his success: 'I was new, clean, spoke well and was not a communist... I looked everyone in the eye, while everyone else read from a sheet of paper... I travelled a lot. This was also new and people came to look at the unknown presidential candidate. The other candidates preferred to stay at home.'[13]

Boris Yeltsin was inaugurated as the first Russian president on 10 July 1991.[14] The ceremony was held at the Kremlin Palace of Congresses without any Communist insignia, just a blessing from Patriarch Alexius II and an address from Gorbachev.[15] Yeltsin could now claim to have what Gorbachev did not – a democratic mandate as a directly elected president. The results were a setback for Gorbachev and the union leadership, who had failed to prevent a Yeltsin victory, even with all the powers of the state on their side. The preference for extremists over moderate candidates reflected the growing polarisation of Russian society, while the overall outcome showed that Russians wanted change – and that they firmly associated this change with Boris Yeltsin.

The democratic candidates were also victorious in the mayoral elections in Moscow and Leningrad. In Moscow, the race was easily won by Gavriil Popov, who took 65.3% of the vote. He immediately embarked on an active programme of privatisation and the renaming of streets, squares and metro stations, although he resigned a year later, in June 1992, over disagreements with the government's economic reforms – and the fear, according to his police chief, 'that the furious population would hang their leaders from the lampposts'.[16] Popov was replaced by his deputy, Yury Luzhkov, starting a trend which saw the democrats step aside in the 1990s as voters preferred a more hands-on 'managerial type' (*khozyaistvennik*) from the old bureaucratic class.

The elections in St Petersburg were a battle between liberal Anatoly Sobchak and Yury Sevenard, a Communist with an exotic family background. Sevenard boasted descent from the French nobility and kinship with Napoleon, while his son Konstantin, who was elected to the city council in 1998, claimed to be the great-grandson of Tsar Nicholas II and his onetime mistress, Mathilde Kschessinska. Sobchak defeated Sevenard in the first round by 66.13% to 25.72%. The turnout was a low 64.89% and 'against all' received an extremely high 7.15%. Sobchak served as mayor for five years and then lost to one of his deputies, Vladimir Yakovlev, when running for a second term in June 1996. Yakovlev, who was another example of the Soviet 'managerial' class, narrowly defeated Sobchak in the second round by 47.5% to 45.8%.[17]

The citizens of Leningrad also voted on 12 June on whether or not to restore the original name of their city, which had been founded as St Petersburg in 1703, changed to Petrograd in 1914 and then renamed Leningrad in 1924. The idea was first proposed in September 1990 by a democratic deputy, Natalia Firsova, but opinions in the city were sharply divided. The Communists and Gorbachev were vehemently opposed. Sobchak sat on the fence, fearing the loss of veteran votes in the mayoral elections if he supported the name change. Those in favour included the anti-communist majority in the city council, Patriarch Alexius II and the exiled writer and Nobel laureate Joseph Brodsky. St Petersburg won by 54.86% to 42.68% and the city officially reverted to its former name on 6 September 1991. That same month, Sverdlovsk city council voted to restore the town's original name of Ekaterinburg.

Yeltsin summed up the day and his election victory: 'The fact that between forty and fifty million people in Russia have voted for a democratic leader shows that a majority of the Russian Federation's population are in favour of the democratisation of society and politics.'[18] However, many of Yeltsin's votes were not so much for him, but a protest against the Communists. As *Kuranty* wrote on 15 June 1991: 'Yeltsin's victory shows the people's hatred of the Communist Party.' While acknowledging that 'power, communications, money and all the structures of the economy are still in the hands of the *nomenklatura*,' the newspaper confidently predicted that 'psychologically, its back has been broken. Russia will be reborn and will no longer be a stepmother, but a real mother to its children.'[19]

Just two months later, an event took place on the Orthodox festival of the Transfiguration which led to Russia being truly reborn. The lawful president was overthrown in a military coup and the citizens took to the streets to defend their freedoms and democracy. For three momentous days in August 1991, the country's fate once again lay entirely in the hands of its people.

The August Coup

'I have returned to another country.'

Mikhail Gorbachev, 22 August 1991

'On 19 August we were in one country, but on 21 August we found ourselves in a completely different one. These three days were the watershed between the past and the future.'

Boris Yeltsin

Gorbachev spent the summer of 1991 negotiating the new union treaty with the heads of all the participating republics. On 29 July, he held the final round of negotiations with Boris Yeltsin and Nursultan Nazarbayev at his residence of Novo-Ogaryovo just outside Moscow. The signing of the treaty was set for 20 August and Gorbachev left Moscow on 4 August for two weeks of holiday at the presidential dacha near the Crimean resort of Phoros. As usual, the Party leadership saw him off at the airport, including the vice-president. Gorbachev told Yanayev: 'I am leaving you in charge.' Raisa, meanwhile, wrote in her diary: 'Irina [their daughter] and I noticed that Yanayev had a rash on his hands.'

Unknown to the Gorbachevs, the KGB had been recording all their private conversations after secretly installing microphones throughout the Kremlin, Gorbachev's residences and even at Raisa's hairdressing salon.[20] The tapes of the negotiations at Novo-Ogaryovo revealed that

Nazarbayev was being lined up as prime minister of the new 'Union of Sovereign States', in place of the current premier, Valentin Pavlov. The vice-presidency of Gennady Yanayev would be abolished, while Dmitry Yazov (defence minister) and Vladimir Kryuchkov (head of the KGB) were also being pensioned off. These officials decided to act before the signing of the treaty by collectively seizing power, declaring a state of emergency and replacing Gorbachev with an eight-member 'state committee', which also included interior minister Boris Pugo.

The coup began at 4:30 pm on Sunday 18 August, when Gorbachev's telephones were cut off. Half an hour later, five co-conspirators – Oleg Baklanov, Oleg Shenin, Valery Boldin, Valentin Varennikov and Yury Plekhanov (the general who had once been ordered around by Raisa) – arrived at Phoros to inform the president that an emergency committee had been set up to stop the slide into disorder. There is confusion over Gorbachev's reaction to the news. The coup leaders later claimed that he shook their hands and asked 'about my role' when they departed at 6 pm. Baklanov was reputedly puzzled by the president's response: 'But he thought that was the only solution! What has changed?'[21] Gorbachev contradicts this by stating that he rudely swore at them. His wife was badly shaken by the news but told him: 'I am with you whatever may happen.'[22]

That evening, in Moscow, Yanayev signed a decree naming himself as acting president of the USSR owing to Gorbachev's inability to perform his duties due to illness. The coup leaders issued their first decree, which introduced a state of emergency for six months in parts of the country and banned demonstrations, strikes and all political parties except the Communist Party. The rest of the country woke up the next morning to find the television showing nothing but *Swan Lake* and hourly broadcasts with the 'appeal to the Soviet people' of the State Committee on the State of Emergency (*GKChP*). Hundreds of tanks were on the streets of Moscow, heading for the centre, while all other soldiers were confined to their barracks.[23]

For once, dual power worked in the country's favour. Gorbachev had been removed, but the conspirators had not taken care of the other legitimate centre of power in Moscow – the Russian president and the Russian parliament. Yeltsin and his team now stepped in to fill the void. He was at his government dacha in Arkhangelskoe to the south-west of Moscow, where he was woken with the news of the coup at 7 am. The decision was taken to move him to the more secure White House, which became the centre of resistance to the coup. Although the route into the city was lined with tanks and the complex had been surrounded by sixty commandos from the elite KGB Alpha unit, their commander, Victor Karpukhin, did not move to arrest Yeltsin. No one stopped his cortege either, as it drove down the Kaluga Highway flying the Russian tricolour. This failure to act would set the tone for the whole coup and the crucial moments the following night outside the Russian parliament building.

Yeltsin arrived at the White House at 9:40 am and issued a joint declaration with the Russian premier (Ivan Silayev) and the chairman of the Russian parliament (Ruslan Khasbulatov), condemning the coup as an illegal act. They formed a defence headquarters headed by vice-president Alexander Rutskoi, who called on all Afghanistan veterans to make their way there to defend democracy. Shortly after midday, Yeltsin climbed onto a tank of the Taman division and read out an appeal to the army not to act against the people. He also called for a general strike in support of democracy.

Throughout the day, several thousand people gathered outside the White House and began to build barricades around it. There was a wide array of famous faces, including politicians Eduard Shevardnadze and Alexander Yakovlev, conductor Mstislav Rostropovich, rock singers Andrei Makarevich and Konstantin Kinchev, a young banker called Mikhail Khodorkovsky and the future co-winner of the Nobel Prize for economics, Esther Duflo. Yuly Rybakov, a human rights activist and future Duma deputy, remembered spotting the Chechen terrorist commander Shamil Basayev with a couple of comrades: 'They brought a box of grenades to defend Russian democracy and, while waiting for the assault, used the box to play chess with the other defenders.' The crowds at the White House were supported from Lefortovo Prison by Valeria Novodvorskaya, who had been imprisoned in May for calling for the armed overthrow of the Soviet system. She recalled: 'I wrote leaflets and appeals right in the investigator's office and my lawyer took them straight to the barricades.'

When the coup leaders gave a press conference at five o'clock, the world's journalists demanded details on Gorbachev's health and whereabouts. Gennady Yanayev told journalists that 'my friend, President Gorbachev' was exhausted after six years and 'needed to restore himself.' The whole press conference was shown directly after the nine o'clock news. Even the state news programme during a military coup was democratic, reflecting just how much the Soviet Union had changed under Gorbachev. Yeltsin was shown standing on a tank and denouncing 'the *coup d'état*', followed by interviews with the defenders of the White House. The hour-long broadcast showed anti-coup demonstrations in Leningrad, calls for resistance in Lithuania, people arguing with soldiers on the streets of Moscow, doubts over the legality of the coup expressed by the Constitutional Oversight Committee and international concern at the 'unconstitutional' development in the USA, UK, Germany, Poland and Japan.

The only non-coup news was a report at the very end on a church service celebrating the Transfiguration, which had been held in the Dormition Cathedral for Russian émigrés. In the final seconds, the camera lingered on the cover of a book entitled *The Abandoned Tsarist Family*. A thousand miles away, in Phoros, Gorbachev and his family felt very much abandoned and cut off from the world after spending the day in complete isolation. Warships had appeared in the surrounding bay and the only way they could get news from outside was by listening to the BBC World Service on a hidden transistor radio.

Raisa, whose grandfather had been shot on that very day in 1937, kept remembering the many 'terrible pages' of Russian history. She wrote in her diary on 19 August: 'I am tormented by bitterness at the betrayal of people... What is happening in the country now?... No mail. No newspapers... "New faces" with machine-guns on the premises. Our doctor and senior guard have stated once more: "We'll stick by you, until the end"... Sub-machine-gunners are deployed at the gates... There are strangers all around... We spent a sleepless night.'[24] In the early hours of 20 August, Gorbachev secretly recorded a ten-minute video with an 'address to the people', calling the coup 'anti-constitutional' and denying that he was ill. They made several copies of the video, which they hid in various places around the house.

Back in Moscow that evening, there were further parallels with the overthrow of the Romanovs. Yeltsin's bodyguard, Alexander Korzhakov, distributed food and drinks among the loyal troops defending them, just as the tsar's wife and daughter had done at the height of the February revolution in 1917. These men were commanded by Alexander Lebed – the same boy who had fallen out of a tree in Novocherkassk in 1962 and had now grown up into a paratrooper general. He had been sent to 'maintain order outside the White House' and, sympathising with the defenders, had arranged his combat vehicles in an outer ring of defence.

The following day, 20 August, events seemed to be coming to a head. Valentin Pavlov resigned due to high blood pressure. A quarter of a million people demonstrated in Leningrad. Estonia declared full independence. At 2 pm, Lebed told Yeltsin that he had been commanded to remove his troops from outside the White House, suggesting that an attack by other forces was imminent. Yeltsin was informed by loyal KGB officers of an approaching assault by the Alpha unit, who were awaiting orders to seize the White House and intern the government. But the crowds defied the curfew introduced from 11 pm to 5 am to stay and defend their parliament.

Later that night, Lebed made his way undercover to the White House and told the defenders that 'Operation Thunder' was scheduled to begin at 3 am. The signal would be the firing of a red rocket. Shortly after Yeltsin and his team lay down to sleep, shots and shouting were heard. They descended to the garage and bundled Yeltsin into a car with the aim of attempting a dash to the nearby US embassy, which had extended an offer of political asylum. But when Yeltsin learnt of the plan, he categorically refused to go and so they barricaded themselves inside the basement, remaining there until five in the morning in the company of Gavriil Popov, Yury Luzhkov and his pregnant wife, Elena Baturina.

The sound of shots had come from the nearby underpass at the intersection of the Garden Ring and New Arbat. Three defenders of the White House were killed there shortly after 1 am, as they attempted to stop the armoured personnel carriers taking up their positions. Their names were Vladimir Usov (aged 37), Ilya Krichevsky (aged 28) and Dmitry Komar (aged 22). Although blood had now been spilled, these three deaths possibly saved the lives of hundreds. The loss of life was the decisive moment for the conspirators, along with the news that the reluctant Alpha and Wimpel units had not moved into place for the planned assault. At 8 am, the tanks of the Taman division started withdrawing from the centre of Moscow. Two hours later, the Russian parliament resumed sitting in the White House.

Later that day – 21 August – Yeltsin was informed that KGB chairman Kryuchkov, who was the main mastermind and leader of the coup, had called the White House and asked to speak to him. This suggested that the ringleaders were faltering and looking for a way out. In a last-ditch attempt to save themselves, they got on a plane and flew to Gorbachev in the Crimea. They set off for the airport at 1:20 pm, but were delayed in a traffic jam caused by the tanks and armoured vehicles returning to their bases.

The Gorbachevs heard this news on the BBC and feared the worst. Raisa suffered a stroke – 'I felt a numbness and a limpness in my arm and the words would not come' – and was put to bed. Their two granddaughters were locked in a room and guards with sub-machine guns were deployed along the stairs and entrance. At 5 pm, three cars drove up with Kryuchkov, Yazov, Baklanov and three others inside. Gorbachev refused to see them and demanded the restoration of his communications. When this was granted, he immediately called Yeltsin, who warmly greeted his political rival: 'Mikhail Sergeyevich, my dear man, are you alive? We have been holding firm here for forty-eight hours!'[25]

A delegation consisting of Alexander Rutskoi, Vadim Bakatin and Yevgeny Primakov also flew to Phoros and brought the Gorbachevs back to Moscow. They took Kryuchkov on their plane to ensure it was not shot down and landed at Vnukovo-2 airport in the early hours of 22 August. This was when the family seemed to succumb to the accumulated stress and tension of the past three days. Gorbachev's daughter Irina had a nervous breakdown, while Raisa was not well again for another two years. Gorbachev wrote of his wife: 'After Phoros, she had certain problems... Not only did she lose the use of one hand, she also went blind.'[26]

The coup leaders were arrested on the morning of 22 August and taken to Matrosskaya Tishina prison. Pugo shot his wife and then himself as the head of the Russian KGB came to detain him at his apartment (the attesting witness was the future Yabloko party leader Grigory Yavlinsky). Gorbachev's military adviser, Marshal Sergei Akhromeyev, hanged himself in the Kremlin on 24 August. All the ringleaders were later tried for treason but granted an amnesty by the Duma in February 1994.

The Funeral of the Soviet Union

'Lord, it is good for us to be here: if thou wilt, let us make here three tabernacles.'

Matthew 17:1-5

The funerals of the three defenders of the White House were held on 24 August, but it was really the funeral of the Soviet Union which was taking place. Gorbachev posthumously awarded the three men the title of 'heroes of the Soviet Union' – the last to ever receive this accolade. Alexander Solzhenitsyn congratulated Yeltsin on 30 August: 'I am proud that the Russian people have found in themselves the strength to throw off the most grasping and long-lasting totalitarian regime on Earth. Only now – and not six years ago – does the genuine liberation of our people begin.'[27]

The triumphant post-coup crowds on the streets headed for the Lubyanka, where they daubed the KGB headquarters and prison with swastikas and kicked in the glass. The statue of Felix Dzerzhinsky, founder of the Soviet secret police, was attacked on the square outside and dismantled by a crane two days later. Yeltsin banned all activities of the Communist Party on Russian territory, and the Russian parliament adopted the old imperial tricolour – symbol of the anti-communist democrats – as the national flag.

A number of unanswered questions remained. Gorbachev later recalled a strange telephone call with Yeltsin before the coup, on 14 August, and said: 'I could not get rid of the feeling that Yeltsin was holding something back.'[28] Grigory Yavlinsky believed that Gorbachev himself was behind the coup and articles appeared the following month suggesting that the Soviet president had either implicitly or explicitly colluded with the conspirators. Gorbachev himself said at his press conference on 22 August: 'I have not told you everything – and never will.' Raisa wrote in her diary on 27 August: 'For the fourth day, I have been reading, rereading and again rereading Mikhail Sergeyevich's letters. That's it. I am saying farewell to them. I am destroying them one by one.' All this aroused suspicions that either he or both of them had something to hide.[29]

The coup sounded the death knell of the political union it was intended to save. While Gorbachev was isolated in the Crimea, the only active and legitimate authorities in the capital – besides the people themselves – had been the Russian president and parliament. In contrast, the union leadership had been either incapacitated (Gorbachev) or usurpers of power (the state committee). As if abandoning a sinking ship, all the other republics declared independence – Lithuania (11 March 1990), Georgia (9 April 1991), Estonia (20 August), Latvia (21 August), Ukraine (24 August), Belarus (25 August), Moldova (27 August), Azerbaijan (30 August), Kyrgyzstan (31 August), Uzbekistan (31 August), Tajikistan (9 September), Armenia (23 September), Turkmenistan (27 September) and Kazakhstan (16 December).

Russia adopted its own programme of economic reforms in October, while Ukrainians voted on 1 December by an overwhelming majority of 90.32% to endorse its August declaration of independence. The final nail was driven into the coffin of the USSR on 8 December, when Gorbachev faced a second – now political – coup. Yeltsin secretly met with Ukrainian president Leonid Kravchuk and Belorussian leader Stanislav Shushkevich at the Belovezha Forest to discuss the creation of a much looser association called the Commonwealth of Independent States (CIS). The 'Agreement on the Creation of the CIS', which was signed later that day in Minsk, began by stating that 'the Union of Soviet Socialist Republics as a subject of international law and geopolitical reality ceases to exist.'[30]

On 12 December, the Supreme Soviet of the RSFSR ratified the Minsk Accords and repealed the Treaty on the Creation of the USSR of 1922. That same day, the three Slavic founders of the CIS were joined by Moldova, Armenia, Azerbaijan and the five Central Asian republics. The fate of the USSR was sealed. Gorbachev signed his last decree on 20 December – awarding pop star Alla Pugacheva the title of People's Artist of the USSR – and resigned as union president on 25 December (he was the only Soviet leader to resign). Previously, two flags had flown over the Kremlin: the red flag and the Russian tricolour. Now the Soviet flag was lowered forever – appropriately enough, given its totalitarian history, at the exact time of 19:37.

Gorbachev went on television on 25 December to address the citizens of a state which no longer existed. Looking back over the past six and a half years, he said: 'I am convinced that the democratic reforms started in the spring of 1985 were historically justified... Free elections, freedom of the press, freedom of worship, representative legislatures and a multi-party system have all become realities.' Although his speech warned that 'we still have not learnt how to use our freedom,' the now former president ended on an optimistic note: 'I am convinced that, sooner or later, our common efforts will bear fruit and our peoples will live in a prosperous and democratic society.'[31]

Gorbachev now had no job, title, office or even a place to live. He was thrown out of his home and his workplace as unceremoniously as he had been removed from power by Yeltsin. The day after his television message, he received a call from his distraught wife to say that 'Kremlin police thugs have appeared at our dacha and demanded that we clear out immediately.'[32] Officials also came to seal his presidential apartment at 10 Kosygin Street and gave him twenty-four hours to move out. He was told that he had until 30 December to vacate his Kremlin office, but when he went there on 27 December to give an interview to Japanese journalists, he was warned by his secretary over the car phone: 'Yeltsin, Poltoranin, Burbulis and Khasbulatov have been sitting all morning in your office. They've drunk a bottle of whisky and are having a party.'[33] Gorbachev never set foot in the Kremlin again.

15

'The Wild Nineties' – Yeltsin

'In a country well governed, poverty is something to be ashamed of. In a country badly governed, wealth is something to be ashamed of.'

Confucius

The 1990s were a period of immense upheaval and unprecedented change, comparable in Russian history only to the Time of Troubles, the rule of Peter the Great and the 1917 revolutions. At no other time did so much change so quickly in the lives of so many people – some of it overnight on a territory covering a sixth of the earth's landmass. Even the Bolsheviks moved slower when initiating the processes which were now being completely reversed. In terms of the sheer pace and extent of the transformations, the 1990s probably rank alongside the French Revolution and the Great Leap Forward in China.

The decade is commonly known in Russia as the 'wild 90s' (*likhie 90-e*), although this term only emerged later, generally among politicians seeking to contrast the 'stable 2000s' – which were equally 'wild' in their own way and only 'stable' thanks to high oil prices – with the general lawlessness, disorder, impoverishment and loss of national identity in the 1990s. The term 'wild nineties' originated in Mikhail Weller's book *Cassandra* (2002) and featured most prominently during the Duma elections of 2007 and when Vladimir Putin was running for a third presidential term in 2012.

The White Knight

'In my view, what we witnessed then was a revolution – one comparable, in terms of its influence on the historical process, to the French Revolution, the 1917 Russian Revolution and the Chinese Revolution of 1949.'

Yegor Gaidar

After Prince Pozharsky liberated Moscow in October 1612, his militia still had to expel the invaders from the rest of the country. In September 1613, he accepted the surrender of the Polish forces defending the 'white fortress' (Belaya) a hundred miles from Smolensk – along with sixty Scottish and Irish mercenaries, who decided to join the service of Tsar Michael. One of them, George Learmont, distinguished himself at the siege of Moscow in 1618, when the Scots repulsed the army of Prince Władysław at the gates of Bely Gorod ('white city'). Learmont settled in Russia, where his descendants included Romantic poet Mikhail Lermontov, prime minister Pyotr Stolypin and Soviet children's writer Arkady Gaidar. The latter's grandson, Yegor Gaidar, was a relatively unknown economist whose life changed forever after he took part in the defence of the White House in August 1991.

A year earlier, Gorbachev had flirted with radical economic reform and adopted Grigory Yavlinsky's '500 Days' plan for a transition to a market economy. This programme, which covered the whole Soviet Union, was later shelved for political reasons, although a law on the privatisation of apartments was passed in July 1991. Yegor Gaidar met Gennady Burbulis in the White House during the coup and told him that he had a ready-made plan for rapid economic transformations – but only in Russia. After the coup, Burbulis arranged for Gaidar to meet Yeltsin, who was taken by the idea of 'Russia first', as this could be used as a battering ram against Gorbachev. Gaidar's plan was adopted on 28 October at the Fifth Congress of People's Deputies, which also granted Yeltsin extraordinary powers for the next thirteen months, including the right to rule by decree and personally head the Russian government.

Yeltsin formed his new cabinet on 5 November. The president headed the government until 15 June 1992, when Gaidar was appointed 'acting prime minister' for the next six months. This radical move was intended to capitalise on Yeltsin's post-coup popularity, allowing him to take personal responsibility for the coming programme of 'shock therapy'. Gaidar was his minister of finance and given *carte blanche* to fill the rest of the cabinet with other young economists, including Anatoly Chubais (minister of state property), Pyotr Aven (foreign economic relations) and Andrei Nechayev (economics).

For half a year, Yeltsin was also Russia's acting defence minister. He planned to appoint the country's first ever civilian defence minister and his initial choice in February 1992 had been Galina Starovoitova (this was before any NATO country had a female defence minister). In the end, he selected General Pavel Grachev as a reward for supporting him during the coup. Andrei Kozyrev, the foreign minister, was nicknamed 'Mr Yes' for his pro-Western policies – in contrast to the Soviet veteran Andrei Gromyko, who had been known as 'Mr No'. Other ministers were Victor Chernomyrdin (fuel and energy), Ella Pamfilova (social security) and Sergei Shoigu (emergency situations). Collectively, Gaidar's cabinet of young reformers became known as the 'kamikaze government' because few believed that they would last long.

An overnight transition from state ownership and central planning to a capitalist market economy was unprecedented in history. But Russia had no choice. Winter was approaching and the country was on the verge of bankruptcy. The newly independent republics had stopped delivering food to Russia and there was no hard currency to pay for foreign imports. The shops were empty and entire cities faced the threat of mass starvation. As Gaidar later wrote of the situation in Russia at the end of 1991, 'we were flying a plane with only one wing, with no guarantee we'd land safely.'[1]

1992 – The Anarchy

'Would you treat your own mother with shock therapy?'
Alexander Solzhenitsyn

The new year traditionally began with televised greetings from the head of state. But Gorbachev was no longer president and Yeltsin was 'incapacitated', so a comedian, Mikhail Zadornov, was asked to stand in at the last moment. He enjoyed himself so much that he overran by one minute on live television. The programmers delayed the midnight chimes of the Kremlin bells and 1992 started a minute later in Russia.

Most Russians were probably glad to spend less time in 1992, especially when the shops reopened on 2 January. For decades, prices in the Soviet Union had stayed the same, but now they were freed and rose by 352% in January alone. Inflation over the entire year was 2,509%. Hyperinflation wiped out any savings people had in Soviet bank accounts, which had been frozen a year earlier as part of Valentin Pavlov's disastrous monetary reforms. Russians were now allowed to own foreign currency and there was a rush to buy US dollars. The dollar exchange rate collapsed in twelve months from 50 roubles in November 1991 to 450 roubles in November 1992.[2]

The state monopoly on trade and all import tariffs were abolished. For the first time since the 1920s, people were allowed to freely buy and sell goods. The shops quickly filled up with imported food, ending the queues and the threat of starvation. Many members of the middle class lost their jobs as a result of the drastic budget cuts and were forced to become 'shuttle traders' (*chelnoki*), travelling to foreign countries to buy food, clothes and electronics for resale in Russia. Enormous street markets (*tolkuchki*) appeared as impoverished citizens sold possessions to feed themselves.

Anatoly Chubais's privatisation programme was based on the Czech model and began in June 1992. Small businesses were sold into private hands – usually their employees – while larger concerns were turned into joint-stock companies. Every citizen was awarded a 'voucher' – Yeltsin preferred the word *check* – which cost twenty-five roubles and had a face value of 10,000 roubles. Many people swapped their checks for a bottle of vodka or invested in 'voucher funds' which vanished overnight. Most vouchers ended up in the hands of criminal authorities or 'red directors' – Soviet managers who now owned the factories they used to run.

The final element in the 'shock therapy' programme was supposed to be foreign assistance and debt relief. But the West refused to provide any help – either to the Soviet Union in 1991 or to Russia in 1992. Margaret Thatcher was a lone supportive voice in 1991, but by then she was out of power.[3] George Bush was afraid of 'being too nice' to Russia in an election year, while Bill Clinton was equally uninterested after 1992.[4] According to Jeffrey D. Sachs, an unpaid American adviser to Gaidar from 1991 to 1993, Washington wanted a 'unipolar world in the twenty-first century that could not be threatened by a resurgent Russia'.[5] At the same time, the West would not help Gaidar trace the billions of dollars that the KGB had secretly transferred to private bank accounts in Europe and the USA (as one former CIA official put it, 'capital flight is capital flight').[6]

Foreign financial assistance was needed to create a social-security net and build political consensus around the reforms. But it never came and predictably, just seven days after Gaidar's economic programme was launched, the Russian parliament called for the government to resign. The opposition to the reforms was led by the chairman Ruslan Khasbulatov and Russian vice-president Alexander Rutskoi. When the Seventh Congress of People's Deputies opened in December 1992, as Yeltsin's term of extraordinary powers came to an end, Gaidar was rejected as prime minister. Yeltsin was forced to nominate the more conservative Victor

Chernomyrdin, who was approved on the final day by a vote of 721 to 172. Gaidar resigned from the government and Chernomyrdin – who had promised the deputies 'a market and not a bazaar' – immediately slowed the pace of reforms.

1993 – President v Parliament

'The tyranny of the legislature is really the danger most to be feared... The tyranny of the executive power will come in its turn, but at a more distant period.'

Thomas Jefferson

At the end of 1992, when the Congress of People's Deputies rejected Yegor Gaidar as prime minister, Yeltsin concluded that 'this democratically elected parliament was itself becoming the chief threat to democracy.'[7] He decided that he had to get rid of it, especially after the Seventh Congress announced that it was planning to write a new constitution.

The problem was that Russia was still partially operating under the old Soviet system – the RSFSR Constitution of 1978 and the Congress of People's Deputies elected in 1990. Yeltsin could have adopted a new constitution and held fresh parliamentary elections in autumn 1991, but he wanted to avoid political unrest. He saw what had happened to Gorbachev, who had engaged in political reforms and neglected the economy. So he did the opposite and devoted all his time and energy to economic matters.

The result was Russia's eternal problem of 'dual power'. Oleg Poptsov, the head of Channel Two (RTR), described the situation in 1993: 'The president publishes decrees, as if there were no Supreme Soviet, while the Supreme Soviet suspends the decrees, as if there were no president.'[8] Two different models were operating side by side: a presidential system introduced in 1991 and a parliamentary system based on the 'soviets'. Both had been popularly elected, but which was more legitimate? This question occupied Russia for the whole of 1993.

In March, Yeltsin informed the nation that he planned to hold a popular 'vote of confidence' in his presidency and was assuming special powers to rule Russia by decree 'until the crisis of power has been overcome.' The Congress of People's Deputies met in emergency session to impeach the president, but the motion fell short of the required 689 votes (617 deputies voted for and 268 voted against). When Yeltsin and Khasbulatov reached a private compromise for early presidential and parliamentary elections in November, the furious deputies held a vote to dismiss Khasbulatov as speaker, which also failed to gain enough support.

Yeltsin pushed forward with his plans for a referendum, which asked four questions:

(1) Do you have confidence in the president Boris Yeltsin?
(2) Do you support the social and economic policies conducted by the president and government since 1992?
(3) Should there be early presidential elections?
(4) Should there be early parliamentary elections?

Yeltsin's supporters were encouraged to remember the correct way to vote by a blitz of television ads employing the catchy formula *Da, da, nyet, da*. The referendum was preceded by an enormous concert on Red Square called 'Rock in Support of the President', which was held on the very spot where Ivan the Terrible had addressed the first Zemsky Sobor in 1549.

The turnout on 25 April was 64.1%, although Chechnya did not take part and a local boycott in Tatarstan rendered the outcome there invalid. The results were (1) 58.7% (2) 53.0% (3) 49.5% (4) 67.2%. The voting showed that the president was more popular than the parliament and there was a much greater desire to re-elect the parliament than re-elect the president. The vote of confidence in Yeltsin (58.7%) was even higher than his results in the 1991 presidential election (57.3%). However, on the eve of the referendum, the constitutional court – which was appointed by the Congress of People's Deputies – ruled that the third and fourth questions were 'constitutional' and required a majority of the entire electorate. When recalculated in these terms, the voting was only 31.7% for early presidential elections and 43.1% for early parliamentary elections. So the referendum had decided nothing.

The impasse continued through the long hot summer of 1993. On May Day, there were violent clashes on the streets of Moscow between riot police and left-wing extremists, resulting in the death of a young policeman. In June, the Supreme Soviet raised the stakes by announcing that the Congress of People's Deputies would vote in November on the proposed constitution being drafted by its own parliamentary commission, which would reduce presidential power in favour of parliament. Yeltsin responded by appointing his own constitutional convention, which met in the Kremlin to draw up a rival document increasing presidential power.

Public anger increased after a chaotic currency reform at the end of July, when it was suddenly announced that old banknotes were being withdrawn from circulation. Members of the public had just two weeks to exchange a very limited sum for new bills – but only at their official place of residence, when many people were away on vacation. The country was furious. Thousands of holidaymakers – including Yeltsin's eldest daughter, Elena Okulova, who had not been told of the plans – were left stranded without funds to return home.[9] As Gaidar observed: 'For the opposition, it was a dream come true.'[10] When asked to explain the disaster at a press conference in August, Chernomyrdin came out with a phrase often used to describe the whole Yeltsin period: 'We wanted the best... but things turned out the way they always do!'

Rutskoi continued to attack the government reforms, saying that they had brought 'anarchy instead of democracy'. On 15 April, Yeltsin replaced the vice-president's Mercedes limousine with a Volga car. The following day, Rutskoi announced that he had 'eleven suitcases' with evidence of corruption committed by government ministers, including Gaidar, Burbulis, Chubais and Kozyrev. Yeltsin launched his own investigation into the vice-president, who was accused of keeping millions of dollars of stolen money in a secret Swiss bank account. This round of mutual mudslinging was the start of a Russian political tradition known as *kompromat*. Rutskoi passed several of the suitcases to the prosecutor's office, which confirmed forty-five of the fifty-one charges. The rest remained in his office at the White House – only to disappear in the course of events which brought revolution back onto the streets in the month of October.

The 'October Revolution' of 1993

'O Liberty, what things are done in thy name!'

Madame Roland, 1793

After the summer ended, Yeltsin moved onto a war footing against his political opponents. On 1 September, he suspended Rutskoi and issued a decree on 23 September which dissolved the Congress of People's Deputies. The president went on national television that evening to announce that new parliamentary elections would be held in December and that this was 'the only way to protect democracy and freedom in Russia... There will be no more sessions of the Congress.'[11]

Rutskoi denounced the move as a *coup d'état* and declared that he was assuming the presidency. He appointed new heads of the military and the security services, while Khasbulatov called for a general strike. The constitutional court ruled that Yeltsin had violated the constitution and he was formally impeached by the deputies, who blockaded themselves inside the White House. They started stockpiling food and weapons and were joined by paramilitary supporters from war zones across the former USSR. Yeltsin responded by cutting off their telephones, electricity and water and surrounded the building with soldiers.

Yeltsin faced divisions inside his own camp over the legitimacy of his actions. Pavel Grachev, the defence minister, asked to be given his commands in writing. The Alpha troops wanted the constitutional court to approve any orders they were given, although their mood changed after a junior lieutenant was shot by a sniper. Patriarch Alexius II chaired peace negotiations at the St Daniel Monastery on 1 October and there was hope that the two sides might agree to a 'zero option' – fresh parliamentary and presidential elections. But on the afternoon of 3 October, a banned demonstration of 10,000 communists and nationalists broke through a police cordon and onto the territory of the White House. Rutskoi appeared on the balcony and urged them to form battalions, while Khasbulatov called for troops and tanks to storm the Kremlin and arrest the 'usurper and criminal' Yeltsin.

A large group of opposition fighters set off towards the centre of Moscow. Led by General Albert Makashov and communist firebrand Victor Anpilov, they captured the mayor's office and raised the red flag above the roof. They also attacked the Ministry of Defence building, which was largely undefended as most of the army had been sent to pick potatoes in September. The rebels then found a dozen military trucks and four armoured personnel carriers, all with the ignition keys still inside. They boarded the vehicles and headed north to attack the television centre at the Ostankino tower, which was only lightly protected by internal troops and police. During the storming of the ground floor, sixty people were killed and over a hundred were injured. Channel One went off the air at 7:26 pm – right in the middle of a football match between Rotor Volgograd and Spartak Moscow to decide first place in the Russian premier league.[12]

Channel Two was still broadcasting from its studio in another part of town. Yegor Gaidar, who had been reappointed first deputy premier on 18 September as a deliberate snub to the opposition, went there to issue a live appeal to Muscovites to take to the streets again in defence of democracy. He recalled the moments before the filming started:

The TV camera lens was already trained on me when I stopped and asked to be left alone in the studio for a minute. Somehow the flush of excitement had suddenly drained away, and in its place came a wave of alarm for those I was about to call out of their quiet apartments and into the streets of Moscow. What a terrible responsibility for their lives I was taking upon myself. But there was no way around it. In reading and rereading documents and memoirs about 1917, I had often caught myself wondering how it was that tens of thousands of cultured, honourable and honest citizens of Petersburg, any number of military officers among them, could have let a relatively small group of extremists seize power so easily. Why did everyone keep waiting for someone else – the Provisional Government, Kerensky, Kornilov, Krasnov – to save them? We all know how the story ended. That thought, probably, is what in the end outweighed my doubts. And so, without hesitation, with a sense that I was in the right, I made my speech.[13]

Grigory Yavlinsky and Yury Luzhkov issued similar appeals to the public. Gaidar said in his broadcast:

We call on those who are ready to support Russian democracy in this difficult moment to come to its assistance, to assemble at the Moscow city council building and join forces to defend our future – and not allow our country to be turned again, for decades, into an enormous concentration camp. Our future is in our hands. If we lose it, we will have no one to blame but ourselves. I believe in our courage, I believe in the common sense of our society, I believe that we simply cannot lose today.

On his way home, he saw the square next to the council building on Tver Street filling up with people, who had heard his appeal and were now building barricades and lighting bonfires (around 15,000 had gathered by nightfall).

Yeltsin flew back to the Kremlin by helicopter and declared a state of emergency. The tanks of the Taman and Cantemir divisions moved into position around the White House and, the following morning, opened fire on the upper floors. As smoke poured from the top of the building, Rutskoi rang the *Echo of Moscow* radio station from a mobile phone and, like Gaidar, issued his own appeal for assistance live on air. He called on the Russian air force to 'take to the skies' and bomb the Kremlin, ending his message with the words: 'I beg you! Save our dying people. Save our dying democracy!'

After the tank bombardment, Yeltsin ordered the Alpha and Wimpel units to storm the White House. But Wimpel refused to carry out the order, while the Alpha commanders independently negotiated with the parliamentary forces and persuaded them to surrender. General Makashov led them to Khasbulatov and Rutskoi, who pleaded for an escort to the US embassy. As the other defenders filed out of the White House with their hands on their heads, Rutskoi, Khasbulatov and Makashov were loaded onto a bus and taken to Lefortovo Prison. They were charged with 'organising mass disorders', although Yeltsin wanted them to stand trial for murder in the first degree, which carried the death sentence. Like the leaders of the 1991 coup, they were all amnestied by the Duma in February 1994.

The total number of casualties was at least 158 dead and 500 injured. Although order was generally restored that day, snipers still remained at large in parts of the city. The anchor on the evening news said that it had been a day the likes of which Muscovites never thought that they would have to live through. Yeltsin suspended several newspapers, including *Pravda* and *Sovetskaya Rossiya*. He removed the guards from Lenin's tomb on Red Square and suspended the Russian Communist Party – even though its leader, Gennady Zyuganov, had gone on television to urge restraint and had left the White House days before the violence began. Rutskoi later recalled that Zyuganov had departed the building on 23 September, telling everyone 'that he was off to raise the proletariat – and that was the last anyone saw of him.'

Russia was now free of the 'Soviet model' which had governed the country since 1917 – and, along with it, a parliament described by Gaidar as 'perhaps one of the most irresponsible in the history of democracy.'[14] When Russia's draft constitution was finally published on 9 November, it capitalised on Yeltsin's victory by providing for a powerful presidency and a weak parliament. The opening words stated that 'Russia is a democratic federal law-bound state with a republican form of government.' Sovereign power belonged to the people, while the president was both head of state and commander-in-chief of the armed forces. Perhaps unsurprisingly, given the recent experience with both Gennady Yanayev and Alexander Rutskoi, the office of vice-president was abolished.

The new Russian parliament ('Federal Assembly') had two chambers – the Federation Council (upper house) and the State Duma (lower house).

The upper house consisted of two representatives from each of the eighty-nine regions or 'subjects' of the Russian Federation (one from its legislative organ and one from its executive body).[15] Parliament had the power to impeach and remove the president from office by a two-thirds majority in each chamber. The president could only appoint a prime minister with the consent of the Duma.

Yeltsin's draft constitution was put to a 'national vote' – not a referendum, as technically the president did not have the right to call a referendum – on 12 December. On the same day, the country also elected the new Duma, a parliament with a name deliberately harking back to the old pre-revolutionary assembly, reflecting Yeltsin's desire to forever bury the Soviet past.

Duma Elections of 1993

'The trouble with free elections is that you never know how they are going to turn out.'

Vyacheslav Molotov

Twenty-one parties and blocs competed for the 450 seats in the State Duma. Half the seats were directly elected by single-member constituencies in a simple majority system. The other half were chosen from national party lists using the Hare quota in a system of proportional representation, although a party had to get at least 5% to qualify for seats.

The turnout was low (54.81%) and the elections were again boycotted in Chechnya and Tatarstan. Most former members of Democratic Russia and the 'kamikaze government' of 1991–92 had joined a bloc called 'Russia's Choice' (*Vybor Rossii*), which was set up in October 1993 and headed by Yegor Gaidar. Although facing competition from other liberal parties, such as Grigory Yavlinsky's Yabloko, Russia's Choice was the clear favourite as the 'party of power' and confidently expected to win at least 50%.

But when the results started coming in from the Far East, Zhirinovsky once again caused a sensation by surging into first place with almost a quarter of the vote. The Liberal Democratic Party of Russia (LDPR) ended on 22.92% (59 seats), way ahead of Russia's Choice, who came second on 15.51% (40 seats). The Communists were third on 12.40% (32 seats). Five other parties passed the 5% threshold – Women of Russia on 8.13% (21 seats), Agrarian Party on 7.99% (21 seats), Yabloko on 7.86% (20 seats), Party of Russian Unity and Accord on 6.73% (18 seats) and the Democratic Party of Russia on 5.52% (14 seats). The option 'against all' got 4.22% (over two million votes) and even came top in thirty-two constituencies, forcing re-runs. The highest result for 'against all' was 38.15% in one part of Kamchatka.[16]

Although the LDPR were the clear winners in the list vote, they only won five constituencies. Russia's Choice took the most constituencies (24), followed by the Agrarians (16), Communists (10), Yabloko (7) and Women of Russia (2). Nevertheless, the results came as a bombshell, both at home and abroad. Ostankino began reporting the returns at 11 pm in a show broadcast live from the Kremlin called 'The New Political Year', which was scheduled to run until six in the morning. No one could believe the outcome, including Yeltsin watching at home – although at least the president was finding out the results this way, just like everyone else. Writer and former deputy Yury Karyakin went up to the microphone and said: 'Russia, you're off your head!' One by one, the special guests left the studio and the programme went off the air at 3:30 am (the official explanation was that the computers were infected with a virus and unable to report the results).

The success of the LDPR can easily be explained. Thirty per cent of the electorate lived below the poverty line and were angry at falling living standards, rampant crime, NATO expansion and the loss of Russia's superpower status. Zhirinovsky had promised to shoot criminals on the spot, restore lost savings, increase pensions, raise military spending, dump nuclear waste next to the Baltic republics, restore the borders of the tsarist empire and invade Central Asia and the Middle East ('Russian soldiers will wash their boots in the warm waters of the Indian Ocean'). He skilfully used television to gain more exposure than any other politician during the five-week campaign. The LDPR participated in all televised debates and bought five half-hour slots on RTR, which they used to target five specific groups – women, young people, pensioners, the military and ethnic Russians living in the 'near abroad'. Zhirinovsky boldly discussed previously taboo themes, such as sexual health, promiscuity and homosexuality, preaching the need for tolerance and comparing gays and lesbians to dissidents in the USSR.

The democrats fought the wrong campaign by attacking the communists and overlooking the nationalists – until it was too late. On the eve of the elections on 11 December – when campaigning was banned – Russian television showed a documentary, *The Hawk*, intended to discredit the LDPR by repeating the long-standing claims that Zhirinovsky had worked for the KGB. While the list vote was generally used as a protest against government policy, the constituency vote tended to be more positive and favoured personalities. This was where the democrats picked up votes and so, when the two results were combined, the LDPR and Russia's Choice were equal on sixty-four seats.

Senator John McCain headed an observation mission from the International Republican Institute, which did not find any evidence of violations and regarded 'the emergence of a multi-party system within two years of the Communists' single-party monopoly to be a truly remarkable development.' Overall, the American monitors hailed the elections as 'a significant, positive step forward in Russia's democratic transition that affirmed a commitment to the democratic process.'[17]

Constitution Referendum

'What kind of an election is it, if there is no fraud?'

Alexander Lebed

On the same day, Russians voted on the draft constitution. The results were 58.43% in favour and 41.57% against. As the turnout was only 54.81%, this meant that only 31.02% of the electorate had voted for Yeltsin's constitution. A minimum turnout of 50% was required for the vote to be valid and claims that the reported figure of 54.81% had been falsified started to emerge in February 1994 in a series of newspaper articles by a former dissident, Kronid Lyubarsky. Suspicions were fuelled by the refusal of the central electoral commission to publish the full results. After the Duma raised the matter on 21 April, the ballot papers were destroyed by order of the chairman, Nikolai Ryabov.

The problem was that Yeltsin had gambled everything on getting a new constitution and parliament. But in almost every region outside the large cities, the turnout was traditionally below 50%. In March 1994, a special working group headed by Alexander Sobyanin analysed the referendum results using computers at the California Institute of Technology and concluded that the turnout had been not 58 million, but only 49 million (46%). Ironically, because the aim was solely to get a turnout above 50%, the votes against the constitution were artificially inflated. But as the Duma elections were being held in parallel, the additional nine million votes had to be distributed somehow among the party lists. There was much greater control of the voting in the cities, so this could only be done in rural areas, which meant inflating the results of the opposition parties, as this is where they were stronger.

The working group believed that six of the nine million votes went to the Liberal Democratic Party and that the proper seat results in the list vote should have been: Russia's Choice – fifty-eight (+18), LPDR – thirty-six (-23), Communists – twenty-eight (-4), Yabloko – twenty-three (+2), Women of Russia – nineteen (-2), Democratic Party of Russia – seventeen (+3) and Agrarian Party – fourteen (-7). The Russian Democratic Reform Movement, which was founded in 1991 by Alexander Yakovlev, Eduard Shevardnadze, Anatoly Sobchak and Gavriil Popov, should have got twelve list seats, but were not awarded any at all (although they won four constituencies). Only the Party of Russian Unity and Accord received the correct number (18 seats). As a result, instead of an unfavourable correlation of reformers to opposition parties of 60 to 112 seats, the true picture should have been 93 to 78 seats.

The consequences – if true – are far-reaching. The election results forced the government to move to the left and pull back the reform programme. On 18 December 1993, Chernomyrdin concluded that 'any "shock" methods must be precluded in the future.'[18] The whole history of the 1990s and Russia might have been very different. There might have been no Chechen War, for example, in 1994. By staking their political futures on shutting down the old Congress, the president and democrats like Gaidar had shackled themselves to the need to quickly adopt a new constitution. Any challenge to the Duma election results would have inevitably raised questions about the legitimacy of the constitution referendum. So both sides – reformers and opposition parties alike – had a direct interest in covering up any falsification.[19]

In any case, when the Duma convened on 13 January 1994, Russia's Choice was the largest faction with seventy-five members. They could also rely on support from their ideological allies in Yabloko (27) and the Party of Russian Unity and Accord (22). Similarly, although the Communists came third with forty-two seats overall, their partners in the Agrarian Party had thirty-seven seats – and held the post of speaker after Ivan Rybkin defeated Yury Vlasov. The final result was thus three large blocs of democrats, communists and nationalists – and the correlation between communists and democrats was still better for Yeltsin than at the Congress of People's Deputies.[20]

The New Duma

'O brave new world, that has such people in't!'

The Duma which sat from 1993 to 1995 proved to be an extraordinarily productive parliament, passing two-thirds of the laws under which Russia lives today. Because the party lists were compiled only a week after the shelling of the White House, few careerists wished to stand, as it was widely believed that Yeltsin would not hesitate to turn his tanks on this new parliament as well. The elected deputies included a large proportion of 'revolutionary romantics' and committed political activists who were genuinely representative of the people. There was very little party discipline and most deputies did and said what they liked.

This Duma is often regarded as Russia's most professional, colourful and entertaining. Two-thirds of the parliamentarians were aged under fifty and 95% had a higher education. Although women only constituted 13% of the total number, this was still an improvement on 5.5% in the Congress of People's Deputies. The Women of Russia faction – whose slogan was 'there is no real democracy without women' – even included a man, Anatoly Guskov, although he was later expelled for not attending debates. This party played an important role in stopping fights in the chamber, especially when their male colleagues were afraid to step in. The environmentalists (Cedar) failed to pass the 5% threshold – despite including Alexander Lebed in their party list without his knowledge – but were still represented after taking one constituency seat (the British parliament, by comparison, did not have a Green MP until 2010).

The political battles began on the very first day when a fight broke out in the canteen. Zhirinovsky jumped the queue and was punched in the face by Mark Goryachev of the Party of Russian Unity and Accord. Later, in March 1997, Goryachev was abducted on the streets of St Petersburg by three masked men. He was forced into a car, driven off and never seen again. The former deputy was believed to have set up a chain of financial pyramids using loans from commercial banks and, on the eve of his disappearance, reportedly transferred a large sum of money belonging to Chernomyrdin into a foreign bank account.

Alexander Nevzorov, whose *600 Seconds* programme was permanently banned after the events of October 1993, won the Central constituency in St Petersburg. He only attended four debates, as he was away the rest of the time fighting in various ethnic conflicts. Another deputy from St Petersburg, Vyacheslav Marychev of the LDPR, always wore a costume reflecting that day's parliamentary business. His various guises included a prisoner, an alcoholic, a bandit, a priest, a soldier and a tramp. During a debate on the Aum Shinrikyo cult, he dressed up as Shoko Asahara. When the Duma tried to impeach Yeltsin, he came as a drunkard. Marychev formed the Duma's first ever faction for 'sexual minorities', but was its only member.

Nikolai Lysenko, who founded the far-right National Republican Party in 1991, ripped up the Ukrainian flag during a heated debate on the Black Sea Fleet in April 1995 – provoking a similar response with the Russian flag the next day in the Ukrainian Rada. He was arrested after a bomb exploded in his Duma office in December 1995. Lysenko claimed it was an assassination attempt, but the Federal Security Service (FSB) suspected him of planting the device himself and arrested him. Although acquitted of the crime in October 1997, he was found guilty of stealing a Duma computer and given a prison sentence of eighteen months.

Lysenko was involved in a mass brawl during a debate on NATO in September 1995. It involved former dissident Father Gleb Yakunin, who had been excommunicated by the Russian Orthodox Church for publishing the names of prominent KGB agents, including Patriarch Alexius II and Metropolitan Philaret of Kiev. Lysenko objected to Yakunin still wearing his priest's vestments in the Duma and ripped off his cross. When a female deputy, Yevgenia Tishkovskaya, tried to intervene, Zhirinovsky dragged her around by her hair; she sued him and he was forced to pay 20,000 roubles in damages. Tishkovskaya only ran for the Duma because she wanted to stop a controversial TV psychic, Anatoly Kashpirovsky, who was standing in her constituency. She won with 24.1% of the vote, although Kashpirovsky was still elected on the LDPR list and once tried to use his psychic powers in the chamber to hypnotise the speaker.

One deputy, Sergei Skorochkin, committed a double murder, shooting a man and a woman from a car with a Kalashnikov rifle in May 1994. Nine months later, he was kidnapped from a bar by four men in camouflage and found dead the next day in a nearby forest. One of his debtors, who supposedly coveted his Duma seat, stood trial for the killing, but was acquitted by a jury. Another deputy, Andrejs Aizderdzis, was murdered in April 1994, leading to a by-election in his constituency of Mytischi in Moscow. This contest was won by possibly the only man in Russia with the power to bring down the state – Sergei Mavrodi.

1994 – 'People's Privatisation'

'I could have thrown crowds at the Kremlin and unleashed a civil war... practically half the country! The authorities did not know what they were doing. They were playing with fire.'

Sergei Mavrodi

After dealing with the communist threat in 1993, Yeltsin faced a potentially greater challenge in 1994 from the forces of capitalism. Once an illegal trader in pirate videocassettes, Sergei Mavrodi had opened one of Russia's first commercial firms (MMM) in 1989. He generated publicity by sponsoring days of free travel on the Moscow underground, running ads for MMM right before the evening news (even during the coup) and appearing on NTV instead of the president to wish everyone a happy new year on 31 December 1993.

In February 1994, MMM started issuing shares offering fantastic returns – 100% over one month, 300% in two months and 700% after three months. But unlike the state, which was then failing to pay wages or index-linked pensions, MMM regularly paid out the promised dividends. As many as fifteen million people invested in MMM shares, including 'the entire Duma' and everyone at the Swiss embassy, right up to the ambassador himself. (When the scheme collapsed, the Swiss diplomats were the only investors to get their money back, as Mavrodi thought that he might have to flee abroad.) In half a year, the price of a share increased by almost 13,000%.

MMM was now becoming a dangerous rival to the state. The company was receiving $50 million a day in cash in Moscow alone, a third of the national budget was invested in the scheme and there were calls from politicians to make Mavrodi the minister of finance. MMM shares resembled Soviet roubles – Lenin's head was replaced by a portrait of Mavrodi – but did not devalue like Russian money. Mavrodi's alternative to Chubais's voucher privatisation – 'people's privatisation' – turned him into a popular hero for creating a scheme which made the poor rich without working and, unlike the state or criminal gangs, did not rob them of their income or savings.

When MMM came under attack from ministers and even Yeltsin himself in July 1994, Mavrodi threatened to hold a national 'vote of confidence' in the government. He planned to collect the required million signatures for a referendum 'in one week' and then ask the country whether it backed him or the Kremlin. Given the state of the nation at that time, it was highly likely that the people would have voted for Mavrodi – and the results of any referendum were constitutionally binding. As he said after these events: 'I had my own army – an army of investors... I could have won that war and quite easily become president myself!'

Mavrodi was summoned to appear before a special sitting of the Russian government on 3 August. He declined to attend and was arrested the next day for tax evasion (the evening news showed special forces abseiling onto the balcony of his seventh-floor apartment in a high-rise block). MMM shares were suspended and thousands of angry investors marched on the White House. In September, despite being in a prison cell, Mavrodi managed to get himself registered as a candidate in the Mytischi by-election. He was released from detention and elected to the Duma on 30 October, taking 27.8% of the vote (the turnout was only 28.3%).[21]

Mavrodi failed to attend a single debate or to meet his election promise to invest $10 million in Mytischi. He was stripped of his mandate in October 1995, but immediately registered as a candidate in the December elections as the leader of the People's Capital Party. Although the opinion polls predicted another victory, he came second last in his constituency with only 1.5% of the vote. After failing to register as a presidential candidate in 1996, he spent the next seven years on the run. In 2003, after being sought by Interpol, he was discovered following a tip-off from his estranged wife. He had been living all the time in Moscow, under everyone's noses, next door to his old address. Mavrodi was sentenced to four and a half years in prison, released in 2007 and died on the street of a heart attack in 2018.

After seeing off the threat from Mavrodi's 'people's privatisation', the government embarked on a second round of its own privatisation scheme, which turned into a scandal known as 'loans for shares'. In March 1995, Chubais found a way to get round a Duma ban on the sale of large state-owned industrial enterprises. The Russian government would borrow money from commercial banks, using shares in oil and gas companies as collateral. Twelve auctions for the right to provide the loans were held at the end of 1995, but the shares were all undervalued and only bankers close to the government were allowed to bid. None of the loans were paid back and all twelve companies became the property of the banks, creating a new class of super-wealthy 'oligarchs', among them Mikhail Khodorkovsky and Boris Berezovsky.[22]

Duma Elections of 1995

'What is the meaning of these disgusting antics?' he asked.

'Oh, they're – what is it they call it? – electioneering. Trying to get us to vote for them, I suppose.'

'Trying to get us to vote for them! Good God!... Is there a Socialist candidate? If so, I shall certainly vote for him.'

George Orwell, *A Clergyman's Daughter*

The 1995 Duma elections coincided with public outrage over the 'loans for shares' scheme, high prices, soaring crime, wage delays and the disastrous war in Chechnya, which claimed around 20,000 lives on both sides and an estimated 80,000 civilian deaths. No one seemed immune from the violence sweeping the country. Grigory Yavlinsky's piano-playing son had a finger cut off and the politician was warned to stop interfering in Chechen affairs – or he would next receive the boy's head. Duma deputy Sergei Markidonov, who was seeking re-election in Chita Region, was shot in the head in his hotel room in November 1995.

Forty-three parties and blocs competed in the 1995 general election. Voting was held on 17 December and the turnout was just under seventy million people (64.76%). The elections were monitored by 993 foreign observers from sixty-one countries, including a 434-member OSCE mission, which 'did not witness irregularities or conscious attempts to alter the election count or unduly influence voters'. A US State Department official described the voting as 'basically free and open, despite some violations of the election law,' while the OSCE Parliamentary Assembly hailed the elections as free and fair.[23]

With so many parties standing, only four managed to pass the 5% barrier in the list vote. The Communists came first with 22.30% – although a third of all left-wing votes went to other parties. The LDPR was second on 11.18%, which was still better than predicted by the opinion polls. As the OSCE report observed, 'Vladimir Zhirinovsky, the *enfant terrible* of Russian nationalist politics... remained the best campaigner in Russia and, when not engaging in fistfights in Parliament, visiting neo-Nazis in Austria or insulting foreign states, he was busily developing his party organisation throughout the country.'[24]

In comparison with 1993, the Communist Party and the LDPR swapped places on the leader board. The Communists swept the south of the country, leaving the Liberal Democrats as the main opposition force in northern Russia and the Far East. Their combined share of the vote was 33.5%. Opposition parties in first and second place did not bode well for Yeltsin's chances in the next year's presidential elections – especially as his approval ratings had slumped from 30% to 14% following several displays of public drunkenness in 1995.

The election results were a disaster for the pro-government parties, showing just how little control the Kremlin had over voters in the middle of the decade. In April 1995, seeking a way to cut off the far left and the far right, Yeltsin had attempted to build a modern two-party system based on the established Western practice. The plan was to create two political blocs loyal to the government. One would be a centre-right 'party of power' headed by Victor Chernomyrdin ('Alexander Hamilton'), while the other would be a centre-left 'loyal and constructive opposition' led by Ivan Rybkin ('Thomas Jefferson').

In May 1995, Chernomyrdin launched 'Our Home is Russia' – which was often ironically called 'Our Home is Gazprom', due to its close financial ties to the Russian gas monopoly. Although the party came a disappointing third on 10.13%, they were first in Moscow (19%) and also did well in St Petersburg (13%), where they were only defeated by Yabloko. They performed horrendously in southern Russia, often coming in tenth place and only polling 0.38% in one part of Dagestan. The party's main problem was being an artificial creation with no real programme at a time when elections were a battleground of different ideas and ideologies. The 'Ivan Rybkin Bloc', which was formed in July 1995, did even worse, coming seventeenth on 1.11% – despite running expensive TV ads featuring a cow (Mashka) and a bull (Ivan) discussing justice, order and peace in a snow-swept field.

Yabloko was the only other party to break the 5% threshold. They won 6.89% overall and came first in Kamchatka (20.43%), St Petersburg (16.03%) and other large cities, including Nizhny Novgorod, Rostov-on-Don, Chelyabinsk, Yaroslavl and Arkhangelsk. The party ran the most original media campaign with TV ads featuring an apple (*yabloko* in Russian) falling from a tree onto Isaac Newton, who says: 'Choose Yabloko – before something worse falls on your head...'

A handful of parties narrowly missed the 5% cut-off point. Women of Russia – who were awarded first number on the list, which ought to have helped them – only got 4.61% this time. The party suffered from running old-fashioned Soviet-style ads and voting for the Chechen War, which lost them the support of the 'Soldiers' Mothers' organisations, although they still won three constituencies. The hard-left bloc 'Communists – Labouring

Russia – For the Soviet Union' headed by Victor Anpilov and former coup leader Vladimir Kryuchkov came just behind them on 4.53%. This was a sensational result for such a radical party, especially as they were competing with Zyuganov for the communist vote. The bloc managed to win one constituency.

Yegor Gaidar's former party, Russia's Choice, had splintered into several small groups, who all ran separately and failed to win any representation. Gaidar headed 'Russia's Democratic Choice', which only got 3.86%, although they took nine constituencies. The party secured 12% of the vote in Moscow and St Petersburg but suffered from Chernomyrdin's party spreading false rumours about them on the eve of the elections, when campaigning was banned. The Agrarians were squeezed out by the other left-wing parties and only received 3.78%, but they did manage to win twenty constituencies (the second best result after the Communists).

The Communists won fifty-eight constituencies and ended up with a total of 157 seats. Left-wing parties now controlled half of the Duma, including the post of speaker, which was won by Gennady Seleznyov, a Communist deputy and former editor of *Pravda*. Our Home is Russia was the second largest faction (55 seats), followed by the LDPR (51 seats) and Yabloko (45 seats). Compared to the previous Duma, the democrats dropped from 34% to 14%, while the nationalists fell from 22% to 11%. The centrists rose slightly from 18% to 24% and the communists climbed from 20% to 32%.

This Duma was clearly going to be a thorn in Yeltsin's side, but it also seemed to rejuvenate him. Three and a half years after declaring to the US Congress that 'communism is dead in Russia' – and just a couple of months after complaining that he was exhausted and did not wish to run for a second term in 1996 – he realised that he would have to square up for one final battle in order to secure his political legacy.

'We Have So Many Parties'

'I'm sure you see how pluralistic Russia has become – too pluralistic, perhaps. We have so many parties.'

Boris Yeltsin to Strobe Talbott, April 1996

The four parties who qualified for the Duma in 1995 on the basis of list seats only got half of all the votes cast (50.5%). The other half went to thirty-nine alternative blocs, who collectively did as well as the mainstream politicians. Twenty-six parties scored under 1%, which included many exotic and unusual candidates, contributing to a diverse and interesting campaign. This was a reflection of the generally high standing of parliamentary democracy in Russia and the way in which multi-party politics had captured the popular imagination after 1993.

The largest 'small party' was the Beer Lovers' Party, which was founded as a libertarian party in 1993 and registered in 1994. The movement was led by Konstantin Kalachyov – who later served as deputy mayor of Volgograd – and attracted several prominent politicians, including Russian justice minister Nikolai Fyodorov. The Beer Lovers' Party spent $300,000 on its 1995 electoral campaign and ran successful TV ads with the message 'Beer unites!' Almost half a million people voted for the party (0.62%), which made it a significant force in the 1996 presidential elections, when every vote counted. Konstantin Kalachyov was persuaded not to stand, and in return Yeltsin's team helped to pay off his electoral debts.

The 'Bloc of Juna' was headed by Yevgenia Davitashvili, a Georgian faith-healer who was the first officially registered psychic in the Soviet Union (she was said to have treated both Leonid Brezhnev and Robert de Niro). Her campaign posters promised: 'A vote for Juna is a vote for your health, prosperity and justice!' Juna only polled 0.47% and retired from politics (she later proclaimed herself 'queen of the Assyrians'). The bloc was formed by a businessman who was facing a criminal investigation for large-scale fraud. Anyone registering as an electoral candidate automatically received immunity from prosecution – so, after failing to get elected via the Bloc of Juna, he immediately attempted to run for president in 1996.

Besides the Beer Lovers' Party – which had a rival in Kazan called the Abraham Lincoln Party of Beer Lovers – Russia also had parties for lovers of saunas, meat dumplings (*pelmeni*), mayonnaise, port wine, cod-liver oil and even spring mattresses. There was a Banana Party and a Poverty Party. 'Subtropical Russia' campaigned for climate change with the aim of raising the annual average temperature in Russia to 20°C (former Soviet dissident Vladimir Pribylovsky was elected its president and unsuccessfully ran for the Duma in 1993 and 1994). The Party of the Seduced and Rejected was founded by a woman called Alisa Lis to 'provide solace' and show that 'even seduced and rejected women can find happiness.'

The boom in small parties was encouraged and assisted by the state. In March 1995, the Duma held a round table for non-traditional parties, inviting such groups as the All-Russian Brownian Movement, the Party of Car Enthusiasts and the Party of the Sun. The Party of Free Love, headed by Soviet sex symbol Elena Kondulainen, was able to secure sponsorship from the Moscow city government. Tiny parties like the 'Union of Housing and Public Utility Workers', who only got 0.14% in the 1995 elections, were still given prime-time slots on national television to present their manifestos and programmes. All this made Russia unique in its plethora of small parties in the 1990s.[25]

16

1996 – The Year of the Rats

'You say that I am a dinosaur? A mammoth? But have you ever stopped to think that after the age of the dinosaurs comes the age of the rats?'

Yegor Ligachev

The 1996 presidential elections were the last great ideological showdown in Russia, when voters were invited to choose between two competing systems – capitalism and communism. They were also the first elections to rely heavily on the media and political spin. Russia could now regard herself as fully integrated with the West, boasting that vital element of modern democracy – the campaign circus – along with celebrity endorsements, smears, illicit funding and foreign interference.

The Davos Pact

Yeltsin began the new year by clearing out his cabinet. Fuming that the disastrous performance of the pro-government parties in the recent Duma elections was 'all Chubais's fault', the president sacked him as first deputy premier. Andrei Kozyrev also lost his job as foreign minister in January to Yevgeny Primakov. By this time, Yeltsin's approval rating had crashed even further from 14% to 5%, potentially placing him fourth or even fifth in the June elections, behind Zyuganov (13%), Lebed (10%), Yavlinsky (9%) and Chernomyrdin (7%). He suffered two heart attacks in July and October 1995 and did not appear in public at all during the Duma election campaign. He also missed the World Economic Forum at Davos in February 1996.

Yeltsin's main political rival, Gennady Zyuganov, did go to Switzerland, where – to the horror of the attending Russian oligarchs – he was feted

228

by the international community as the likely future president. Fearing the seizure of their assets and possible prosecution or imprisonment, they met on the sidelines to discuss how to prevent a communist victory in June. Boris Berezovsky dashed round to the hotel room of his bitter business rival Vladimir Gusinsky – whom, according to press reports, he had recently considered having murdered – and suggested that they call a temporary truce and work together.[1] Berezovsky contacted five other beneficiaries of the privatisation scheme and invited the now unemployed Chubais to act as their general coordinator.

The result was a loose group of oligarchs who became known in the press as the 'seven bankers' (*semibankirschina*) – in reference to the 'seven boyars' who had deposed Vasily Shuisky and assumed power themselves in 1610.[2] The other five were Mikhail Khodorkovsky, Vladimir Potanin, Vladimir Vinogradov, Alexander Smolensky and Mikhail Friedman. Besides having access to vast sums of money and controlling almost half the Russian economy, the group could also dictate what was shown on national television. Berezovsky owned a controlling stake in Channel One (ORT), while Gusinsky had bought the rights to the fourth channel (NTV). Channel Two (RTR) had been critical of Yeltsin, particularly over the Chechen War, but was brought into line after Oleg Poptsov was dismissed in February 1996.

The only remaining problem was Yeltsin's existing campaign team, which was headed by first deputy prime minister Oleg Soskovets and his two close allies, bodyguard Alexander Korzhakov and FSB chief Mikhail Barsukov.[3] Their strategy of co-opting the policies of Yeltsin's communist and nationalist rivals had little positive effect on his ratings and, convinced of the likelihood of defeat, they had already discussed a number of alternative options, ranging from cancelling or postponing the elections to turning Russia into a constitutional monarchy with Yeltsin as regent for life.

The members of the 'Davos Pact' realised that they had to sideline this ineffective team. The only way to get around Alexander Korzhakov, who controlled all access to the president, was to find someone even closer to him – and so they approached Yeltsin's favourite and younger daughter, Tatyana Dyachenko. A computer engineer by profession, she was now hired by the Davos team as her father's 'image consultant'. She combined this role with looking after her infant son Gleb, who was born in 1995 with Down's Syndrome. He later became an international swimming champion, winning medals at the Special Olympics World Summer Games in Los Angeles in 2015.

'Yanks to the Rescue'

Yeltsin's campaign team included three American political consultants –
George Gorton, Joe Shumate and Richard Dresner – who had been hired
by Soskovets in February 1996. They were paid $250,000 plus unlimited
expenses to run a Western-style campaign, but they were kept hidden at the
President-Hotel in Moscow to prevent accusations of foreign interference.
Time magazine later described how the three spin doctors 'used polls, focus
groups, negative ads and all the other techniques of American campaigning
to help Boris Yeltsin win'. The story even inspired a comedy film, *Spinning
Boris* (2003), starring Jeff Goldblum.[4] However, Yeltsin's former aide,
Georgy Saratov, claimed that the trio were 'whack-job idiots' better
suited to 'the elections of a collective-farm chairman'.[5] The Americans
nearly killed their client after they urged Yeltsin to dance onstage at a pop
concert and he suffered a heart attack two weeks later (ironically, one of
his campaign slogans was 'vote with your heart').

Further American assistance came from Bill Clinton, who confessed to
his deputy secretary of state, Strobe Talbott: 'I want this guy to win so bad
it hurts.'[6] Clinton was also seeking a second term of office in 1996 and the
two presidents did all they could to support each other's bids. When visiting
Moscow for a nuclear summit in April 1996, Clinton agreed to 'swallow
hard and say nothing as Yeltsin lectured him about Russia's great-power
prerogatives'. As an American official explained: 'The idea was to have
Yeltsin stand up to the West, just like the communists insisted they would
do if Zyuganov won. By having Yeltsin posture during that summit without
Clinton's getting bent out of shape, Yeltsin portrayed himself as a leader to
be reckoned with. That helped Yeltsin in Russia, and we were for Yeltsin.'[7]

Having refused to support Gaidar's reform programme in the early
1990s, the United States now lobbied the IMF to approve a $10.1 billion
loan to Russia in March 1996, in addition to $2.4 billion in credits from
France and Germany. But the money was slow to arrive and, as the
transcript of a telephone conversation released by Bill Clinton's Presidential
Center shows, Yeltsin had to urgently ask for more cash on 7 May:

Yeltsin: Bill, for my election campaign, I urgently need for Russia a loan
of $2.5 billion.

Clinton: Let me ask this: didn't it help you a lot when the Paris Club
rescheduled Russia's debt? I thought that would have caused several
billions of dollars to flow into your country.

Yeltsin: No. It will be coming in the second half of the year. And in the first half of the year, we will only have $300 million due to conditions set by the IMF... But the problem is I need money to pay pensions and wages. Without resolving this matter of pensions and wages, it will be very difficult to go into the election campaign. You know, if we could resolve this subject in a way with him providing the $2.5 billion in the first half, we could perhaps manage. Or if you could do it under your banks with Russian government guarantees.

Clinton: I'll check on this with the IMF and with some of our friends and see what can be done. I think this is the only way it can be done, but let me clarify this. I had understood that you would get about $1 billion from the IMF before the election.

Yeltsin: No, no, only $300 million.

Clinton: I'll check.

Yeltsin: Okay.[8]

'Choose or Lose'

'Yeltsin's election teams launched a high-cost, large-scale agitation and propaganda campaign with bands, singers and dancers and all the other razzmatazz, complete with catchy slogans previously honed on American voters: "Choose or Lose", "Vote with Your Heart!"'

Mikhail Gorbachev

One of the contributing factors to Bill Clinton's win in 1992 was the largest turnout of young voters in twenty years, thanks mainly to an MTV campaign called *Choose or Lose*. MTV refused to get involved with Yeltsin's re-election battle, fearing that he would lose and 'tarnish their brand', so his team created their own Russian version (*Golosui ili proigraesh*). It was run by Sergei Lisovsky, one of the suspects in the 1995 contract killing of a popular TV host, Vladislav Listyev. Lisovsky organised a string of pop and rock concerts across Russia, starting in Tomsk on 17 May and ending in Nizhny Novgorod on 15 June. The musicians were offered as much as $120,000 for taking part, although they all claimed to be performing for free.[9]

Russian electoral law capped the campaign budgets at $2.9 million, but Yeltsin is believed to have spent almost $2 billion. Some of the money was spent on a free weekly newspaper called 'God Forbid!' (*Ne dai bog!*), which was sent to ten million homes between April and June and warned of the threat of civil war, mass arrests, empty shops and famine in the event of a communist victory. Articles compared Zyuganov to Hitler ('Zyug Heil!') and interviewed certified lunatics who planned to vote for him. There was an anti-communist 'Stars on Reds' section featuring Brigitte Bardot, Gérard Depardieu and Adolfo Larrue Martínez III, who played Cruz Castillo in the popular soap opera *Santa Barbara*. A weekly 'anti-communist crossword' offered a holiday in Prague as the first prize.[10]

Zyuganov did not have the financial resources of Yeltsin, but he could rely on half a million members of the Communist Party, who held rallies and distributed leaflets. He was backed by four national newspapers, forty of the eighty-nine regional governors, former vice-president Alexander Rutskoi and several high-ranking members of the Russian Orthodox Church. Zyuganov had his own musical support – Yegor Letov of Siberian punk-rock band Civil Defence (*Grazhdanskaya oborona*) and, at the other end of the musical spectrum, Tender May (*Laskovy mai*). The first ever group for teenagers in the USSR, Tender May was specially reformed in 1996 by producer and vocalist Andrei Razin – allegedly because his grandmother liked Zyuganov – and held a benefit gig for the communists in April.[11]

'Vanity of Vanities: All is Vanity'

'This Fair is no new-erected business, but a thing of ancient standing... And moreover, at this Fair there is at all times to be seen Jugglings, Cheats, Games, Plays, Fools, Apes, Knaves, and Rogues, and that of every kind.'

John Bunyan, *The Pilgrim's Progress*, 1678

As Mikhail Gorbachev observed during the election campaign: 'Public opinion is being persuaded that it has only the option of a lesser evil, as if besides the "party of power" that wants to see Yeltsin re-elected and the Communist Party, there are no other forces able to rule Russia today.'[12] He was correct. While the media presented the elections as a binary choice – Yeltsin or Zyuganov, market capitalism or Soviet communism, the future or the past, choose or lose – there were far more options on the ballot paper. In the end, eight other candidates competed in the first round.[13]

Vladimir Zhirinovsky ran on a pro-Russian and anti-Chechen platform. He might have won a presidential election held in 1993 or 1994, but his nationalist electorate largely deserted him for Alexander Lebed, who once described him as 'God's ape'.[14] Lebed was a national hero for protecting ethnic Russians and preventing bloodshed in 1992, when he commanded the Fourteenth Army in Moldova. As a sober non-communist authoritarian figure, he was a dangerous rival to both Yeltsin and Zyuganov. In his political ads, which showed junkies shooting up in an underpass and deputies fighting in the Duma, he vowed to introduce 'truth and order'. His campaign was partially financed by Berezovsky after polling suggested that a strong Lebed showing would split the Zyuganov vote. Lebed received free advertising thanks to a series of popular comedy films, starting with *Peculiarities of the National Hunt* (1995), in which the hero, General Ivolgin, was largely based on the 'iron general'.[15]

Grigory Yavlinsky competed for Yeltsin's electorate and so was marginalised by the Russian media. According to a study by Yabloko, Yeltsin received 800 times as much coverage on television as Yavlinsky. US ambassador Thomas Pickering suggested to him that he withdraw from the race, otherwise he risked becoming unwelcome 'in all civilised countries' and 'not a hero, just a footnote in history'. Yavlinsky was supported by several famous dissidents (Sergei Kovalyov and Sakharov's widow Elena Bonner), many democrats and two national newspapers, but ran a dismal campaign. Although his TV ads were directed by Bakhyt Kilibayev, who had created Mavrodi's highly successful MMM adverts, his lightweight videos in the same style, featuring break-dancing traffic cops and singing conscripts, did not match the politician's serious image. Yavlinsky aimed to finish third and strike a deal with Yeltsin in return for his share of the vote.

Mikhail Gorbachev ran against the better advice of friends and former colleagues, such as Alexander Yakovlev. He recalled: 'Raisa was also opposed, but I could not reconcile myself to the election being a choice between Yeltsin and Zyuganov.'[16] Like Yavlinsky, Gorbachev suffered from a lack of media coverage and accused Yeltsin of acting like Brezhnev: 'We are watching the presidential campaign of a single candidate.'[17] He travelled all over the country, but faced 'a conspiracy of silence on the part of the media under government control, and wild, venomous misconduct by extreme communist and nationalist groups'.[18]

When visiting Omsk in April, Gorbachev was punched in the face by 'a sinister-looking young man' who 'struck a blow on a part of my head that paratroopers are trained to strike'. He later heard that 'Zhirinovsky's "Liberal Democratic" Party had been behind the incident. A drunken LDP official let that slip at Zhirinovsky's birthday party, saying, "What a reception we gave Gorbachev in Omsk!" When I heard about that, I forwarded my information to the Prosecutor General's Office, only to receive a meaningless bureaucratic non-response.'[19] Zhirinovsky denied the claim and demanded a million roubles from Gorbachev in compensation. The case only went to court in 2015 and was won by Zhirinovsky, although Gorbachev was only ordered to pay 6,300 roubles ($100).

In an effort to update his image for the campaign, Gorbachev and his wife recorded a dream-trance composition which became a megahit at raves and discos. The history of the track dates back to their first meeting with Margaret Thatcher at Chequers in December 1984. Thatcher's daughter Carol recalled: 'Denis showed Mrs Gorbachev the Long Library after lunch. She browsed the shelves of more than five thousand leather-bound books dating back to the seventeenth century, and showed such an interest in the English classics that, when she returned to Moscow, Mum and Dad gave her a first edition of Thackeray's *Vanity Fair*.'[20] Raisa mentions the present in her own memoirs: 'Here is one of the gifts that I hold very dear – *Vanity Fair* by Thackeray. It's a first edition, published in London in 1848. It was presented to me by Mrs Margaret Thatcher. This work of an outstanding novelist ends with the question: "Which of us is happy in this world?"'[21] Yevgeny Rudin (DJ Groove) put a sample of the couple discussing the book's ending to a techno backing-track and Raisa's repeated affirmation that 'happiness exists' (*schastye yest*) became, in many ways, a slogan for the post-communist hedonism of the 1990s. But most voters were unaware of the couple's involvement, as they were not featured in the video, so Gorbachev failed to capitalise on the song's popularity.[22]

Two other candidates competed with Gorbachev on social-democratic platforms. Svyatoslav Fyodorov was a famous eye surgeon who had been considered for the post of Russian premier in October 1991. He founded and headed the Party of Workers' Self-Government, which pursued policies inspired by Franklin D. Roosevelt's New Deal and Louis O. Kelso and Mortimer J. Adler's *Capitalist Manifesto* (1958). Martin Shakkum was a centre-left moderate whose television ads featured actors impersonating his opponents under the slogan 'Everyone talks, while he acts' – although he himself acted little when elected to the Duma in 1999.

The Russian Socialist Party was led by a brash billionaire who declared that 'money is man's greatest invention.' Vladimir Bryntsalov was Russia's 'vodka and pharmaceutical king' and at one point sold 30% of all medicines in Russia. He was elected in 1993 to the Duma, where he gave out pills for male potency and his attendance record was under 5% (his most memorable appearance was when he head-butted a Communist deputy in 2001). Bryntsalov campaigned under the slogan 'Less democracy and more socialism.' His policies included raising the minimum wage to $1,000 a month and protecting Russian industry by closing the country's borders. Bryntsalov was supported by the thrash-metal group Metal Corrosion (*Korroziya metalla*), which headlined a tour of other heavy-metal bands in aid of his campaign in May.

Former weightlifting champion Yury Vlasov was elected to the Duma in 1993 and unsuccessfully ran against Ivan Rybkin for the post of speaker. He was an independent candidate in 1996 and now abandoned the liberal values he had espoused at the Congress of People's Deputies in 1989, campaigning on a platform of nationalist, protectionist and authoritarian policies. Vlasov was supported by writer Eduard Limonov, a former ally of Zhirinovsky and founder of the National Bolshevik Party. He also had the personal backing of Arnold Schwarzenegger, who was inspired to become a bodybuilding champion after meeting Vlasov at the World Weightlifting Championships in Vienna in 1961.

Several other politicians considered running for president but did not make it onto the final ballot paper. Without Yeltsin's knowledge, Victor Chernomyrdin collected almost half a million signatures in support of his bid, but then changed his mind. Galina Starovoitova – a potentially dangerous challenger to Yeltsin, who could also have counted on at least 10% of the female vote – was rejected for supposedly submitting too many false signatures with her application. Sergei Mavrodi was refused on similar grounds. Aman Tuleyev withdrew his candidacy on 8 June in support of Zyuganov, but still received 308 votes in advance polling, when his name was still on the ballot paper.

The Two Rounds of Voting

The campaign reached its climax in the final week. A bomb exploded in the Moscow underground on 11 June, killing four passengers, but there was no day of mourning and the canvassing continued. The television stations poured out a constant stream of anti-communist films, while Yeltsin's ads 'showed black-and-white footage of Stalin voting at a Communist Party ballot in the forties; in case anyone missed the point, the narrator asked whether Russians wanted to return to this sort of "democracy" in the near future.'[23] On the final day of the campaign, NTV quizzed a number of celebrities about their voting plans. They sent a television crew to Switzerland to interview Alla Pugacheva, who said that she would be flying home the next day specially to vote for Yeltsin.

A total of 75,587,139 people (69.81% of the electorate) voted in the first round on 16 June. A polling station was created at an hotel near Wigan in England, where the Russian football team was staying during the European championships (voting took place a day early, as Russia was due to play eventual champions Germany on 16 June). When the votes were counted, Yeltsin was first on 35.28%, narrowly ahead of Zyuganov on 32.03%, but still short of the 50% needed to win outright. Alexander Lebed came third on 14.52%, while Yavlinsky was fourth on 7.34% and Zhirinovsky was fifth on 5.70%. The other five candidates got less than 1% – Fyodorov (0.92%), Gorbachev (0.51%), Shakkum (0.37%), Vlasov (0.20%) and Bryntsalov (0.16%). 1.54% voted 'against all' and 1.43% of the ballot papers were declared invalid.

As in previous elections, Yeltsin was popular in the large cities, northern Russia and Siberia, while Zyuganov won in rural areas and the 'red band' running along the southern borders. The highest figures were 65.1% for Zyuganov in Dagestan and 63.2% for Yeltsin in neighbouring Chechnya, where the head of the OSCE observation mission wrote: 'The Chechnya situation was of great concern. It was a very unstable region and few observers went there.'[24] Gorbachev's representative, Arthur Umansky,

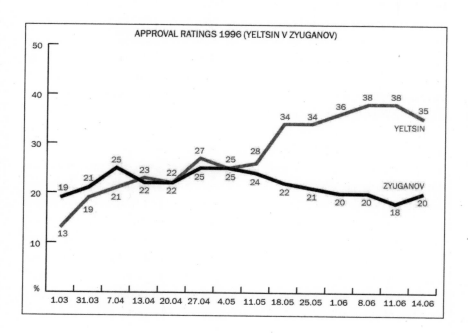

told him 'over the telephone from Chechnya that he was coming to Moscow with documents about serious falsification of the election results. We learnt that shortly afterwards armed men burst into his house and took him away. He was never seen again.'[25]

A second round between Yeltsin and Zyuganov was scheduled for 3 July – the only time this has happened in a Russian presidential election. As the top two candidates scrambled for the remaining 30% of the vote, the most interesting events in the campaign took place. On 18 June, Lebed was appointed secretary of the Security Council and secured the dismissal of his long-standing enemy, Pavel Grachev. Lebed had clashed with the defence minister over his handling of events in Moldova and Chechnya and said of his former commanding officer in October 1995: 'I don't like prostitutes, whether they are wearing a skirt or trousers.' In exchange for his promotion, Lebed called on his supporters to vote for Yeltsin. After Yavlinsky failed to receive any similar offers – although Yeltsin had dangled the post of prime minister before the vote – Yabloko urged its electorate to vote 'against all' in the second round. Zhirinovsky avoided openly endorsing Yeltsin and simply advised his supporters to vote against Zyuganov.

On 19 June, Sergei Lisovsky was arrested along with Chubais's assistant, Arkady Yevstafiev, while carrying half a million dollars in cash out of the White House in a Xerox copy-paper box. They were detained on the orders of Korzhakov and Barsukov, who wanted to discredit the rival campaign team by showing their use of illicit funding. The arrests led to a hurried exchange of phone calls between the members of the 'Davos Pact' and Yeltsin's family. Tatyana Dyachenko rang Korzhakov and demanded the release of the two men. When this was refused, they decided to act through the media. In the early hours of Saturday morning, NTV interrupted Artyom Troitsky's music programme *Cafe Oblomov* for a special news broadcast. NTV anchor Yevgeny Kiselyov announced that the arrests were part of a plan to cancel the second round of elections, carry out a *coup d'état* and roll back democracy. Later that day, at a meeting of the Security Council, Yeltsin sided with Chubais's team and sacked Korzhakov, Barsukov and Soskovets.[26]

Six days later and exactly one week before the second round of voting, on 26 June, Yeltsin suffered his third heart attack. He did not attend the G7 summit in France at the end of June and vanished from the television screens. When the country started noticing his absence, the media announced that he had caught a cold and lost his voice. Finally, two days before the vote, NTV ran a fake report of Yeltsin holding a meeting with Chernomyrdin in his Kremlin office. The video was filmed at his government dacha in Barvikha, where NTV journalists had Yeltsin dressed in a shirt, tie and jacket and propped up in bed with pillows. It was Chernenko in February 1985 all over again – but just enough to pull Yeltsin over the finishing line. He defeated Zyuganov in the second round on 3 July by 53.82% to 40.31% on a turnout of 68.88% (4.82% voted 'against all' and 1.05% of the papers were invalid).

The following day, *The New York Times* announced that Yeltsin's win was 'a victory for Russian democracy'. Speaking at an Independence Day rally in Ohio, Bill Clinton declared that in 'a free and fair election... the Russian people chose democracy.' Michael Meadowcroft, who headed the OSCE observation mission, wrote in his final statement that the election was generally well-run and the results accurately reflected the voters' wishes on polling day. The relatively high turnout was commended as 'a further consolidation of the democratic process in Russia', although concern was expressed about the pre-election period, particularly the media imbalance and the use of administrative resources in favour of Yeltsin, whose 'campaign overspent the legal limits'.[27]

In a personal statement issued almost two decades later, Michael Meadowcroft revealed: 'The OSCE was more concerned with the political consequences of a potential Zyuganov victory; the quality of the electoral underpinning of a Yeltsin victory was a lesser concern.' Some of Meadowcroft's 'more trenchant comments' were moderated under pressure from the OSCE office in Warsaw, which tried to get him 'to tone down, or, in some cases, to omit, critical comments'.[28] Thomas Graham, chief political analyst at the US embassy in Moscow from 1994 to 1997, thought it was

...imperative that Yeltsin win or that someone like Yeltsin win in June 1996, in order to continue the reform process... this was a classic case of the ends justifying the means, and we did get the result that we wanted... it's after we got that result that a lot of this began to unravel very visibly for people both in Russia and the West.[29]

Time magazine took a similarly pragmatic stance on 15 July 1996: 'Last week Russia took a historic step away from its totalitarian past. Democracy triumphed – and along with it came the tools of modern campaigns, including the trickery and slickery Americans know so well.

If those tools are not always admirable, the result they helped achieve in Russia surely is.'[30] When asked 'if he had any compunction about the extent to which the Yeltsin campaign was violating election spending laws by many orders of magnitude, Dresner's answer was "No," because "Yeltsin was for democracy, and whatever it takes to win is OK."'[31]

The most far-reaching legacy of Russia's second presidential election was the use of political spin. The experience of 1996 showed that a combination of administrative resources, media access and unlimited cash could elevate a candidate from nowhere, even one with rock-bottom ratings, to the highest office in the land. This was demonstrated at Davos in 2000, when American journalist Trudy Rubin asked a panel of top Russian officials: 'Who is Mr Putin?' None of them could answer her question. All they could say was: 'He is the president of Russia.'

Yeltsin's inauguration was held in Moscow on 9 August. The entire ceremony lasted sixteen minutes and the recitation of the oath took just forty-five seconds. Political commentator Lilia Shevtsova recalled:

> Slowly, with an absent-minded air, Yeltsin shuffled across the stage of the State Kremlin Palace towards the microphone, like someone afraid of falling over. His voice shook as he read from a screen the oath, which consisted of a few dozen words. He then shuffled off backstage, like a sleepwalker, without noticing anyone.[32]

Yeltsin immediately took a two-month break, citing 'colossal exhaustion'. He underwent a seven-hour, multiple-bypass heart operation in November, when Chernomyrdin was appointed acting president for exactly twenty-three hours.

17

Boyar Rule

Search for an Heir

On 1 September 1997, Yeltsin announced: 'My term ends in 2000. I will not run again.' The search for a successor now began in earnest. The young regional governor of Nizhny Novgorod, Boris Nemtsov, had been appointed joint deputy premier along with Chubais in March 1997 and seemed for a time to be the favoured candidate. But they were both brought down by the oligarchs after war broke out in the camp of the 'seven bankers'.

The armistice between the oligarchs collapsed in July 1997 over the privatisation of Svyazinvest, a holding company for Russia's telecommunications network. Berezovsky and Gusinsky were both interested in acquiring the conglomerate and expected a repeat of the rigged auctions of 1995, especially after helping Yeltsin to victory in 1996. But the government was in desperate need of $1.2 billion to pay wages and Chubais announced that there would be a fair and open competition, which was won by Vladimir Potanin's bid. In response, Berezovsky and Gusinsky launched an information war against Chubais and the other members of Yeltsin's second 'government of young reformers'.

In November 1997, media outlets controlled by Gusinsky and Berezovsky reported that Chubais and four other ministers had each received 'advances' of $90,000 from a Potanin-owned publishing house for an unwritten book on the history of privatisation. In the ensuing scandal, both Chubais and Nemtsov lost their portfolios, although they remained as first deputy premiers until March 1998, when Yeltsin unexpectedly dismissed the entire cabinet. Chernomyrdin was replaced as premier by the thirty-five-year-old Sergei Kirienko, who became Russia's youngest ever prime minister. Because he was virtually unknown and looked so boyish, he was nicknamed 'Kinder Surprise'.

In 1997, for the first time in a decade, Russia experienced economic growth (1.4%). But the budget problems continued as oil prices fell below $10 a barrel and, as the Communist-controlled Duma refused to allow any spending cuts, the government financed the deficit by issuing more and more short-term rouble-denominated bonds (GKOs). Demand was maintained by constantly hiking the rate of return, which reached as high as 150% in June 1998. As the bonds were guaranteed by the state, everyone started investing in them, from banks and pension funds to scientific institutes and even the Russian Orthodox Church. The result was a financial pyramid which Sergei Mavrodi called 'a carbon copy of MMM'.[1]

As rumours spread of an impending default, Yeltsin declared 'firmly and clearly' on Friday 14 August that there would be no devaluation of the rouble. When the markets reopened on Monday 17 August, Russia defaulted on its domestic debt and declared a moratorium on repayment of its foreign debt. This led to what has been described as 'the most catastrophic and complete financial collapse in modern history'. The dollar exchange rate soared from 6.29 roubles on 17 August to 50 roubles on 7 September. Trade was paralysed, prices rocketed as in 1992 and shops either closed their doors or were stripped bare in panic buying. The annual inflation rate for 1998 was over 80% and the economy contracted by at least $100 million.

Yeltsin sacked Kirienko a week later and nominated Chernomyrdin again as prime minister, but he was twice rejected by the Duma. Yavlinsky suggested Yevgeny Primakov, who was approved in September. Primakov was most remembered for turning his plane around mid-flight over the Atlantic, while on his way to the USA in March 1999, in protest against the start of NATO air strikes against Yugoslavia. By May 1999, he had an approval rating of 70% and looked set to become the next president, but he was suddenly fired by Yeltsin on 12 May. The reason was a Duma vote the next day on impeaching Yeltsin which, if successful, would result in Primakov becoming the acting president. Yeltsin did not want to end his career this way and so he got rid of Primakov.

The Communist opposition launched five impeachment charges against Yeltsin. The only one likely to get the required two-thirds majority (301 votes) was launching an illegal war in Chechnya in 1994, as this charge was also supported by Yabloko, but still only got 283 votes. Yeltsin survived the impeachment attempt, but rarely turned up for work at the Kremlin. At one stage, he was away for six months.[2] In the absence of a functioning president, power now devolved to a small core of officials based around his daughter Tatyana and her third husband, Valentin Yumashev, who took over from Chubais as head of the presidential administration in March 1998.[3] This group of people was heavily backed by Berezovsky and ORT and became known as 'The Family' – especially on Gusinsky's rival NTV channel, which supported the political ambitions of Primakov, Luzhkov and Yavlinsky.

As the search for a successor continued, Russia entered a period of 'prime-ministerial leapfrog' – just like on the eve of the February revolution. At one meeting with Bill Clinton in 1999, Yeltsin could not even remember the name of his current premier: 'He started to use a Russian expression that means what's-his-name, thought better of it and turned to [foreign minister Igor] Ivanov, who whispered in his ear, "Stepashin!"'[4] Sergei Stepashin was tried out as premier in May, but was sacked after less than three months, reportedly telling *The Times*: 'They threw me out because I am not for sale.'[5] On 9 August 1999 – two days before the total solar eclipse which many believed heralded the end of the world – Yeltsin went on national television to announce that his chosen successor to take Russia into the twenty-first century was Vladimir Putin.

'Energy and Brains'

'Odd,' said Arthur, 'I thought you said it was a democracy.'

'I did,' said Ford. 'It is.'

'So,' said Arthur, hoping he wasn't sounding ridiculously obtuse, 'why don't people get rid of the lizards?'

'It honestly doesn't occur to them,' said Ford. 'They've all got the vote, so they all pretty much assume that the government they've voted in more or less approximates to the government they want.'

'You mean they actually vote for the lizards?'

'Oh yes,' said Ford with a shrug, 'of course.'

'But,' said Arthur, going for the big one again, 'why?'

'Because if they didn't vote for a lizard,' said Ford, 'the wrong lizard might get in.'

Douglas Adams, The Hitchhiker's Guide to the Galaxy

Vladimir Putin seemed to be an ideal candidate. In St Petersburg, he had been a capable and efficient deputy mayor to Anatoly Sobchak, who disliked getting involved in the day-to-day running of the city. More importantly, he had proven his loyalty to his superiors when they fell from power. After Sobchak's defeat in the 1996 election, Putin was the only former member of his team to refuse to work for the new governor. When a criminal investigation was opened into Sobchak in 1997, he helped him to escape to Paris and made no secret of it. Putin was fanatical about loyalty and is said to have tested his former wife, Lyudmila, shortly before they were married, by arranging for a colleague to chat her up on the street to see if she responded to his advances or not.

In August 1996, Putin was offered a job in Moscow by Pavel Borodin, who headed the presidential property administration. He was then appointed director of the FSB in July 1998 and helped Yeltsin to get rid of the prosecutor general, Yury Skuratov, after he opened a corruption investigation into the contract to renovate the Kremlin (the 'Mabetex affair'), which threatened to expose 'The Family'. In the early hours of 18 March 1999, RTR broadcasted a film of 'someone who looked like the prosecutor general' naked in bed with two prostitutes. As the head of the FSB, Putin authenticated the recording and the identity of Skuratov, which allowed Yeltsin to safely sack him.

Two days before Putin's nomination as prime minister, the problem of Chechnya suddenly reared its head again. On 7 August, Chechen radicals led by Shamil Basayev invaded Dagestan and declared an independent Sharia state. The following month, Russia was rocked by a series of explosions in apartment blocks, killing 307 people in four separate incidents, including 224 deaths in Moscow. There were suspicions that the security services were behind the bombings after confusion over an FSB 'training exercise' in Ryazan on 22 September and a yanked news report of a lorry packed with explosives stopped by police outside St Petersburg. On 13 September, Duma speaker Seleznyov announced that there had been a terrorist attack on a residential building in Volgodonsk – three days before it actually happened. This was a separate incident, linked to a local contract killing, but when Zhirinovsky raised the matter in the chamber on 17 September, he had his microphone cut off and was deliberately provoked by another deputy, who threw a folder at him. In the ensuing chaos, Zhirinovsky was suspended from the Duma for a month.

Against this background of fear and paranoia, a politician like Putin was a comforting and protective figure. He vowed at a press conference on 24 September: 'We will track down terrorists everywhere. In an airport? That means in an airport. If we catch them in a toilet, then – you will forgive me – we will soak them in the dunny.' His approval rating soared from 1% in August and 4% in September to 22% in October and 45% in November. That month, Yeltsin met Bill Clinton in Istanbul and shared his thoughts on Putin: 'He will continue the Yeltsin line on democracy and economics and widen Russia's contacts. He has the energy and the brains to succeed.'[6]

Duma Elections of 1999

'In a democracy, the real rulers are the dexterous manipulators of votes, with their henchmen, the mechanics who so skilfully operate the hidden springs which move the puppets in the arena of democratic elections.'

Konstantin Pobedonostsev

The only potential threat to Putin's ascendancy was a new party set up by powerful regional leaders opposed to the Kremlin. In November 1998, Moscow mayor Yury Luzhkov had founded the 'Fatherland' (*Otechestvo*) party. Then, in April 1999, Tatarstan president Shaimiev and St Petersburg governor Yakovlev created 'All Russia' (*Vsya Rossiya*). On 3 August, the two parties merged in a centre-left bloc called 'Fatherland-All Russia'. The following day, they offered first place on their list in the forthcoming Duma elections to Yevgeny Primakov. This was a clear indication that Primakov was their chosen candidate for the 2000 presidential elections, with Luzhkov lined up as prime minister.

In September, Berezovsky helped to set up a rival pro-Kremlin 'party of power' known as 'Unity' (*Yedinstvo*). Tapping into the popular image of 'three *bogatyrs*' – epic heroes of strength and courage who protected the Russian people in olden times – the bloc was led by emergency situations minister Sergei Shoigu, Olympic wrestler Alexander Karelin and police crime-fighter Alexander Gurov. This started a vogue for sports stars and showbiz celebrities with no interest in politics appearing on party lists – as well as for virtual parties with no ideology or programme beyond supporting whoever was president.

Throughout autumn 1999, Primakov and Luzhkov were mercilessly attacked on Channel One (ORT). Luzhkov was accused of illegally acquiring land, mansions and thoroughbred horses, laundering money in foreign bank accounts and even of links to scientology. Photographs showed Luzhkov meeting criminal authorities in restaurants, while a helicopter filmed footage of his estate outside Moscow. On 24 October, ORT presenter Sergei Dorenko claimed that the seventy-year-old Primakov was seriously ill and secretly undergoing a series of major operations in

Switzerland. An outraged Primakov immediately rang up NTV and rejected the claims live on air on Yevgeny Kiselyov's programme.

By the time the Duma elections came around on 19 December, the smear campaign in Berezovsky's media seemed to have worked. The Communists were again first on 24.29%, but Unity was a very close second on 23.32%. Fatherland-All Russia came a disappointing third on 13.33%. Only three other parties passed the 5% threshold for list seats – the pro-Putin democrats in the Union of Rightist Forces (8.52%), the Zhirinovsky Bloc (5.98%) and Yabloko (5.93%).

The election was a catastrophe for Our Home is Russia, which finished in tenth place (1.19%), behind Women of Russia (2.04%) and even the Party of Pensioners (1.95%). Zhirinovsky's party had its worst ever result and had to stand under a different name after the LDPR was banned from running in October, due to grave concerns in the electoral commission over the backgrounds of fifty-two of its candidates. Two days later, Zhirinovsky and his sister Lyubov created a new party called the 'Zhirinovsky Bloc' with a different list of candidates, which now included billionaire Suleiman Kerimov.

The last year of the twentieth century seemed to be finally bidding farewell to the revolution. The Communists lost control of the Duma and their left-wing comrades did even worse. Victor Anpilov's 'Stalinist Bloc for the Soviet Union' only got 0.61% – despite having Stalin's grandson, Yevgeny Jugashvili, on its list and the novelty of Stalinists participating in a democratic election. They were closely followed by the 'Movement in Support of the Army' led by Victor Ilyukhin and Albert Makashov (0.58%). Sazhi Umalatova's Party of Peace and Unity only got 0.37%, while Bryntsalov's Russian Socialist Party was twentieth on 0.24% (although he still won a constituency seat). Ivan Rybkin's Socialist Party of Russia came second last on 0.09%.

The Communist Party won the greatest number of constituencies (46), followed by Fatherland-All Russia (29), Unity (9), Union of Rightist Forces (5) and Yabloko (4). Boris Berezovsky won a seat in Karachay-Cherkessia in the northern Caucasus, while his business partner Roman Abramovich was elected in Chukotka. No elections were held in Chechnya. The Communists remained the largest faction, but the two newly formed pro-Kremlin parties – Unity and the Union of Rightist Forces – won a larger share of the vote (32%). The only bright news for the left was the election of Yeltsin's arch-enemy, the seventy-nine year-old Yegor Ligachev, as the oldest deputy and father of the house.

18

'Managed Democracy' – Putin

The End of the Century
'Russia must enter the new millennium with new faces, new intelligent, strong and energetic people. As for those of us who have been in power for many years, we must go.'

Boris Yeltsin, 31 December 1999

On 31 December 1999, just as Russia was preparing to celebrate the new millennium, Boris Yeltsin suddenly announced his resignation. This was a deliberate ploy to capitalise on Putin's sky-high ratings before they could drop back down again by the summer. Yeltsin's resignation meant that the presidential elections would now be brought forward by three months – greatly disadvantaging Putin's main rivals, who had all depleted their financial, emotional and physical reserves in the Duma campaign. Putin took over as acting president and immediately signed a decree 'on guarantees to the former president of the Russian Federation and the members of his family', which included lifetime immunity from prosecution.

Yeltsin said in his address on national television:

Today I am speaking to you for the last time as Russian president... I want to ask you for forgiveness, because many of our hopes have not come true, because what we thought would be easy turned out to be painfully difficult. I ask you to forgive me for not fulfilling some hopes of those people who believed that we should be able to jump from the grey, stagnating, totalitarian past into a bright, rich and civilised future in one go. I myself believed this. But it could not be done in one fell swoop. In some respects I was too naive... A new generation is taking my place, the generation of those who can do more and do it better... I have always had confidence in the amazing wisdom of Russian citizens. Therefore, I have no doubt what choice you will make at the end of March 2000.[1]

The Bonfire of the Vanities

Bill Clinton: 'Who will win the election?'
Boris Yeltsin: 'Putin, of course. He will be the successor to Boris Yeltsin. He's a democrat, and he knows the West.'

Vladimir Putin returned to work straight after the holiday. On the first working day of the new year, 3 January 2000, he dismissed Tatyana Dyachenko as presidential adviser and vetoed a law criminalising cruelty to animals, which had been passed by parliament and was only awaiting the president's signature. He announced that he would not campaign during the presidential elections and did not even issue a manifesto. Dmitry Medvedev, the head of his campaign team, explained two weeks before the election that, 'at this time, Mr Putin does not feel it appropriate to present the components of his programme.'[2]

There was none of the razzmatazz of 1996. Yevgeny Primakov announced on 4 February that he would not be standing ('I sensed how far our society is from being a civil society and from being a true democracy').[3] Zhirinovsky was initially barred after submitting a false property declaration but was reinstated on 6 March. Ella Pamfilova ran as the first ever female candidate. The only 'colourful' figure in the race was Umar Dzhabrailov, a Chechen businessman who had been romantically linked to Sharon Stone and Naomi Campbell and was suspected of several contract killings.

Putin was supported by Unity and the Union of Rightist Forces, including Boris Nemtsov. This time around, the pro-Kremlin media focused its attacks on Grigory Yavlinsky, who threatened to take enough urban and middle-class votes away from Putin to prevent him from immediately winning in the first round. In the final week of campaigning, ORT ran endless reports claiming that Yavlinsky was financed by George Soros and generally supported by 'Jews, foreigners and homosexuals'.[4] He was accused of exceeding the limits on campaign spending and illegal electioneering at military units.

The turnout on 26 March was 68.70% and Vladimir Putin won the election in the first round on 52.94%. Gennady Zyuganov came second on 29.21%, followed by Grigory Yavlinsky (5.80%), Aman Tuleyev (2.95%) and Vladimir Zhirinovsky (2.70%). The option 'against all' received 1.90%. Below that figure came Konstantin Titov (1.47%), Ella Pamfilova (1.02%), Stanislav Govorukhin (0.45%), Yury Skuratov (0.43%), Alexei Podberyozkin (0.14%) and Umar Dzhabrailov (0.08%).

RTR broke the law by broadcasting the results of an exit poll at 8 pm in Moscow, when voting was still taking place in Kaliningrad Region. *The Moscow Times* later claimed evidence of large-scale fraud and ballot-box stuffing, reporting that over a million new voters appeared on the electoral register between the Duma and presidential elections.[5] International observers found no indication of significant fraud, although an American official noted that

> ...the OSCE offered symbolic endorsement to Putin... in violation of its organisational rules. After an election campaign that drew almost exclusively on Putin's handling of the war in Chechnya, which included heavily documented instances of war crimes, the leader of the OSCE election observation mission and former member of the Danish Parliament, Helle Degn, accompanied Putin to the polling station in a show of solidarity, smiling behind him within camera range as he voted.[6]

The elections of December 1999 and March 2000 were the last occasions in Russia when no one could be sure of the results until the very end and there was still an element of competition – albeit between 'corporations', rather than traditional political parties. In 2001, Unity merged with its rivals in Fatherland-All Russia to form a new bloc called 'United Russia' (*Yedinaya Rossiya*) – and won every subsequent general election in Russia.[7]

The Tsar Back on the Throne
'Democracy means compliance with and respect for laws, rules and regulations.'

Vladimir Putin, 20 December 2012

On 7 May 2000, Vladimir Putin was officially sworn in as president, observing at the ceremony that 'for the first time in all of Russian history, supreme power is being handed over in the most democratic and simplest possible way – through the will of the people, legitimately and peacefully.'[8] This time, the event was held at the Grand Kremlin Palace, the former residence of the tsars. After his inauguration, Putin lost no time in implementing what he described as 'the dictatorship of the law'. Just four days later, armed men in masks raided the Moscow headquarters of Vladimir Gusinsky, who was arrested for embezzling state funds and thrown into prison. He was released three days later and moved abroad after signing away ownership of his media company.

All the other oligarchs were targeted in quick succession. Vladimir Potanin was accused of robbing the state of $140 million in the rigged privatisation of Norilsk Nickel. Masked policemen raided a business owned by Pyotr Aven and Mikhail Friedman, while Vagit Alekperov of Lukoil was charged with tax evasion. Even the UES electricity monopoly run by Chubais was accused of illegally selling shares to foreigners in 1992. Putin then invited the country's top businessmen to the Kremlin in July. He promised not to overturn the privatisations of the 1990s, as long as they all maintained an equal distance from power. Most of them toed the line, but some did not – and immediately paid the price. After ORT was sharply critical of Putin's response to the sinking of the *Kursk* submarine in August 2000, Berezovsky was advised to sell his 49% stake in the company 'or follow Gusinsky'. He sold his business interests to Roman Abramovich and settled in England, where he committed suicide in 2013. When Mikhail Khodorkovsky started financing opposition parties, he was arrested for tax evasion in 2003 and spent the next ten years in prison.

Putin neutralised the powerful regional governors by dividing the country into seven 'federal districts', each of which was managed by a 'presidential representative'. The north-west region was governed by Victor Cherkesov, a KGB colleague from Leningrad who had still been prosecuting dissidents in 1988, including Irina Turkova, the last person to be imprisoned for a political joke in the USSR. The Federation Council was weakened by removing the governors and heads of regional parliaments from the chamber and replacing them with their proxies. The governors fought the proposals tooth and nail, as this meant an end to their parliamentary immunity and extended visits to Moscow, but backed down under threat of criminal investigations.

Putin ended his first year in power by urging the Duma to pass a law replacing the national anthem introduced by Yeltsin in 1993 – Mikhail Glinka's *Patriotic Song* – with the old Soviet melody set to different words.[9] This was duly done on 8 December and signed into law by Putin on 25 December – just in time for the New Year celebrations. Exactly one year ago, in his television address announcing his resignation, Yeltsin had promised that 'Russia will never return to the past.' Now he was forced to listen at home to the anthem of the totalitarian state which he thought he had buried.

In just under a year, Vladimir Putin had managed not only to tame the 'boyars', but also subjugate the elected representatives of the 'land'. The tsar was back on the throne.

Notes

1 'Sovereign Democracy' – Medieval Rus

1. *Procopius in Seven Volumes*, with an English translation by H. B. Dewing, Vol. 4, London: William Heinemann, 1924, pp. 269-273.
2. 'Lavrent'evskaya letopis'', *Polnoe sobranie russkikh letopisei*, Vol. 1, Moscow: Yazyki slavyanskoi kul'tury, 1997, columns 377-378.
3. *Povest' vremennykh let*, translated and commentated by Dmitry Likhachev, St Petersburg: Nauka, 2007, p. 186. Olga acted as regent from 945 to circa 960 during the minority of her son Svyatoslav (who was not a Christian).
4. This would happen many times in Russian history. As Alexander Solzhenitsyn observed, 'the Crimean War, and the Japanese War, and our war with Germany in the First World War – all those defeats brought us freedom and revolution,' whereas victory over Napoleon allowed the strengthened monarchy to defeat the Decembrists and delayed the emancipation of the serfs by half a century. Alexander Solzhenitsyn, *The Gulag Archipelago, 1918–1956*, London & Glasgow: Collins-Fontana Books, 1974, p. 272.
5. *The Chronicle of Novgorod, 1016–1471*, translated from the Russian by Robert Michell and Nevill Forbes Ph.D., London: Offices of the Society, 1914, p. ix.
6. Ibid.
7. The chronicle reports: 'The same autumn, great rain came down day and night, on our Lady's Day [Assumption], and till St Nicholas Day [19 December], we saw not the light of day' (ibid., p. 71).
8. Ibid., p. 162.
9. Ibid., p. 50.
10. Beazley, Raymond; Forbes, Nevill; Birkett, G. A., *Russia from the Varangians to the Bolsheviks*, Oxford: Clarendon Press, 1918, p. 37.
11. Karamzin, N. M., *Istoriya Gosudarstva Rossiiskogo: XII tomov v 3-kh knigakh*, Book 2, Vols. V-VIII, Moscow: Olma-Press, 2002, p. 249.
12. Ibid.
13. Elizabeth married Harald III of Norway, Anna married Henri I of France and Anastasia married Andrew I of Hungary. A possible fourth

daughter, Agatha, may have married Edward the Exile, son of Edmund Ironside – and so have been the mother of St Margaret of Scotland, wife of Malcolm III, who slayed Macbeth in 1057.

14. *Osmosmysl* means 'eight-minded' and referred either to Yaroslav's great wisdom or possibly his fluency in eight languages.

15. *The Chronicle of Novgorod, 1016–1471*, translated from the Russian by Robert Michell and Nevill Forbes Ph.D., London: Offices of the Society, 1914, p. 64.

16. Beazley, Raymond; Forbes, Nevill; Birkett, G. A., *Russia from the Varangians to the Bolsheviks*, Oxford: Clarendon Press, 1918, p. 40.

17. *The Chronicle of Novgorod, 1016–1471*, translated from the Russian by Robert Michell and Nevill Forbes Ph.D., London: Offices of the Society, 1914, p. 216.

18. The fate of the *veche* bell is unknown. Nikolai Karamzin suggests that it was taken to the Dormition Cathedral in the Moscow Kremlin, while others believe that it now hangs from the Spassky Gates overlooking Red Square.

19. *Polnoe sobranie russkikh letopisei. Tom XXV. Moskovskii letopisnyi svod kontsa XV veka*, Moscow & Leningrad: Izdatel'stvo Akademii nauk SSSR, 1949, p. 318.

2 The Sixteenth Century – Muscovy

1. Beazley, Raymond; Forbes, Nevill; Birkett, G. A., *Russia from the Varangians to the Bolsheviks*, Oxford: Clarendon Press, 1918, p. 96.

2. Kovalensky, Mikhail, *Khrestomatiya po russkoi istorii*, Vol. 2, Moscow: Gosudarstvennoe izdatel'stvo, 1922, p. 23.

3. *Readings in Russian Civilization, Volume I: Russia Before Peter the Great, 900–1700*, second edition, edited by Thomas Riha, Chicago & London: University of Chicago Press, 1969, pp. 91-93.

4. Belov, Ye. A., *Russkaya istoriya do reformy Petra Velikogo*, St Petersburg: Login Fyodorovich Panteleyev, 1895, p. 214.

5. The *Stoglav* included matters of family law. For example, the minimum age for marriage was now set at twelve for a girl and fifteen for a boy, while marrying for a fourth time was considered a crime. For the first time in Russian history, homosexual acts between men were condemned – although the Stoglav only required 'sodomites' to repent of their ways. Many foreign visitors to Russia in the sixteenth century were amazed at the prevalence of homosexuality and the tolerance shown towards such behaviour; Ivan the Terrible himself held orgies with young men dressed as women. Homosexuality was only criminalised in 1706, when Peter the Great adopted the Saxon military codex to regulate life in the army and navy (the punishment was death by burning, although this was reduced in 1716 to flogging or eternal exile).

6. The resolution of the Sobor lists the names of all 374 participants and shows that it was divided into four groups. There were thirty-two clergymen, sixty-two boyars and government officials, 205 members of the military-service class and seventy-five merchants and industrialists (including forty-one traders from Moscow).

7. *Tsar' Ivan IV Groznyi. Samoderzhavnyi i samovlastnyi. Svidetel'stva prizhiznennye. Da vedayut potomki...*, Moscow: Russkii mir, 2005, p. 217.

8. See *Russia at the Close of the Sixteenth Century. Comprising the Treatise 'Of the Russe Common Wealth' by Dr Giles Fletcher; and The Travels of Sir Jerome Horsey, Knight, now for the first time printed entire from his own manuscript*, edited by Edward A. Bond, London: Printed for the Hakluyt Society, 1856, p. 270.

9. An *oprichnik* was a personal bodyguard of Ivan the Terrible who used terror to rule the tsar's personal fiefdom, the *Oprichnina*.

3 Interregnum

1. Pushkareva, Natalia, *Women in Russian History: From the Tenth to the Twentieth Century*, translated and edited by Eve Levin, New York: M. E. Sharpe, Inc., 1997, p. 78.

2. Tikhomirov, M. N., 'Soslovno-predstavitel'nye uchrezhdeniya (zemskie sobory) Rossii XVI veka', *Voprosy istorii*, 1958, No. 5, p. 65.

3. The oath of loyalty to Boris Godunov included a specific vow 'not to see Simeon Bekbulatovich or his offspring or anyone else as tsar of Muscovy'. Bekbulatovich was later stripped of his titles and possessions – and possibly also blinded by Godunov.

4. Kliuchevsky, V. O., *A Course in Russian History: The Seventeenth Century*, translated from the Russian by Natalie Duddington, Chicago: Quadrangle Books, 1968, pp. 23-24.

5. Ibid., p. 55.

6. Smirnov, I. I., *Vosstanie Bolotnikova, 1606–1607*, 2nd edn., Moscow, 1951, p. 63.

7. Kliuchevsky, V. O., *A Course in Russian History: The Seventeenth Century*, translated from the Russian by Natalie Duddington, Chicago: Quadrangle Books, 1968, p. 30.

8. Ibid., p. 34.

9. Ibid., p. 36.

10. Ibid., p. 36.

11. Ibid., p. 38.

12. *Akty vremeni pravleniya tsarya Vasiliya Shuiskogo (1606 g. 19 maya – 17 iyulya 1610 g.)*, Moscow: Imperatorskoe Obschestvo istorii i drevnostei rossiiskikh pri Moskovskom universitete, 1914, pp. 1, 3.

13. Kliuchevsky, V. O., *A Course in Russian History: The Seventeenth Century*, translated from the Russian by Natalie Duddington, Chicago: Quadrangle Books, 1968, p. 44.

14. The rest of Moscow had been stormed two days earlier, on 22 October, which was also the feast day of the icon of Our Lady of Kazan. By the twenty-first century, 22 October (Old Style) had become 4 November (New Style), which has been celebrated since 2005 in Russia as National Unity Day as a replacement for the former Soviet holiday marking the Bolshevik revolution on 7 November.

15. After the election of Michael Romanov, Maryna Mniszech tried to raise an army and march on Moscow, but was betrayed and captured in 1614.

She was either drowned or strangled in a dungeon, while the three-year-old 'tsarevich' was hung from the Kremlin walls.

16. 'Povest' o zemskom sobore 1613 g.', *Voprosy istorii*, 1985, No. 5.
17. Ibid.
18. Ibid.
19. *Sbornik Novgorodskogo obschestva lyubitelei drevnosti*, Vol. V, Novgorod, 1911, p. 30.
20. 'Povest' o zemskom sobore 1613 g.', *Voprosy istorii*, 1985, No. 5.

4 The Seventeenth Century – The Age of the Zemsky Sobor

1. Philipp Johann von Strahlenberg, who was a Swedish prisoner in Russia from 1709 to 1721; see Kliuchevsky, V. O., *A Course in Russian History: The Seventeenth Century*, translated from the Russian by Natalie Duddington, Chicago: Quadrangle Books, 1968, pp. 80-81.
2. Ibid., p. 208.
3. Ibid., p. 209.
4. Ibid., p. 216.
5. Ibid., p. 219.
6. Ibid., pp. 218-219.
7. Kotoshikhin, G. O., *O Rossii, v tsarstvovanie Alekseya Mikhailovicha*, St Petersburg: Archaeographic Commission, 1840.
8. A delegate of the Kursk gentry caused a storm at the Zemsky Sobor of 1648 by complaining to the tsar about his fellow townsmen, 'saying all manner of evil things' against the people of Kursk and accusing them of spending church festivals in an unseemly way. This led to angry protests from the citizens of Kursk, who threatened their representative with 'every kind of harm'; Kliuchevsky, V. O., *A Course in Russian History: The Seventeenth Century*, translated from the Russian by Natalie Duddington, Chicago: Quadrangle Books, 1968, p. 208.
9. Collins, Samuel, *The Present State of Russia, in a Letter to a Friend at London; Written by an Eminent Person residing at the Great Czars Court at Mosco for the space of nine years*, London: Dorman Newman, 1671, p. 116.
10. Avrich, Paul, *Russian Rebels, 1600–1800*, New York & London: W. W. Norton & Company, 1976, p. 60.
11. Back in 1669, Fyodor had been one of the candidates for the Polish throne, alongside his own father and the Duke of York (future King James II) but lost the election to Michał Korybut Wiśniowiecki.
12. Massie, Robert K., *Peter the Great: His Life and World*, London: Victor Gollancz Ltd., 1981, p. 214.
13. Peter I faced three major waves of discontent during his reign – the Bashkir uprising from 1704 to 1711, a revolt at Astrakhan in 1705 and the rebellion of the Don Cossacks under Kondraty Bulavin from 1707 to 1708.
14. Tavernise, Sabrina, 'Interview with Mikhail Khodorkovsky: Money, Power and Politics', *Frontline/World*, 31 October 2003.
15. Peter did introduce an element of democracy into local government, which was reformed along European lines. He granted municipal autonomy to the

towns in 1699, when the administration of trade and industry passed into the hands of elected burgomasters, similar to the guildhall system he had seen in the West. After capturing Riga and Reval (Tallinn) from Sweden in 1710, he introduced their system of provincial self-government (*Landrats*), which were briefly elected by the local nobility in 1714, although later reduced to Senate appointees and then abolished entirely in 1720.

5 Imperial Russia

1. Beazley, Raymond; Forbes, Nevill; Birkett, G. A., *Russia from the Varangians to the Bolsheviks*, Oxford: Clarendon Press, 1918, pp. 258-259.
2. A rephrasing of the parable of the king's banquet in Matthew 22:8: 'The wedding is ready, but they which were bidden were not worthy.'
3. There is evidence that Count Panin later conspired with playwright Denis Fonvizin to overthrow Catherine and replace her with her son Paul, who promised to observe their planned constitution. The plot included Princess Ekaterina Dashkova and Paul's first wife, Grand Duchess Natalia Alexeyevna, but was betrayed to the empress, who forced her son to confess and provide a list of the conspirators (although none of them suffered or was arrested).
4. Massie, Robert K., *Catherine the Great: Portrait of a Woman*, London: Head of Zeus Ltd., 2012, p. 335.
5. Ibid., pp. 572-573.
6. Ibid., p. 404.
7. Finnish women were not the first to actually cast votes in Europe. This also happened on the territory of the Russian Empire, in Latvia, when electing municipal delegates in local elections in December 1905. Every twenty-year-old resident was allowed to vote, regardless of nationality or sex (the state of Latvia did not exist in 1905 and was spread over three provinces of the Russian Empire).
8. Rudakov, Vladimir, 'Vybory prezidenta', *Istorik*, No. 3 (39), March 2018.
9. Anisimov, Yevgeny, *Romanovs in Peterhof and Oranienbaum 1705–1917*, St Petersburg: Petronius, 2011.
10. Ibid.
11. *The Times* wrote that 'Russia is in a strange predicament of having two self-denying emperors and no active ruler'; Sutherland, Christine, *The Princess of Siberia*, London: Robin Clark Ltd., 1984, p. 98.
12. Anisimov, Yevgeny, *Romanovs in Peterhof and Oranienbaum 1705–1917*, St Petersburg: Petronius, 2011.
13. Many Russian liberals of the nineteenth century opposed a constitution or any other limitations on supreme power, believing that only an autocrat could implement liberal reforms in a country where 90% of the population were illiterate serfs.
14. The document became known in Russia as the 'Pineapple (*Ananas*) Manifesto' because the first paragraph contained the unusual construction 'and on Us [Russian: *a na Nas*] to lay the holy duty of autocratic rule'.
15. Mazour, Anatole G., *Russia Past and Present*, New York, Van Nostrand, 1951, p. 36.

16. Pobedonostsev, Konstantin Petrovich, *Reflections of a Russian Statesman*, translated from the Russian by Robert Crozier Long, London: Grant Richards, 1898, pp. 34-35.
17. King Christian IX wrote to his daughter on 14 April 1882: 'I do not intend to recommend that your beloved Sasha form a representative body with a deciding voice, no, only one with a consultative voice, which might serve as a bridge for moving onto the former'; State Archives of the Russian Federation, F. 642, Op. 1, D. 3001, L. 184 verso. In his memoirs, Pavel Milyukov recalls 'the liberal influence of Fredensborg' during the early reign of Nicholas II; Milyukov, P. N., *Vospominaniya*, Moscow: Sovremennik, 1990, Vol. 2, p. 75.
18. *Pravitel'stvennyi vestnik*, 18 January 1895, No. 14, p. 1. There is speculation that the words pronounced by Nicholas II at the Winter Palace differed from the text published the following day in the official government herald – and that the nervous emperor misspoke and said 'senseless' instead of the planned 'groundless' or 'unfeasible' daydreams. The draft proposal submitted to the tsar by Konstantin Pobedonostsev originally had the adjective 'mad'.
19. The Social Democrats split in 1903 into a *Bolshevik* faction led by Vladimir Ulyanov (Lenin) and a *Menshevik* faction headed by Julius Martov.
20. Rothstein, Andrew, *A History of the U.S.S.R.*, Harmondsworth: Penguin, 1950, pp. 16-17.

6 'Dress Rehearsal' – 1902–06

1. Rothstein, Andrew, *A History of the U.S.S.R.*, Harmondsworth: Penguin, 1950, p. 35.
2. Uratadze, Gregory, *Reminiscences of a Georgian Social Democrat*, Stanford CA: Hoover Institution on War, Revolution and Peace, 1968, p. 41.
3. *L. N. Tolstoi. Sobranie sochinenii. V 22 tomakh*, Vol. 22, Moscow: Khudozhestvennaya literatura, 1985, p. 192.
4. *L. N. Tolstoi. Put' zhizni*, Moscow: Respublika, 1993, pp. 211-230.
5. Lee, Eric, *The Experiment: Georgia's Forgotten Revolution 1918–1921*, London: Zed Books, 2017, p. 16.
6. Suny, Ronald Grigor, *The Making of the Georgian Nation*, Bloomington and Indianapolis: Indiana University Press, 2nd edition, 1994, p. 166.
7. Villari, Luigi, *Fire and Sword in the Caucasus*, London: T. F. Unwin, 1906, p. 98.
8. Ibid., p. 94.
9. Ibid., pp. 95-96.
10. Ibid., pp. 96-97.
11. *Mogzauri*, 1905, No. 1, p. 99.
12. Villari, Luigi, *Fire and Sword in the Caucasus*, London: T. F. Unwin, 1906, p. 98.
13. Nikolai Sultan-Krym-Girei was the grandson of the Scottish inventor James Beaumont Neilson, who disinherited his daughter, Anne Neilson, after she married Alexander Sultan-Krym-Girei at St Cuthbert's Church in Edinburgh in 1820.

14. Lang, David Marshall, *A Modern History of Soviet Georgia*, New York City: Grove Press, 1962, p. 153.
15. Villari, Luigi, *Fire and Sword in the Caucasus*, London: T. F. Unwin, 1906, pp. 98-99.
16. Staroselsky joined the Bolsheviks in 1907 and fled to France to avoid arrest in 1908.
17. The Democratic Republic of Georgia is not covered in this book as readers are better directed to Eric Lee's wonderful work, *The Experiment: Georgia's Forgotten Revolution 1918–1921* (London: Zed Books, 2017).
18. Antip Knyazev was arrested in August 1938 and sentenced to eight years in a concentration camp in March 1939. He died in 1941.
19. Zarkhy, S., *Prezident 'Ruzaevskoi respubliki'*, Moscow: Profizdat, 1968, p. 78.
20. Kostamarov, G., *Moskovskii Sovet deputatov v 1905 godu*, Moscow: Moskovskii rabochii, 1948, p. 80.
21. *Zabaikal'skii rabochii*, No. 1, December 1905.
22. *Krasnyi arkhiv*, No. 4, 1925, pp. 339-343.
23. *Russkoe slovo*, 10 January 1906.
24. *V. I. Lenin. Collected Works*, Moscow: Progress Publishers, Vol. 23, 1964, pp. 236-253.

7 The Imperial Duma

1. Russia was on the gold standard from 1897 to 1914 and the rouble was worth approximately 10½ British pence or 51½ US cents.
2. Marie, Grand Duchess of Russia, *Education of a Princess*, New York: Viking Press, 1930, p. 84.
3. Diary entry of Grand Duke Konstantin Konstantinovich on 17 April 1906; see *K. R. Velikii Knyaz' Konstantin Romanov. Dnevniki. Vospominaniya. Stikhi. Pis'ma*, Moscow: Iskusstvo, 1998, p. 284.
4. Gurko, Vladimir, *Features and Figures of the Past. Government and Opinion in the Reign of Nicholas II*, translated by Laura Matveev, New York: Russell and Russell, 1939, p. 470.
5. Nicholas II, 'The Speech from the Throne', *Readings in Russian Civilization, Volume II: Imperial Russia, 1700–1917*, edited by Thomas Riha, Chicago & London: University of Chicago Press, second edition, 1969, pp. 445-446.
6. Vladimir Nabokov's own father, Dmitry Nabokov, had been the Russian minister of justice from 1878 to 1885. After the overthrow of the tsar in 1917, Vladimir served in the Provisional Government, while his brother Konstantin was appointed ambassador to London. He emigrated in 1919 and died defending Pavel Milyukov from an assassination attempt at a Cadet conference in Berlin in 1922.
7. Vladimir Nabokov was held in the Kresty Prison and spent his time reading books, performing gymnastics, studying Italian and writing letters to his wife on toilet paper. The first thing he did upon entering the detention centre was to ask for an English bath.

Notes

8. Shevyrin, V. M., *Rytsar' rossiiskogo liberalizma: graf Petr Aleksandrovich Geiden*, Moscow: Premier Press, 2007, p. 182.

9. Dowager Empress Maria Fyodorovna to sister Queen Alexandra, Gatchina, 12/25 May 1907 (Hoover Institution, Stanford. Maria Fyodorovna, Empress, Box 3, Folder 17).

10. *The Secret Letters of the Last Tsar, Being the Confidential Correspondence between Nicholas II and his Mother*, edited by Edward J. Bing, New York & Toronto: Longmans, Green and Co., 1938, p. 228.

11. Pares, Bernard, *The Fall of the Russian Monarchy: A Study of the Evidence*, London: Cassell, 1988, pp. 120-121; Guchkov's opponent, Colonel Sergei Myasoyedov, was hanged as a traitor in 1915. Duels were a regular event among Russian parliamentarians. In 1907, the assistant minister of the interior, Vladimir Gurko, challenged Cadet deputy Fyodor Rodichev to a duel after Rodichev accused him of corruption in a debate (Rodichev backed down). In 1908, another Cadet member, Osip Pergament, duelled with the monarchist Nikolai Markov II (both failed to hit each other and patched up their quarrel over champagne). In 1911, Vladimir Nabokov challenged newspaper editor Mikhail Suvorin to a duel (Suvorin also backed down).

12. Dowager Empress Maria Fyodorovna to sister Queen Alexandra, Anichkov Palace, 27 February/11 March 1912 (Hoover Institution, Stanford. Maria Fyodorovna, Empress, Box 5, Folder 12).

13. Kokovtsev, Count V. N., *Iz moego proshlogo. Vospominaniya. 1903–1919 g.g.*, Vol. II, Paris: Illyustrirovannaya Rossiya, 1933, p. 35.

14. Smith, Douglas, *Rasputin: Faith, Power, and the Twilight of the Romanovs*, London: Macmillan, 2016, pp. 256-257.

15. Savich, N. V., *Vospominaniya*, St Petersburg: Logos, 1993, p. 83.

16. *The Reign of Rasputin: An Empire's Collapse. Memoirs of M. V. Rodzianko, President of the Russian State Duma*, translated by Catherine Zvegintzoff, London: A. M. Philpot Ltd., 1927, p. 75.

17. Hanbury-Williams, Major-General Sir John, *The Emperor Nicholas II as I Knew Him*, London: Arthur L. Humphreys, 1922, pp. 75-76.

18. Purishkevich, V. M., *Dnevnik chlena Gosudarstvennoi Dumy*, Riga, 1924, p. 6; *Gosudarstvennaya Duma, 1906–1917. Stenograficheskie otchety*, Vol. 4, Moscow, 1995, pp. 89-97.

19. Smith, Douglas, *Rasputin: Faith, Power, and the Twilight of the Romanovs*, London: Macmillan, 2016, p. 265.

20. *The Complete Wartime Correspondence of Tsar Nicholas II and the Empress Alexandra. April 1914–March 1917*, edited by Joseph T. Fuhrmann, Westport & London: Greenwood Press, 1999, pp. 674-675.

21. *The Reign of Rasputin: An Empire's Collapse. Memoirs of M. V. Rodzianko, President of the Russian State Duma*, translated by Catherine Zvegintzoff, London: A. M. Philpot Ltd., 1927, p. 263.

22. St Petersburg was renamed the more 'patriotic' and Slavic-sounding Petrograd on 18 August 1914.

8 1917

1. Pares, Bernard, *The Fall of the Russian Monarchy*, New York: Vintage Books, 1961, p. 443.
2. Evidence of Count Woldemar Freedericksz given to the Extraordinary Commission of Investigation of the Provisional Government on 2 June 1917; quoted from *Padenie tsarskogo rezhima*, edited by Pavel Schyogolev, Moscow & Leningrad: Gosudarstvennoe izdatel'stvo, 1926, Vol. 5, p. 38.
3. Shub, David, *Lenin: A Biography*, Harmondsworth: Penguin Books, 1966, p. 190.
4. Russia made further history in the field of women's political rights when the Provisional Government appointed the first ever female cabinet member. This was Countess Sofia Panina, who served as deputy minister for welfare from May and education from August 1917. She was the great-great-granddaughter of Count Pyotr Panin, whose elder brother, Nikita, had attempted to introduce a constitution in 1762.
5. Pitcher, Harvey, *When Miss Emmie was in Russia*, London: Eland Publishing Ltd., 1977, p. 139.
6. Kerensky, Alexander, *The Crucifixion of Liberty*, London: Arthur Baker Ltd., 1934, p. 244.
7. State Archives of the Russian Federation, F. 601, Op. 1, D. 1151, L. 500 & verso.
8. State Archives of the Russian Federation, F. 601, Op. 1, D. 2100 a, L. 7.
9. *Dnevniki Nikolaya II i imperatritsy Aleksandry Fedorovny: v 2 t.*, Moscow: PROZAiK, 2012, Vol. 1, p. 290.
10. *Rech'*, No. 121 (3863), 26 May 1917, p. 5.
11. Klyuchevsky stood as a Cadet candidate for the First Duma but was not elected. He was briefly a member of the State Council in 1906 as a representative of the Academy of Sciences and universities.
12. *Revolyutsionnoe dvizhenie v Rossii posle sverzheniya samoderzhaviya*, Moscow: Izdatel'stvo Akademii nauk SSSR, 1957, p. 188.
13. Sukhanov, N. N., *Zapiski o revolyutsii*, Moscow: Respublika, 1991, Vol. I, Parts 1-2, p. 142.
14. *Pervyi Vserossiiskii s'ezd Sovetov rabochikh i soldatskikh deputatov. Tom II*, Moscow & Leningrad: Gosudarstvennoe sotsial'no-ekonomicheskoe izdatel'stvo, 1931, p. 153.
15. Originally printed in part in *Pravda*, No. 99, 5 July 1917 and in full in *Rabochii i soldat*, No. 4, 27 July 1917. I. Stalin. *Sochineniya. Vol. 3: 1917 mart–oktyabr'*, Moscow: OGIZ; Gosudarstvennoe izdatel'stvo politicheskoi literatury, 1946, pp. 149-155.
16. *Sed'maya (aprel'skaya) Vserossiiskaya konfederatsiya RSDRP (bol'shevikov); Petrogradskaya obschegorodskaya konfederatsiya RSDRP (bol'shevikov). Aprel' 1917 goda. Protokoly*, Moscow: Gospolitizdat, 1958, p. 252.
17. V. I. Lenin, *Polnoe sobranie sochinenii*, Vol. 34, Moscow: Izdatel'stvo politicheskoi literatury, 1969, p. 343.
18. Polikarpov, V. D., *Voennaya kontrrevolyutsiya v Rossii. 1905–1917*, Moscow: Nauka, 1990, p. 185.

19. Sablin, Ivan & Kukushkin, Kuzma, 'Zemskii Sobor: Historiographies and Mythologies of a Russian 'Parliament'', *SocArXiv*, 22 November 2019, p. 32.
20. *V. I. Lenin, Polnoe sobranie sochinenii*, Vol. 34, Moscow: Izdatel'stvo politicheskoi literatury, 1969, p. 392.
21. Trotsky, Leon, 'Breaking Up the Constituent Assembly', *Lenin*, New York: Blue Ribbon Books, 1925.

9 *The Constituent Assembly Elections*

1. Some Muslim women had already voted in the spring; see Chapter 11, Section 2 on the Crimean Democratic Republic.
2. Women in Russia received the same voting rights as men ahead of all Western countries, including the United States (1920), Great Britain (1928), France (1944) and Switzerland (1971).
3. *Vserossiiskoe soveschanie Sovetov rabochikh i soldatskikh deputatov: Stenograficheskii otchet*, Moscow & Leningrad: Gosudarstvennoe izdatel'stvo, 1927, p. 113.
4. *Yuzhnye vedomosti*, Simferopol, 27 September 1917.
5. The age limit of twenty was a compromise between the four largest parties. The Cadets wanted the European voting age of twenty-one, the SRs and Mensheviks proposed twenty and the Bolsheviks wanted eighteen. This was still lower than in other European countries, except for Switzerland, where twenty-year-olds could also vote.
6. These figures show that the Cadets were the most efficient and the Bolsheviks were the least efficient. The average numbers were Cadets – 3.8, SRs – 4.1, Mensheviks – 4.7, Popular Socialists – 5.6, Bolsheviks – 6.0. The number of times a party was listed first was Cadets – 18, SRs – 15, Mensheviks – 4, Bolsheviks – 1; Protasov, L. G., *Vserossiiskoe Uchreditel'noe sobranie: istoriya rozhdeniya i gibeli*, ROSSPEN, Moscow, 1997, p. 123.
7. The ex-emperor and his family were exiled to Siberia in August 1917 and would have been in the Tobolsk electoral district, where the turnout was a low 33.5% and nine of the ten seats went to the SRs (who got 78.53% of the vote). The tenth seat went to the Popular Socialists (10.27%). This district was one of only two in the country where the Mensheviks and Bolsheviks ran together (the other was Vologda) – although they still only got 2.44% and were defeated by the Muslims (5.22%) and Cadets (2.79%). The Left SRs came last in Tobolsk on 0.75%.
8. *Anarkhiya*, Moscow, 6 November 1917.
9. *Svobodnoe slovo soldata i matrosa*, Reval, 28 November 1917.
10. *Yuzhnyi Ural*, Orenburg, 6 December 1917.
11. *Kavkazskoe slovo*, 14 November 1917.
12. *Nasha bor'ba*, Ekaterinoslav, 24 October 1917.
13. Rybakov, I. Ya., '1917 god v Aleksandrovskom uezde (Iz vospominanii)', *Nashe khozyaistvo (Vladimir)*, 1927, Nos. 10-11, p. 114.
14. *V. I. Lenin, Polnoe sobranie sochinenii*, Vol. 35, Moscow: Izdatel'stvo politicheskoi literatury, 1974, p. 111.
15. Russian State Archives of Social and Political History, F. 275, Op. 1, D. 27, L. 1.

16. Znamensky, O. N., *Vserossiiskoe Uchreditel'noe sobranie. Istoriya sozyva i politicheskogo krusheniya*, Leningrad: Nauka, 1976, pp. 201, 210.
17. As Edvard Radzinsky writes, 'the founding father of Russian Marxism lived to see the triumph of his ideas'; Radzinsky, Edvard, *Stalin*, translated from the Russian by H. T. Willetts, London: Hodder and Stoughton, 1996, p. 121.
18. Unity ran candidates in twelve districts, getting 27,000 votes but no seats. Plekhanov left Russia shortly afterwards and died in Finland in 1918.
19. Translated from the Russian by Jon Stallworthy and Peter France.
20. Russia was not divided into eleven time zones until 1919 and before then used a system of local solar time.
21. *Znamya revolyutsii*, Tomsk, 16 November 1917.
22. Two SRs, one Menshevik, one republican democrat and two independents (one of whom was a woman) stood in Kamchatka. The winner was one of the two SRs, a man called K. P. Lavrov.
23. *Trudovoe slovo*, No. 4, 15 November 1917.
24. *Vperyod!*, 21 November 1917.
25. *Izvestiya TsIK i Petrogradskogo Soveta*, 22 November 1917.
26. *Sotsial-demokrat*, Kharkiv, 17 November 1917.
27. On 23 November 1917, a group led by Stalin arrested the members of *Vsevybory* 'for sabotage', but this move was even criticised by some Bolsheviks and they were released four days later.
28. State Archives of the Russian Federation, F. 1810, Op. 1, D. 428, L. 17.
29. *Soyuznaya mysl'*, Chelyabinsk, 9 December 1917.
30. State Archives of Tambov Region, F. 1068, Op. 1, D. 85, L. 48.
31. Protasov, L. G., *Vserossiiskoe Uchreditel'noe sobranie: istoriya rozhdeniya i gibeli*, ROSSPEN, Moscow, 1997, p. 254.
32. *Svobodnyi krai*, Irkutsk, 25 November 1917.
33. State Archives of Tomsk Region, F. R-240, Op. 1, D. 878, L. 23-25.
34. State Archives of Tambov Region, F. 1068, Op. 1, D. 85, L. 36.
35. Dmitriyenko, N. M., Vybory vo Vserossiiskoe Uchreditel'noe sobranie v Tomske v 1917 g.', *Vestnik Tomskogo gosudarstvennogo universiteta*, No. 357, April 2012, pp. 75-79.
36. The best source for information is considered to be Oliver H. Radkey's book *Russia Goes to the Polls: The Election to the All-Russian Constituent Assembly, 1917* (Ithaca: Cornell University Press, 1989).
37. State Archives of the Russian Federation, F. 1810, Op. 1, D. 26, L. 9; *Tiflisskii listok*, 17 November 1917.
38. Protasov L. G. & Miller, V. I., 'Vserossiiskoe Uchreditel'noe sobranie i demokraticheskaya alternativa: dva vzglyada na problemu', *Otechestvennaya istoriya*, No. 5, 1993, p. 12.
39. *Svobodnaya rech'*, 28 November 1917.
40. State Archives of the Russian Federation, F. 1810, Op. 1, D. 79, L. 72.
41. *Luch*, 20 November 1917.
42. The Old Believers (*starovery*) were a group of Russian Orthodox Christians who had broken away from the main church over reforms introduced in the 1660s and continued to follow the old versions of the liturgical rites and texts.

43. *Byulleten' Osoboi armii*, 24 November 1917.
44. Vorobyov, A. A., 'Zhenskii udarnyi batal'on i vybory vo Vserossiiskoe uchreditel'noe sobranie', *Belorusskie zemli v sostave Rossiiskogo gosudarstva (1772–1917 gg.): Materialy Respublikanskoi nauchno-tekhnicheskoi konferentsii, Minsk, 2 dekabrya 2013 g.*, Belarusian National Technical University, Minsk, 2013, pp. 113-114; Bochkaryova's battalion was with the Tenth Army on the Western Front during the October revolution and did not participate in the defence of the Winter Palace – this was done by another female unit, the First Petrograd Women's Battalion.
45. Wildman, Allan K., *The End of the Russian Imperial Army, Volume II: The Road to Soviet Power and Peace*, New Jersey: Princeton University Press, 1987, p. 29.
46. *Narod*, Petrograd, 6 November 1917.
47. *Proletariat Povolzh'ya*, Saratov, 19 December 1917.
48. *Vlast' naroda*, 22 November 1917.

10 1918

1. There had been a battle over which city would host the Constituent Assembly. On 7 March 1917, the Moscow City Duma declared that it should sit in 'the heart of Russia – Moscow'. Four days later, the Petrograd Soviet countered that their town was the home of the revolution and better placed to defend the assembly from any attempts at counter-revolution. In the end, the Provisional Government decided that it would be cheaper just to use the Tauride Palace, now vacant after they relocated to the Winter Palace and the Petrograd Soviet moved into the Smolny Institute. In November 1917, the Smolny became the seat of the Bolshevik government – until they themselves transferred the capital of Russia to Moscow in March 1918 and moved into the Kremlin.
2. *Dekrety Sovetskoi vlasti. T. I. 25 oktyabrya 1917 g. – 16 marta 1918 g.*, Moscow: Politizdat, 1957, p. 278.
3. Merezhkovsky, D., *Bol'naya Rossiya*, Leningrad: Izdatel'stvo Leningradskogo universiteta, 1991, p. 223.
4. *Nashi vedomosti*, 30 December 1917.
5. *Vol'naya Sibir'*, Petrograd, 14 & 21 January 1918.
6. A second demonstration of anarchists set off for the Tauride Palace from the offices of the *Burevestnik* newspaper on Nicholas (now Marat) Street, carrying banners which read 'Down with the Constituent Assembly!' and 'Long live anarchy!'
7. *Novaya zhizn'*, No 6 (220), 9 January 1918; Gorky, Maxim, *Untimely Thoughts: Essays on Revolution, Culture and the Bolsheviks, 1917–1918*, translated from the Russian and with notes by Herman Ermolaev, New Haven & London: Yale University Press, 1968, p. 125.
8. Ibid., p. 126.
9. Trotsky, Leon, 'Breaking Up the Constituent Assembly', *Lenin*, New York: Blue Ribbon Books, 1925.
10. Raskolnikov, F. F., 'Rasskaz o poteryannom dne', *Utro strany Sovetov*, Leningrad: Lenizdat, 1988, pp. 311-312.

11. Chernov, Victor, 'Russia's One-Day Parliament', *Readings in Russian Civilization, Volume III: Soviet Russia, 1917–1963*, edited by Thomas Riha, Chicago & London: University of Chicago Press, second edition, 1969, p. 514.

12. V. I. Lenin. *Collected Works*, Moscow: Progress Publishers, Vol. 26, 1972, pp. 431-433.

13. Chernov, Victor, 'Russia's One-Day Parliament', *Readings in Russian Civilization, Volume III: Soviet Russia, 1917–1963*, edited by Thomas Riha, Chicago & London: University of Chicago Press, second edition, 1969, p. 515.

14. *Vperyod!*, 12 January 1918.

15. Russian State Archives of Social and Political History, F. 274, Op. 1, D. 49, L. 22.

16. Mawdsley, Evan, 'Sea Change in the Civil War', *Was Revolution Inevitable? Turning Points of the Russian Revolution*, edited by Tony Brenton, New York: Oxford University Press, 2017, p. 213.

17. Chernov, V. M., *Pered burei*, Moscow: Direct-Media, 2016, p. 429.

18. *A Long Journey: The Autobiography of Pitirim A. Sorokin*, New Haven, Connecticut: College and University Press, 1963, p. 132.

19. Mawdsley, Evan, 'Sea Change in the Civil War', *Was Revolution Inevitable? Turning Points of the Russian Revolution*, edited by Tony Brenton, New York: Oxford University Press, 2017, p. 213.

20. *Petrogradskii golos*, 11 January 1918.

11 Civil War

1. The conservative wing, which supported religious orthodoxy and Sharia law, broke away from the party in June 1917 to form *Shura-i Ulema* (Council of Clergy). This group of traditionalists declined to join the provisional government.

2. Russian Soviet Federative Socialist Republic.

3. Back in the days of the independent Crimean Khanate (1441–1783), women had participated in politics and even affairs of state. Queen Nur Sultan corresponded with Ivan III and influenced diplomatic and political life during the reign of her husband, Meñli I Giray (1466–1515). The demand for political equality between men and women began long before 1917 among the Muslims of the Russian Empire and can be traced back to the rise of Jadidism in the 1880s. Jadidism developed from support for a new (*jadid*) educational method into a social and cultural movement among young Muslim intellectuals which advocated democracy and equality.

4. Qandım, Yunus, 'Kurultai. Kak eto bylo', *Avdet*, 12 April 1991; Şefiqa Gaspıralı was the daughter of Ismail Gaspıralı, one of the founders of the Jadidist movement. In 1906, she married Nasib Yusifbeyli, who became prime minister of the Azerbaijan Democratic Republic in March 1919. After the Red Army invaded Azerbaijan in April 1920, her husband was murdered and she fled with their children to Turkey.

Notes

5. The Bolsheviks only got 5% in the elections to the Constituent Assembly in November 1917.
6. The Crimea was subsequently occupied at various stages of the Civil War by the Reds and Whites, Germans and Allies, Ukrainians and Russians, until the final defeat of the last White Army there in December 1920.
7. *Idel* means 'Volga' in the Tatar language, implying that the state was based around the River Volga and the Ural Mountains.
8. The people from the River Konda were originally called the 'Kondinsky' in Russian, from which the famous abstract artist Wassily Kandinsky takes his name. Kandinsky's ancestors came from Kyakhta in Buryatia and he himself claimed descent from a Manchurian (or Mongolian) princess.
9. The 'three worlds' were the sky, water and earth.
10. Sablin, Ivan, *Governing Post-Imperial Siberia and Mongolia, 1911–1924: Buddhism, Socialism and Nationalism in State and Autonomy Building*, New York & London: Routledge, 2016, p. 127.
11. Ibid., p. 128.
12. According to another legend, the lama is still alive and materialised in front of a group of Buddhologists in Moscow in the 1970s.
13. Goldman, Emma, *My Disillusionment in Russia*, London: C. W. Daniel Company, 1925, pp. 148-149.
14. Wolff, Marc Mikhailovich, 'In the Crimea', *The Other Russia*, edited by Michael Glenny & Norman Stone, London: Faber and Faber, 1990, p. 142.
15. Kropotkin returned to Russia from exile at the age of seventy-four. He was greeted at the Finland Railway Station on 30 May 1917 by Kerensky, who on 20 July offered him any ministerial position he wanted in the Provisional Government. Kropotkin declined the offer, saying that 'a boot cleaner is a more honest and useful profession.'
16. Paz, Abel, *Durruti: The People Armed*, Montreal: Black Rose Books, 1976, p. 89.
17. Although Makhno was a bank robber, the National Bank of Ukraine issued a commemorative coin on the 125th anniversary of his birth in October 2013.
18. The Bolsheviks added the word 'Communist' to the name of their party at the Seventh Congress in March 1918.
19. Matyushina, Margarita, 'Antologiya bunta, ili Vzglyad iz XXI veka', *Tambovskaya zhizn'*, No. 118 (25540), 18 August 2010.
20. Russian State Archives of Social and Political History, F. 17, Op. 112, D.108, L. 21-21 reverse; Hoover Institution Archives, B. I. Nicolaevsky collection, Box No. 18-28, typewritten copy.
21. Radzinsky, Edvard, *Stalin*, translated from the Russian by H. T. Willetts, London: Hodder and Stoughton, 1996, p. 168.
22. According to the official figures, 1,155 children were imprisoned in ten concentration camps on 1 August 1921. 758 of them were aged under five and 397 were younger than three.
23. The reports mention, for example, the use of seventy-nine chemical shells near Lake Ramza on 20 August, eighty-five near the village of Inzhavino on 22 August and fifty near the village of Kipets on 23 August

(State Archives of Tambov Region, F. R.-1832, Op. 1, D. 943, L. 3). Tukhachevsky was shot exactly sixteen years later, on 12 June 1937, after confessing 'in a bloodstained deposition' to being a German spy.

24. Sennikov, B. V., *Tambovskoe vosstanie 1918–1921 gg. i raskrest'yanivanie Rossii 1929–1933 gg.*, Moscow: Posev, 2004.

25. Grand Duke Michael had already been shot in Perm on the night of 12/13 June 1918.

26. The *Petropavlovsk* was later renamed the *Marat* and represented the USSR in the Coronation Fleet Review at Spithead in May 1937.

27. During the First World War, the *Petropavlovsk* had been based at Naissaar (the name means 'island of women' in Estonian). In December 1917, the crew seized power on the island and proclaimed the Soviet Republic of Naissaar. Petrichenko was appointed chairman of the Council of People's Commissars, which had commissars of war, home affairs, labour, finance, public health and education. The republic had its own constitution, capital (the village of Lõunaküla), national anthem (*The Internationale*), flag (the black and red banner of the anarcho-syndicalists) and planned to issue its own currency. The Soviet Republic of Naissaar ended after just two months, in February 1918, when the island was occupied by German troops.

12 Soviet Union

1. Trotzky, Leon, 'The Principles of Democracy and Proletarian Dictatorship', *The Class Struggle*, New York City: Socialist Publication Society, Vol. III, No. 1, February 1919, p. 88.

2. Stalin, I., 'O diskussii, o Rafaile, o stat'yakh Preobrazhenskogo i Sapronova i o pis'me Trotskogo', *Pravda*, No. 285, 15 December 1923; quoted from *I. Stalin. Sochineniya. Vol. 5: 1921–1923*, Moscow: OGIZ; Gosudarstvennoe izdatel'stvo politicheskoi literatury, 1947, pp. 371-387.

3. The Soviet secret police was known as the Cheka (1917–22), GPU (1922–23), OGPU (1923–34), NKVD (1934–43), NKGB (1943–46), MGB (1946–53) and KGB (1954–91).

4. Bazhanov, Boris, *Bazhanov and the Damnation of Stalin*, translation and commentary by David W. Doyle, Athens: Ohio University Press, 1990, pp. 56-57.

5. Trotsky, Leon, *The Revolution Betrayed: What Is the Soviet Union and Where Is It Going?* translated by Max Eastman, Detroit: Labor Publications, 1991, p. 246.

6. Bazhanov, Boris, *Bazhanov and the Damnation of Stalin*, translation and commentary by David W. Doyle, Athens: Ohio University Press, 1990, p. 92.

7. Radzinsky, Edvard, *Stalin*, translated from the Russian by H. T. Willetts, London: Hodder and Stoughton, 1996, p. 297.

8. *J. V. Stalin, Works, Vol. 14: 1934–1940*, London: Red Star Press Ltd., 1978, p. 179.

9. FSB RF Central Archives, F. 3, Op. 4, D. 1955, L. 6-14.

10. Ibid., L. 11-14.

11. *J. V. Stalin, Works, Vol. 14: 1934–1940*, London: Red Star Press Ltd., 1978, pp. 307-309.

Notes

12. UFSB RF Sverdlovsk Regional Archives, F. 1, Op. 1, D. 259, L. 175.
13. Hryciuk, Grzegorz, 'Wyborcza farsa w stylu ZSRS: 22 października 1939', *Polacy we Lwowie 1939–1944*, Warsaw: Książka i Wiedza, 2000.
14. *Partizany Bryanschiny. Sbornik materialov i dokumentov BPA*, Vol. 2, compiled by T. M. Shulzhenko et al., Bryansk: Bryanskii rabochii, 1962, p. 66.
15. State Archives of Bryansk Region, F. 2608, Op. 1, D. 3, L. 44.
16. Sokolov, B. V., *Okkupatsiya. Pravda i mify*, Moscow: AST-Press Kniga, 2005, p. 205.
17. Klimenko, O. O., *Bofoni: groshovi dokumenti OUN i UPA*, Kiev: UBS NBU, 2008, pp. 7-9.
18. Khruschev, Sergei, *Reformator*, Moscow: Veche, 2016.
19. Scamell, Michael, *Solzhenitsyn: A Biography*, New York: Hutchinson, 1984, p. 406.
20. Dora Lazurkina said in her speech on 30 October 1961: 'I always carry Ilich in my heart and always, comrades, in the most difficult moments, survived only because I had Ilich in my heart and consulted with him on what to do. Yesterday I consulted with Ilich and it was as if he were standing before me alive.' Stalin was secretly reburied the following night, which was Halloween. In a further mystical twist, Lazurkina died at the age of ninety on 24 January 1974 – exactly fifty years to the day that Lenin had died.
21. *Programme of the Communist Party of the Soviet Union*, Moscow: Foreign Languages Publishing House, 1961, p. 91.
22. Communist Union of Youth (*Kommunisticheskii soyuz molodezhi*).
23. Russian State Archives of Contemporary History, F. 5, Op. 32, D. 39, L. 140.
24. Ibid., Op. 30, D. 383, L. 30-102.
25. Russian State Archives of Contemporary History, F. 5, Op. 30, D. 383, L. 1.
26. *Memoirs of Nikita Khrushchev, Volume 3: Statesman, 1953–1964*, edited by Sergei Khrushchev, University Park, PA: Pennsylvania State University, 2007, p. 379.
27. Khrushchev lived for the next seven years as a pensioner and died of a heart attack in 1971. He was denied a state funeral and burial at the walls of the Kremlin and was laid to rest in the Novodevichy Cemetery, with an avant-garde tombstone designed by nonconformist sculptor Ernst Neizvestny.
28. Taubman, William, *Khrushchev: The Man and His Era*, New York: W. W. Norton & Co., 2003, p. 13.
29. Kirov Regional State Archives of Social and Political History, F. P-1290, Op. 70, D. 106, L. 140-150.
30. Soviet figures made a return under Vladimir Putin, who took over 90% of the vote in five regions in the 2012 presidential elections, including 99.76% in Chechnya on a turnout of 99.61%.
31. Gorbachev, Raisa, *I Hope. Reminiscences and Reflections*, translated by David Floyd, London: Fontana, 1992, p. 125.
32. Gorbachev, Mikhail, *Memoirs*, London: Doubleday, 1996, p. 155.
33. Ibid., p. 164.
34. Dowd, Maureen, 'Where's the Rest of Him?', *New York Times*, 18 November 1990.

13 *Perestroika – Gorbachev*

1. Brown, Archie, *The Human Factor: Gorbachev, Reagan, and Thatcher, and the End of the Cold War*, Oxford: Oxford University Press, 2020, p. 3.
2. Thatcher, Margaret, *The Downing Street Years*, London: HarperCollins, 1993, pp. 459-463.
3. Ibid., p. 461.
4. Moore, Charles, *Margaret Thatcher: The Authorized Biography*, Vol. 2, London: Penguin Press, 2016, p. 240.
5. *The Diary of Anatoly S. Chernyaev 1991*, donated by A. S. Chernyaev to The National Security Archive, translated by Anna Melyakova.
6. Gorbachev, Mikhail, *Memoirs*, London: Doubleday, 1996, p. 547.
7. Brown, Des, 'When Margaret Thatcher and Mikhail Gorbachev Changed the World', *The Moscow Times*, 22 October 2015.
8. During the interview, Thatcher inadvertently revealed to Soviet viewers that the USSR possessed the world's largest stockpiles of nuclear weapons and missiles – a fact which had previously been kept secret from them.
9. Thatcher, Margaret, *The Downing Street Years*, London: HarperCollins, 1993, p. 453.
10. Interview with L. M. Zamyatin, *Kommersant*, 3 May 2005; quoted from Service, Robert, *The End of the Cold War: 1985–1991*, London: Pan Books, 2016, p. 491.
11. Gorbachev, Mikhail, *Memoirs*, London: Doubleday, 1996, p. 545.
12. Ibid., p. 165.
13. Ibid., p. 46.
14. Alexeyeva, Lyudmila, 'Gorbachev i dissidenty', *SSSR: Vnutrennie protivorechiya*, No. 19, Benson, VT: Chalidze Publications, 1987, p. 51.
15. Gorbachev's younger brother, Alexander, who died aged fifty-four in 2001, was also rumoured to be an alcoholic.
16. Gorbachev, Raisa, *I Hope. Reminiscences and Reflections*, translated by David Floyd, London: Fontana, 1992, p. 26.
17. Reagan, Nancy, *My Turn: The Memoirs of Nancy Reagan*, New York: Random House, 1989, p. 160.
18. Gorbachev, Mikhail, *Memoirs*, London: Doubleday, 1996, p. 407.
19. Ibid., p. 198.
20. Ibid., p. 258.
21. *XIX Vsesoyuznaya konferentsiya Kommunisticheskoi partii Sovetskogo Soyuza: 28 iyunya–1 iyulya 1988 goda: stenograficheskii otchet v dvukh tomakh*, Vol. 1, Moscow: Politizdat, pp. 56-57.
22. The Romanovs got their revenge on Yeltsin in 2018 – the hundredth anniversary of their deaths – when a gas cylinder exploded in his childhood home and it burnt down on the eve of his birthday.
23. See Chapter 2, note 9.
24. The quotation was published without any footnotes or source notes and has subsequently found its way into other books. The sentence appears to originate from Isaac Deutscher's book *Russia After Stalin*, published in London in 1953, which states: 'The core of Stalin's genuine historic

achievement lies in the fact that he found Russia working with the wooden plough and left her equipped with atomic piles.'

25. Gorbachev, Mikhail, *Memoirs*, London: Doubleday, 1996, p. 256.
26. Ibid., p. 259.
27. Ibid., p. 278.
28. Ibid., p. 270.
29. Ibid., p. 498.
30. Alexius II was the first patriarch in Soviet history to be chosen without government interference and was elected to the post by secret ballot in June 1990.
31. *Ogonyok*, No. 9, February 1989.
32. Minayev, Boris, *El'tsin*, Moscow: Molodaya gvardiya, 2010, p. 56.
33. Zubok, Vladislav, *The Idea of Russia: The Life and Work of Dmitry Likhachev*, I. B. Tauris & Co. Ltd., London & New York, 2017, p. 142.
34. The Communists still won general elections in Russia in 1990, 1995 and 1999 without the help of Article 6.
35. Garthoff, Raymond L., *The Great Transition: American-Soviet Relations and the End of the Cold War*, Washington DC: The Brookings Institution, 1994, p. 442.
36. Gorbachev, Mikhail, *Memoirs*, London: Doubleday, 1996, p. 367.
37. Ibid., p. 368.
38. Chechnya declared independence in November 1991 under its elected president, Dzhokhar Dudayev, while Tatarstan declared itself a 'sovereign state' after holding a referendum in March 1992.
39. After spending a year in detention, Shmonov was sentenced to four years in a psychiatric clinic. He unsuccessfully stood for the Duma in 1999 and became a human-rights advocate specialising in victims of forced psychiatric treatment. The brightest moment for Gorbachev in 1990 was possibly being awarded the Nobel Peace Prize in November for ending the Cold War.

14 1991 – *Transfiguration*

1. Gorbachev, Mikhail, *Memoirs*, London: Doubleday, 1996, p. 347.
2. 80.2% voted in favour of the second question, compared to 70.2% for the first question.
3. Email from Ralph Murphine to the author, 20 May 2020.
4. Alternatively, if the countdown began from the dissolution of the Constituent Assembly in January 1918, then the end of the period would be August 1991.
5. Alexander Korzhakov alleges in his memoirs that Popov exasperated Yeltsin with his 'intellectual talk', while Burbulis ruined his chances by getting drunk and vomiting in the presence of Yeltsin's wife and daughter.
6. Yakovlev, Alexander, *Sumerki*, Moscow: Materik, 2005, pp. 560-561.
7. Graf Lambsdorff, Dr. Otto, 'Den Demagogen ernst nehmen', *Liberale Depesche*, No. 3, 1994, p. 30.
8. Friedrich-Naumann-Stiftung für die Freiheit, ADL, Bestand Otto Graf Lambsdorff, N103-293, p. 55.

9. 'Narody Rossii sdelali svoi vybor', *Rossiiskaya gazeta*, No. 124 (170), 14 June 1991.

10. Agumava, Fidel, 'Kak zarozhdalas' demokratiya v nashei strane', *Parlamentskaya gazeta*, 12 June 2019.

11. Yeltsin Center, F. 6, Op. 1, D. 68, L. 37-154.

12. Sobyanin, A. A. & Sukhovolsky, V. G., *Demokratiya, ogranichennaya fal'sifikatsiyami. Vybory i referendumy v Rossii v 1991–1993 gg.*, Moscow: Proektnaya gruppa po pravam cheloveka, 1995, pp. 71-73, 100.

13. Andreyev, Alexander & Andreyev, Maxim, *Neistovyi Zhirinovskii. Politicheskaya biografiya lidera LDPR*, Moscow: Tsentrpoligraf, 2016.

14. As Yeltsin was now president, his place as chairman of the Supreme Soviet of the RSFSR was taken by his first deputy, Ruslan Khasbulatov.

15. The Kremlin Palace of Congresses, a modernist building commissioned by Khrushchev, was renamed the State Kremlin Palace in 1992 and used again for Yeltsin's second inauguration in August 1996.

16. Proskurnina, Olga & Rozhkova, Maria, 'Luzhkov dopustil nepopravimuyu oshibku – pozvolil poiti v prezidenty Primakovu', *Vedomosti*, 28 September 2010.

17. Sobchak's electoral campaign was headed by his first deputy mayor, Vladimir Putin, who tried to help Sobchak by getting the first round brought forward by a month (to no avail). This was the third successive defeat for Putin as an electoral agent. He led the unsuccessful campaign of the pro-Sobchak 'All Petersburg' bloc for the St Petersburg Legislative Assembly in 1994 (which only won four of twenty-four seats) and was the regional chairman of the party of power, Our Home is Russia, in the 1995 Duma elections (they were defeated by Yabloko). Like the fall of the Berlin Wall in 1989, the 1996 mayor elections left him temporarily with no job and with a healthy distrust of the unpredictability of democracy.

18. 'Reaction of Yeltsin on Election Results, 1991', *Current Digest of the Soviet Press*, Vol. XLIII, No. 24, 17 July 1991, p. 1.

19. Ibid., p. 4.

20. O'Clery, Conor, *Moscow, December 25th, 1991: The Last Day of the Soviet Union*, New York: PublicAffairs, 2012, pp. 221-222.

21. Ogushi, Atsushi, *The Demise of the Soviet Communist Party*, London: Routledge, 2007, p. 146.

22. Gorbachev, Mikhail, *Memoirs*, London: Doubleday, 1996, p. 631.

23. One soldier told me that he spent the whole day watching *Swan Lake* on television; then, in the evening, his unit was taken to the theatre – to see a performance of *Swan Lake*.

24. Gorbachev, Mikhail, *Memoirs*, London: Doubleday, 1996, pp. 633-636.

25. Ibid., p. 639.

26. Ibid., p. 641.

27. Medvedev, Roy & Zhores, *Solzhenitsyn i Sakharov. Dva proroka*, Moscow: Vremya, 2005.

28. Gorbachev, Mikhail, *Memoirs*, London: Doubleday, 1996, p. 629.

29. As the possibility of direct presidential elections approached, Gorbachev may have believed that this was the only way to stay in power and hold the union together, given his falling ratings and Yeltsin's growing authority after his election victory in June 1991.
30. Yeltsin hoodwinked Gorbachev by telling him that he was flying to Minsk for negotiations 'to try and persuade Ukraine to join the union'. Gorbachev later heard from an eyewitness that, when Yeltsin returned from Minsk, he 'broke into a forty-minute tirade, telling excitedly how he had managed to "dupe" Gorbachev just before leaving for Minsk, misleading him about the purpose of his trip, when in reality he intended to do the exact opposite of what he said. "We had to get Gorbachev out of the way," Yeltsin added.' See Gorbachev, Mikhail, *Memoirs*, London: Doubleday, 1996, p. 658.
31. Ibid., pp. xxvi-xxix.
32. Vodolazskaya, Yevgenia, *Raisa Gorbacheva*, Rostov-on-Don: Phoenix, 2000, p. 96.
33. Gorbachev, Mikhail, *The New Russia*, translated by Arch Tait, Cambridge: Polity Press, 2016, p. 19.

15 'The Wild Nineties' – Yeltsin

1. Gaidar, Yegor, *Days of Defeat and Victory*, translated by Jane Ann Miller, Seattle & London: University of Washington Press, 1999, p. 115.
2. By 1994, Gorbachev's presidential pension of 4,000 roubles a month was worth less than $2. Although he earned a substantial income from lecture fees, this was still not enough to cover the running of his foundation and other living costs, so he filmed a television ad for Pizza Hut in 1997 – only for his fee to be wiped out in the crash of 17 August 1998.
3. Gorbachev recalled his meeting with Thatcher in London on 19 July: 'Shortly before I was due to leave after the London G7 summit in July 1991, she asked to meet me at the Soviet Embassy and, without warning, started laying into other Western leaders for failing to genuinely support Perestroika... "As politicians they are not worth tuppence! They are incompetent. They have let you down!"'; Gorbachev, Mikhail, *The New Russia*, translated by Arch Tait, Cambridge: Polity Press, 2016, p. 383.
4. Email from Jeffrey D. Sachs to the author, 29 January 2020.
5. Sachs, Jeffrey D., 'Geography, Geopolitics and Policy in the Performance of Transition Economies', *Economics of Transition*, Vol. 26 (4), 2018, p. 844.
6. Foer, Franklin, 'How Kleptocracy Came to America', *The Atlantic*, March 2019.
7. Gaidar, Yegor, *Days of Defeat and Victory*, translated by Jane Ann Miller, Seattle & London: University of Washington Press, 1999, pp. 233-234.
8. Turovsky, Valery, 'Prezident gotov sam prinyat' reshenie o dosrochnykh parlamentskikh vyborakh', *Izvestiya*, 13 August 1993.
9. Yeltsin, Boris, *The Struggle for Russia*, translated from the Russian by Catherine A. Fitzpatrick, London: HarperCollins, 1994, p. 219.
10. Gaidar, Yegor, *Days of Defeat and Victory*, translated by Jane Ann Miller, Seattle & London: University of Washington Press, 1999, p. 229.

11. Jeffries, Ian, *The New Russia: A Handbook of Economic and Political Developments*, London: RoutledgeCurzon, 2002, pp. 456-457.

12. Two weeks later, *Moskovskie novosti* published an article entitled 'Parliament Fell for the President's Bait', which quoted an anonymous intelligence officer responsible for pro-Soviet coups and military provocations in the Third World: 'Motor vehicles with ignition keys "abandoned in a panic" are a trick used by special forces in banana republics.' Suspicions were also raised over the ease with which the rebels broke through the police lines and over who shot the Alpha lieutenant, while it was claimed that the transmission of the football match was interrupted at the direct request of Chernomyrdin. See 'Parlament klyunul na prezidentskuyu blesnu', *Moskovskie novosti*, 17 October 1993, No. 42, pp. 4-5.

13. Gaidar, Yegor, *Days of Defeat and Victory*, translated by Jane Ann Miller, Seattle & London: University of Washington Press, 1999, pp. 246-247.

14. Ibid., p. 220.

15. The two representatives were initially directly elected on 12 December 1993. The first term of office for both houses was two years and, thereafter, four years.

16. The record result for 'against all' was 65.55% in the vote to elect the head of Kurganinsk district in Krasnodar Region in 2004 – which is possibly why the option was removed from the ballot paper shortly afterwards, in 2006.

17. *Russia Election Observation Report, December 12, 1993*, International Republican Institute, 27 January 1994.

18. Jeffries, Ian, *The New Russia: A Handbook of Economic and Political Developments*, London: RoutledgeCurzon, 2002, p. 473.

19. Lyubarsky, Kronid & Sobyanin, Alexander, 'Golos', *Novoe vremya*, No. 15, 1995.

20. Sixty-eight former members of the Congress of People's Deputies were elected to the Duma in 1993.

21. The by-election was held soon after 'Black Tuesday', 11 October 1994, when the rouble fell by 27.5% against the US dollar, bringing the resignations of the chairman of the Russian central bank and the acting finance minister.

22. Chubais later defended the scheme as a necessary evil to prevent a return to communism: 'We did not have a choice between an "honest" privatisation and a "dishonest" one... Our choice was between bandit communism or bandit capitalism'; Ostrovsky, Arkady, 'Father to the Oligarchs', *Financial Times*, 13 November 2004.

23. Commission on Security and Cooperation in Europe, *The Russian Duma Elections, December 17, 1995: A Report Prepared by the Staff of the Commission on Security and Cooperation in Europe*, June 1996, p. 9.

24. Ibid., pp. 3-4.

25. The only parallels elsewhere in Europe were the similar 'beer lovers' parties' in Ukraine, Belarus and Poland and the Partito dell'Amore founded in Italy by Cicciolina and Moana Pozzi.

16 1996 – The Year of the Rats

1. Remnick, David, *Resurrection: The Struggle for a New Russia*, London: Picador, 1998, p. 330.
2. Fadin, Andrei, 'Semibankirschina kak novorusskii variant semiboyarschiny', *Obschaya gazeta*, 14 November 1996.
3. Barsukov was appointed director of the FSB in July 1995 precisely because he did not have any background in intelligence work. This echoed Khrushchev's similar reasons for appointing Vladimir Semichastny as head of the KGB in 1961. Yeltsin then went against this principle and his next three appointees – Nikolai Kovalyov, Vladimir Putin and Nikolai Patrushev – were all former KGB agents.
4. Kramer, Michael, 'Rescuing Boris: The Secret Story of How Four U.S. Advisers Used Polls, Focus Groups, Negative Ads and All the Other Techniques of American Campaigning to Help Boris Yeltsin Win', *Time*, 15 July 1996, p. 28.
5. Abarinov, Vladimir, 'Yanki pri dvore tsarya Borisa', *Sovershenno sekretno*, 1 November 2003.
6. Talbott, Strobe, *The Russia Hand: A Memoir of Presidential Diplomacy*, New York: Random House, 2002, p. 205.
7. Kramer, Michael, 'Rescuing Boris: The Secret Story of How Four U.S. Advisers Used Polls, Focus Groups, Negative Ads and All the Other Techniques of American Campaigning to Help Boris Yeltsin Win', *Time*, 15 July 1996, pp. 34-35.
8. National Security Council and NSC Records Management System, 'Declassified Documents Concerning Russian President Boris Yeltsin,' *Clinton Digital Library*, accessed 6 November 2020, Case number 2015-0782-M, Document ID 9603149, Row 45, Section 1, Shelf 3, Position 1, Stack V.
9. One of the groups, The Untouchables (*Neprikasayemye*), was dropped on the first day of the tour after their vocalist, Garik Sukachov, told journalists that he planned to vote for Gorbachev.
10. The newspaper was resurrected in the run-up to the Russian presidential election in March 2012, when it targeted the democratic opposition to Vladimir Putin and the potential threat of a 'colour revolution'.
11. Andrei Razin claimed – completely separately – that he was Gorbachev's nephew and even recorded a pop song on the subject (*Uncle Misha*). He was really an orphan whose foster-grandmother had been the Gorbachevs' cook in the 1970s. Through her, he got to know Gorbachev's mother, Maria Gopkalo, and later bought her house in Stavropol (the deal was contested in court and the stress possibly contributed to her death in 1993).
12. Gorbachev, Mikhail, *Memoirs*, London: Doubleday, 1996, p. 695.
13. Two of these eight candidates were later killed in helicopter crashes – Svyatoslav Fyodorov in June 2000 and Alexander Lebed in April 2002.
14. When speaking these words in October 1995, Lebed was quoting early Christian writer Tertullian, whose concept of *simia dei* meant the way in which the devil imitates God.
15. The word *lebed'* means 'swan' in Russian, while *ivolga* is 'oriole'.
16. Gorbachev, Mikhail, *The New Russia*, translated by Arch Tait, Cambridge: Polity Press, 2016, p. 102.

17. Thornhill, John, 'Gorbachev resurrects glasnost banner', *Financial Times*, 13 May 1996, p. 2.
18. Gorbachev, Mikhail, *The New Russia*, translated by Arch Tait, Cambridge: Polity Press, 2016, p. 108.
19. Ibid., pp. 109-110.
20. Thatcher, Carol, *A Swim-on Part in the Goldfish Bowl: A Memoir*, London: Headline Publishing Group, 2008.
21. Gorbachev, Raisa, *I Hope. Reminiscences and Reflections*, translated by David Floyd, London: Fontana, 1992, p. 193.
22. DJ Groove was also involved in the *Choose or Lose* tour and composed the title-track of the same name.
23. Remnick, David, *Resurrection: The Struggle for a New Russia*, London: Picador, 1998, p. 337.
24. Commentary by Michael Meadowcroft dated 8 January 2013 on an article originally published in *The Exile* on 30 November 2007, https://beemeadowcroft.uk/currentaffairs/russiacommentary.pdf
25. Gorbachev, Mikhail, *The New Russia*, translated by Arch Tait, Cambridge: Polity Press, 2016, p. 114.
26. Korzhakov took revenge by claiming in his 1997 memoirs that Yevgeny Kiselyov was a KGB agent with the code name of 'Alexeyev'. This could neither be proven nor disproven, as secret services never publicly acknowledge their employees. Several Russian books have also named Kiselyov's boss, Vladimir Gusinsky, as an ex-KGB agent with the code name of 'Denis'.
27. Meadowcroft, Michael, 'Election of President of the Russian Federation 16th June 1996 and 3rd July 1996: Report on the Election', *Organization for Security and Co-operation in Europe Office for Democratic Institutions and Human Rights*, 12 July 1996.
28. Commentary by Michael Meadowcroft dated 8 January 2013 on an article originally published in *The Exile* on 30 November 2007, https://beemeadowcroft.uk/currentaffairs/russiacommentary.pdf
29. Interview to *Frontline*, season 2000, episode 9, *Return of the Czar*, aired on 9 May 2000.
30. Kramer, Michael, 'Rescuing Boris: The Secret Story of How Four U.S. Advisers Used Polls, Focus Groups, Negative Ads and All the Other Techniques of American Campaigning to Help Boris Yeltsin Win', *Time*, 15 July 1996, p. 37.
31. Domrin, Alexander N., 'Something Wicked Comes This Way: Sad Story of U.S. Aid to Russian "Reformers"', *Nezavisimaya gazeta*, 22 March 2001.
32. Shevtsova, Liliya, *Rezhim Borisa El'tsina*, Moscow: ROSSPEN, 1999.

17 Boyar Rule

1. Mavrodi testified that the architect of the GKO scheme, Bella Zlatkis, had once approached him to ask how the MMM model might be adopted by the ministry of finance.
2. Boris Nemtsov revealed that in 1997 Margaret Thatcher wrote a letter to Boris Yeltsin about the harm caused to others by alcoholism, saying that her

own husband drank, which caused a lot of problems for the family – while, under Yeltsin, the whole country was suffering. Nemtsov was afraid to pass on the letter himself, so she sent it via diplomatic channels.

3. Valentin Yumashev had been a journalist with *Ogonyok* in the late 1980s and helped to write Yeltsin's two books of memoirs in the early 1990s. Before then, he had been a janitor at the Peredelkino dacha of dissident writer Lydia Chukovskaya, suggesting that he may have been a KGB agent sent to spy on whoever visited her – and was later attached to Yeltsin in the same way that Vladimir Putin was also allegedly 'attached' to another democratic leader, Anatoly Sobchak, in St Petersburg in 1990 (Putin had first asked to work for Galina Starovoitova, but she had turned him down).

4. Talbott, Strobe, *The Russia Hand: A Memoir of Presidential Diplomacy*, New York: Random House, 2002, p. 351.

5. *The Times*, 14 August 1999, p. 15.

6. National Security Council and NSC Records Management System, 'Declassified Documents Concerning Russian President Boris Yeltsin', *Clinton Digital Library*, accessed 6 November 2020, Case number 2015-0782-M, Document ID 9908997, Row 46, Section 5, Shelf 6, Position 2, Stack V.

18 'Managed Democracy' – Putin

1. Jeffries, Ian, *The New Russia: A Handbook of Economic and Political Developments*, London: RoutledgeCurzon, 2002, pp. 536-537.

2. Mendelson, Sarah E., 'Democracy Assistance and Political Transition in Russia: Between Success and Failure', *International Security*, Vol. 25, No. 4 (Spring 2001), Cambridge, MA: MIT Press, p. 98.

3. Jeffries, Ian, *The New Russia: A Handbook of Economic and Political Developments*, London: RoutledgeCurzon, 2002, p. 540.

4. *International Herald Tribune*, 28 March 2000, p. 7.

5. The electoral commission countered this claim by suggesting that nearly half a million Chechens displaced by the war had failed to vote in December, but voted for Putin in March; Jeffries, Ian, *The New Russia: A Handbook of Economic and Political Developments*, London: RoutledgeCurzon, 2002, p. 559.

6. Mendelson, Sarah E., 'Democracy Assistance and Political Transition in Russia: Between Success and Failure', *International Security*, Vol. 25, No. 4 (Spring 2001), Cambridge, MA: MIT Press, pp. 100-101.

7. United Russia was helped by sometimes being awarded figures exceeding 100%. For example, in the Duma elections of 2007, the party officially polled 104% and 109% in parts of Mordovia. The record for a single candidate was 117% in the Polyustrovo municipal elections in St Petersburg in 2014. During the Duma elections in 2011, TV channel *Russia-24* was allegedly informed of the results for United Russia by telephone from the Kremlin but told to give the true figures for all other parties, resulting in total numbers over 100% being reported live on air (including, famously, 146% in Rostov Region).

8. Jeffries, Ian, *The New Russia: A Handbook of Economic and Political Developments*, London: RoutledgeCurzon, 2002, p. 543.

9. The melody was originally written by Alexander Alexandrov in 1938 as *Anthem of the Bolshevik Party*. Stalin liked the tune and it was chosen to replace *The Internationale* as the Soviet anthem in 1943.

Bibliography

Aksyutin, Yu. V., *Khruschevskaya 'ottepel'' i obschestvennye nastroeniya v SSSR v 1953–1964 gg.* (Moscow: ROSSPEN, 2010)

Aleshkin, Pyotr; Vasilyev, Yury, *Krest'yanskaya voina za Sovety protiv kommunistov (1918–1922 gg.): Stat'i* (Ekaterinburg: Izdatel'skie resheniya, 2016)

Anarkhiya rabotaet. Primery iz istorii Rossii (Common place, 2014)

Avrich, Paul, *Russian Rebels, 1600–1800* (New York & London: W. W. Norton & Company, 1976)

Beazley, Raymond; Forbes, Nevill; Birkett, G. A., *Russia from the Varangians to the Bolsheviks* (Oxford: Clarendon Press, 1918)

Belash, A. V.; Belash, V. F., *Dorogi Nestora Makhno* (Kiev: 'Proza' Advertising and Publishing Centre, 1993)

Belyaev, I. D., *Sud'by zemschiny i vybornogo nachala na Rusi* (Moscow: Obschestvo rasprostraneniya poleznykh knig, 1905)

Belyaev, I. D., *Zemskie sobory na Rusi* (Moscow: A. D. Stupin, 1902)

Blotsky, Oleg, *Vladimir Putin. Istoriya zhizni* (Moscow: Mezhdunarodnye otnosheniya, 2002)

Chekin, S. N., *Staryi Buyan, Samara, Pechorlag: Povestvovanie vracha Trudnikova* (Moscow: AIRO-XXI, 2013)

Gaidar, Yegor, *Days of Defeat and Victory*, translated from the Russian by Jane Ann Miller (Seattle & London: University of Washington Press, 1999)

Gessen, Masha, *The Man without a Face: The Unlikely Rise of Vladimir Putin* (London: Granta, 2013)

Golovko, Sergei, 'Partizanskaya respublika', *Belaruskaya Dumka* (No. 4, 2015, pp. 26-33)

Gorbachev, Mikhail, *Memoirs* (London: Doubleday, 1996)

Gorbachev, Mikhail, *The New Russia*, translated from the Russian by Arch Tait (Cambridge: Polity Press, 2016)

Gorbachev, Raisa, *I Hope. Reminiscences and Reflections*, translated from the Russian by David Floyd (London: Fontana, 1992)

Hedlund, Stefan, *Russia's 'Market' Economy: A Bad Case of Predatory Capitalism* (London: UCL Press Limited, 1999)

Bibliography

Jeffries, Ian, *The New Russia: A Handbook of Economic and Political Developments* (London: RoutledgeCurzon, 2002)

Jones, Stephen F., *Socialism in Georgian Colors: The European Road to Social Democracy, 1883–1917* (Cambridge, Mass.: Harvard University Press, 2005)

Karatsuba, Irina; Kurukin, Igor; Sokolov, Nikita, *Vybiraya svoyu istoriyu. Razvilki na puti Rossii: ot Ryurikovichei do oligarkhov* (Moscow: AST, 2014)

Khrushchev, Sergei, *Nikita Khruschev: Reformator* (Moscow: Vremya, 2010)

Kliuchevsky, V. O., *A Course in Russian History: The Seventeenth Century*, translated from the Russian by Natalie Duddington (Chicago: Quadrangle Books, 1968)

Korzhakov, Alexander, *Boris El'tsin: ot rassveta do zakata* (Moscow: Interbook, 1997)

Kostomarov, Nikolai, *Russkaya respublika (Severnorusskie narodopravstva vo vremena udel'no-vechevogo uklada. Istoriya Novgoroda, Pskova i Vyatki)* (Moscow: Direct Media, 2014)

Kramola: Inakomyslie v SSSR pri Khruscheve i Brezhneve. 1953–1982 gg. Rassekrechennye dokumenty Verkhovnogo suda i Prokuratury SSSR, compiled by V. A. Kozlov, O. V. Edelman, E. Yu. Zavadskaya (Moscow: Materik, 2005)

Kutsenko, Y. I.; Latkin, V. F., 'K istorii vooruzhennogo vosstaniya v Sochi v dekabre 1905 g.' *Istoricheskii arkhiv* (1955, No. 6, pp. 47-74)

Lee, Eric, *The Experiment: Georgia's Forgotten Revolution 1918–1921* (London: Zed Books, 2017)

Levchik, D. A., 'Politicheskii 'kheppening", *Sotsiologicheskie issledovaniya* (No. 8, 1996, pp. 51-56)

Liseytsev, Dmitry Vladimirovich, 'Zemsky Sobors of the late 16th–early 17th century in Russia: Historiographical stereotypes in the reflection of historical sources', *Studia historica, Historia moderna* (37, 2015, pp. 71-91)

Massie, Robert K., *Catherine the Great: Portrait of a Woman* (London: Head of Zeus Ltd., 2012)

Massie, Robert K., *Nicholas and Alexandra* (New York: Atheneum, 1967)

Mendelson, Sarah E., 'Democracy Assistance and Political Transition in Russia: Between Success and Failure', *International Security* (Vol. 25, No. 4, spring 2001, Cambridge, MA: MIT Press, pp. 68-106)

Mokeyev, A. B., 'Vybory vo Vserossiiskoe Uchreditel'noe sobranie v Petrograde', *Vestnik Sankt-Peterburgskogo universiteta* (Ser. 2, 2009, Edn. 2, pp. 182-186)

Motrevich, V. P., 'Vybory v Verkhovnyi Sovet SSSR 1946 g.', *Dokument. Arkhiv. Istoriya. Sovremennost'* (Vol. 10, Ekaterinburg: Izdatel'stvo Ural'skogo universiteta, 2009, pp. 372-380)

Novodvorskaya, Valeriya, *Po tu storonu otchayaniya* (Moscow: Novosti, 1993)

Obolensky, Dmitri, *The Byzantine Commonwealth: Eastern Europe, 500–1453* (London: Sphere Books Ltd, 1974)

Popova, O. G., 'Ideya uchreditel'nogo sobraniya v rossiiskoi istorii i ego rol' v popytke sozdaniya pravovogo gosudarstva v 1917–nachale 1918 g.', *Problemy istorii Rossii* (Edn. 2, Ekaterinburg: Volot, 1998, pp. 146-175)

Protasov, L. G., *Vserossiiskoe Uchreditel'noe sobranie: istoriya rozhdeniya i gibeli* (Moscow: ROSSPEN, 1997)

Radzinsky, Edvard, *Ivan IV Groznyi* (Moscow: AST, 2012)

Radzinsky, Edvard, *Stalin*, translated from the Russian by H. T. Willetts (London: Hodder and Stoughton, 1996)

Readings in Russian Civilization, Vols. I-III, second edition, edited by Thomas Riha (Chicago & London: University of Chicago Press, 1969)

Remnick, David, *Resurrection: The Struggle for a New Russia* (London: Picador, 1998)

Rothstein, Andrew, *A History of the U.S.S.R.* (Harmondsworth: Penguin, 1950)

Sablin, Ivan, *Governing Post-Imperial Siberia and Mongolia, 1911–1924: Buddhism, Socialism and Nationalism in State and Autonomy Building* (New York & London: Routledge, 2016)

Schuyler, Eugene, *Peter the Great. Emperor of Russia. A Study of Historical Biography*, Vol. 1, New York: Charles Scribner's Sons, 1884

Shanin, Teodor, *Russia, 1905–07: The Roots of Otherness: Volume 2: Revolution as a Moment of Truth* (New Haven: Yale University Press, 1986)

Shevyakin, Alexander, *KGB protiv SSSR. 17 mgnovenii izmeny* (Moscow: Eksmo, 2018)

Smirnov, I. I., *'Markovskaya respublika'. Iz istorii krest'yanskogo dvizheniya 1905 goda v Moskovskoi gubernii* (Moscow: Moskovskii rabochii, 1975)

Smith, Douglas, *Rasputin: Faith, Power, and the Twilight of the Romanovs* (London: Macmillan, 2016)

Sokolov, B. V., *Okkupatsiya. Pravda i mify* (Moscow: AST-Press Kniga, 2005)

Talbott, Strobe, *The Russia Hand: A Memoir of Presidential Diplomacy* (New York: Random House, 2002)

Thatcher, Margaret, *Statecraft: Strategies for a Changing World* (London: HarperCollins, 2002)

Thatcher, Margaret, *The Downing Street Years* (London: HarperCollins, 1993)

The Chronicle of Novgorod, 1016–1471, translated from the Russian by Robert Michell and Nevill Forbes Ph.D., with an introduction by C. Raymond Beazley D.Litt. and an account of the text by A. A. Shakhmatov (London: Offices of the Society, 1914)

Tsyrempilov, N., 'Konstitutsionnaya teokratiya Lubsan-Samdana Tsydenova: popytka sozdaniya buddiiskogo gosudarstva v Zabaikal'e (1918–1922)', *Gosudarstvo, religiya, tserkov' v Rossii i za rubezhom* (No. 4 [33], 2015, pp. 318-346)

Tufar N. Kh.; Tufar, N. N.; Kinayatuly Z., *Ocherki istorii gagauzov. Komratskaya Respublika. 1906 god. Oguzskoe gosudarstvo IX-X v.v.* (Comrat: Centrul de Cercetări Ştiinţifice al Găgăuziei 'M. V. Marunevici', 2015)

Villari, Luigi, *Fire and Sword in the Caucasus* (London: T. F. Unwin, 1906)

Vodolazskaya, Yevgenia, *Raisa Gorbacheva* (Rostov-on-Don: Phoenix, 2000)

Vybory vo Vserossiiskoe Uchreditel'noe sobranie v dokumentakh i vospominaniyakh sovremennikov, edited by Yu. A. Bedeneyev and I. B. Borisov (Moscow: ROIIP, 2009)

Yakovlev, Alexander, *Sumerki* (Moscow: Materik, 2005)

Yeltsin, Boris, *The Struggle for Russia*, translated from the Russian by Catherine A. Fitzpatrick (London: HarperCollins, 1994)

Yermolov, Igor, *Tri goda bez Stalina. Okkupatsiya: sovetskie grazhdane mezhdu natsistami i bol'shevikami. 1941–1944* (Moscow: Tsentrpoligraf, 2010)

Index

Lyubarsky, Kronid 217
Lyubotin Republic 75
Mabetex Affair 243
Magazines: *Economist* 55; *Novy mir*
 168; *Time* 230, 238
Makarevich, Andrei 199
Makarov, Alexander 87
Makashov, General Albert 190, 191,
 195, 212, 214, 245
Makharadze, Gerasim 84
Makhno, Nestor 134-136, 142
Maklakov, Nikolai 88
Makukhin, Lieutenant Colonel
 Vladimir 129
Manchuria: Chinese-Eastern Railway
 100, 101, 112; Harbin 71;
Manifesto of Unshakable Autocracy
 61
Maqsudí, Sadrí 130, 131
Margeret, Jacques 43
Maria Fyodorovna, Empress
 (Princess Dagmar of Denmark)
 61-62, 83, 87
Markidonov, Sergei 223
Markovo Republic 68-69
Martha, Great Nun (born Xenia
 Shestova) 43
Martínez, Adolfo Larrue III 232
Martynovsky 150, 151
Marychev, Vyacheslav 219-220
Mavrodi, Sergei 220, 221-222, 233,
 235, 241
Maximus the Greek 27, 29
May Day 83, 168, 183, 210
Mayoral elections 189, 196, 243
McCain, John 217
Meadowcroft, Michael 238
Medals and awards: St George's
 Cross 75; Hero of the Soviet
 Union 190, 202; People's Artist of
 the USSR 204
Medici, Catherine de' 25
Medieval chronicles: Chronicle
 of Novgorod 22, 25; Nikon
 Chronicle 14; Suzdal Chronicle
 13; Piskaryov Chronicle 33;
 Primary Chronicle 12, 13
Medvedev, Dmitry 176, 247

Medvedev, Roy 160, 177, 179
Menshevik Party 63, 64, 73, 81, 88,
 100, 102, 104, 105, 107, 111, 112,
 114, 115, 138, 144
Mestnichestvo ('place position') 26,
 50
Metropolitan Macarius of Moscow
 27
Metropolitan of Kiev 15, 220
Mexico 144
Michael Romanov, Tsar 34, 41-48,
 87, 93, 123, 206
Michael, Grand Duke 93, 115,
 140, 151; Brasova, Natalia (née
 Sheremetievskaya) 151
Middle East 216
Mikoyan, Anastas 159
Miloslavskaya, Maria 50
Milyukov, Pavel 80, 86, 89, 92, 95,
 115
Minin, Kuzma 40
Mlynář, Zdeněk 166
MMM 221, 222, 233, 241
Mniszech, Maryna 37, 38, 41
Moderates 58, 81, 85, 95-96, 104,
 126, 190, 195, 234
Moldova 75-76; Moldavian
 Democratic Republic 113; Soviet
 republic 169, 187; independent
 republic 176, 203, 204, 233, 237;
 Gagauz Autonomous SSR 76;
 Gagauz Republic 76
Molotov-Ribbentrop Pact 123, 148,
 179
Mongol invasion 22-23, 24, 26;
 Golden Horde 23
Mongol khans 23, 26; Genghis
 Khan 128; Öz Beg Khan 23
Mongolia 133
Montesquieu 55
Moore, Charles 164
Mordovia 71, 185
Moscow 19, 21, 23-30 and passim
Moscow Kremlin 26, 36, 37, 39,
 40, 41, 42, 46, 48, 50-51, 62, 168,
 170, 180, 184, 190, 197, 202,
 204, 207, 210, 212, 213, 216, 238,
 241, 243, 249; Grand Kremlin